PENGUIN BOOKS

GOD'S DOG

Hope Ryden grew to love wildlife during the summers she spent as a girl in the woods of northern Wisconsin. In 1961 she began writing and producing documentary films for television, several of which were about wildlife. Her articles and photographs have appeared in *Reader's Digest, Time, National Geographic, The New York Times,* and other publications; in addition to the present book, she is the author of *America's Last Wild Horses, The Wild Colt, The Wild Pups,* and *The Little Deer of the Florida Keys.* Ms. Ryden is also the author of *Mustangs: A Return to the Wild,* published by Penguin Books, and she has been quite active on the wild horses' behalf, taking part in court action and testifying before U.S. Senate and House Committees. Ms. Ryden lives in New York City.

Also by Hope Ryden

America's Last Wild Horses (revised edition)
Mustangs: A Return to the Wild
The Wild Colt
The Wild Pups
The Little Deer of the Florida Keys

HOPE RYDEN

GOD'S DOG
A Celebration
of the North American Coyote

Photographs by Hope Ryden

Penguin Books

Penguin Books Ltd, Harmondsworth,
Middlesex, England
Penguin Books, 625 Madison Avenue,
New York, New York 10022, U.S.A.
Penguin Books Australia Ltd, Ringwood,
Victoria, Australia
Penguin Books Canada Limited, 2801 John Street,
Markham, Ontario, Canada L3R 1B4
Penguin Books (N.Z.) Ltd, 182–190 Wairau Road,
Auckland 10, New Zealand

First published in the United States of America by Coward, McCann & Geoghegan, Inc., 1975
Published in simultaneous hardcover and paperback editions by The Viking Press and
Penguin Books 1979

LIBRARY OF CONGRESS CATALOGING IN PUBLICATION DATA
Ryden, Hope.
God's dog.
Bibliography: p. 299.
Includes index.
1. Coyotes—Behavior.   2. Mammals—Behavior.
I. Title.
QL737.C22R92 1979   599'.74442   78–13336
ISBN 0 14 00.5071 X

Printed in the United States of America by
The Book Press, Brattleboro, Vermont
Set in Linoterm Baskerville

Pages 148–163 appeared originally
in *The New York Times Magazine*
in slightly different form.

In memory of Sitka and Huggy,
two special dogs

I wish to thank former government trapper Vern E. Dorn and rancher Lloyd Tillett for lessons in the tracking of coyotes, Abbie Tillett for a particularly timely word of encouragement, biologist Franz Camenzind for some valuable discussions, employees of Yellowstone National Park and the National Elk Refuge for their help and cooperation during the periods of time I made field observations in those areas, Helenette Silver and employees of the New Hampshire State Fish and Game Department for information about and assistance in finding the New Hampshire wild canid, the Paul Maxwells, the Everett McConahays and JoAnn Spiegelberg for acquainting me with their hand-raised coyotes, Ed Park, Dick Randall and Bill Hobbs for photographs of victims of predator control, Jean Ris for her patience in typing and retyping copy, my father for his comments on early drafts of this book and my editors Peggy Brooks and Barbara Burn for being so sensitive to wild animals.

I am indebted to Yellowstone Park biologist Dr. Mary Meagher for her helpful criticisms, to Cynthia Wilson, Washington representative for the National Audubon Society, for her careful scrutiny of all material relating to predator control, and to psychologist Dr. Michael W. Fox for his review of the manuscript prior to publication.

H.R.

Preface

Coyotes intrigued and mystified me long before I set out to make a serious study of them. During one period of my life, while I was tracking wild horses in remote places across the West, the nightly rhapsodizing of coyotes sometimes relieved the silence of my isolated campsite, and occasionally I caught a tantalizing glimpse of one furtively traveling behind vegetative cover. The coyote wisely makes himself inconspicuous whenever the species to which I belong is about. Once, however, while I was camped on a remote desert in southern Nevada, I was surprised to discover *Canis latrans* was likewise trying to obtain a look at me! I had bedded down for the night beside a piñon pine and at daybreak woke abruptly with an eerie feeling that I was being watched. My remote location (a restricted military test site) all but precluded anyone short of a space visitor from happening upon me, and so I experienced a moment of preternatural terror until I spotted two quizzical faces topped by large stand-up ears peering at me from behind a small rise. Without stirring, I observed the pair of curious coyotes out of the corner of my eyes as they continued to study me with grave attention. Perhaps they had come to feast on the piñon nuts I was lying among, become fascinated by the strange misshapen lump they found stretched out on top of their trove, and lingered to investigate. When I shifted slightly, they vanished like magical creatures.

During those wild-horse years, I picked up what information I could about these appealing wild dogs who are native only to our own continent. But though coyote lore abounds, I found hard facts difficult to come by. There even seemed to be a lack of consensus as to how the creature's name should be pronounced. In the Southwest, people spoke to me of *coy-o-tees*. However, in Wyoming, Idaho, Montana, and parts of Colorado, anybody who dragged the word into three syllables revealed himself an outsider! In the northern states, *Canis latrans* is known as *ky-oht.*(For a time I was able to adjust my pronunciation accordingly, but eventually, after conducting two years of fieldwork in Wyoming, the habit of saying *ky-oht* became too deeply ingrained for me to change.)

As my interest in the coyote grew, I also became increasingly conscious of literary references to the animal, and I tried to discover in them clues to the true nature of this enigmatic creature. More often than not, these allusions cast *Canis latrans* in a stereotyped role more descriptive of human weakness than animal behavior. Aphorisms about "lone" coyotes, "cowardly" coyotes, "sneaky" coyotes, and "dirty" coyotes told me more about the writer's penchant for moralizing than about *Canis latrans* himself. Ironically, the people who maligned the coyote's "character" often also insisted he personified the spirit of the West!

At one point, while I was still only casually rummaging for information, I went so far as to track the coyote into the past, where I was surprised to find him enjoying the good opinion of the white men who first encountered him. Anglo explorers who saw him on the Great Plains named him "prairie wolf." He might, however, as logically have been given the title of "desert wolf" or "little wolf of the mountain," for early records show him simultaneously thriving in southern Mexico and the northern Rockies. To a limited degree he also occupied areas east of the Mississippi—in Illinois, Indiana, Minnesota, and Wisconsin. There the French in 1765 saw fit to christen their frontier settlement "Prairie du Chien" in honor of his abundant presence. That they did so suggests that the coyote might have been as estemed by them as by the many different Indian tribes who venerated the animal.

In Crow mythology Old Man Coyote's position was supreme. That Northwestern tribe not only regarded him as "First Worker," creator of the earth and all living creatures, but also believed him to be the founder of human customs. Yet because life on earth was so obviously full of error, it naturally followed that Old Man Coyote himself must be fallible and, though inordinately clever, capable of being duped. The Crows saw no inconsistency in casting the coyote in the various roles of transformer, trickster, and fool. They relished stories in which their hero received his come-uppance from lesser animals. Mankind, then as now, delighted in the fall of the mighty. Nevertheless, the coyote was no less venerated for being vulnerable.

Even tribes that did not cast the coyote as the ultimate symbol of the Universal Principle gave him a special place in their view of creation. In the Southwest, the Navajos referred to him as "God's dog." They set the coyote over the wolf, calling the latter *ma'ii tosh*, which means "big coyote," as opposed to the white man, who tends to refer to the coyote as a "small wolf." The Indians were not so prone to equate physical size with relative importance.

Even the high civilizations that flourished in Mexico deified the coyote. Coyotlinauatl was an Aztec god whose worshipers dressed in coyote skins. Tezcatlipoca, another Aztec deity, could transform himself into a coyote at will. Heuheucoyotl, or "Old Coyote," was a mischief-maker like his counterpart, "Trickster," to the north. And Coyolxauhqui was the moon goddess, who, as J. Frank Dobie points out, was appropriately named for the chief native bayer-at-the-moon. Today, despite efforts of early Anglo explorers to call him a "prairie wolf," *Canis latrans*'s sacred Aztec title, "coyotl," has prevailed.

Perhaps because of uncertainty over the way it is pronounced, the English-speaking North American still concocts nicknames for the coyote. In Minnesota, where intensive agriculture has driven an indigenous subspecies from the state's southern prairies northward into third-growth forest now heavily trussed with undergrowth, *Canis latrans* is being called a "brush wolf." So well has the animal adapted to what, in fact, is an alien environment, that onlookers naively describe him as a product of it! And in New York's Adirondacks, where coyotes have appeared in recent years, "bush wolf" is a similar misnomer.

I was to come to realize that it is to a large extent this ability of the coyote to adapt to diverse conditions that makes him so difficult to define. At the same time, this versatility is undoubtedly what has enabled the species to survive man's every effort to extirpate him. For the adaptable coyote not only is capable of bivouacking where he pleases, but seems able to adopt any number of life-styles. He can hunt either by day or by night, dine on fresh meat or survive off carrion, raid town garbage pits or feast on wild fruits and berries, den in burrows or whelp in conduit pipes, run in packs or operate as a loner. Bold coyotes can be observed in the alleyways of Los Angeles. But shy ones may be heard only in the wilderness, where they fill their private haunts with soulful cadenzas. Even the coyote's physical body reflects his protean quality. In *The Mammals of North America*, E. Raymond Hall and Keith R. Kelson identify nineteen subspecies of *Canis latrans*.

It would appear from this that the coyote may still be in the process of becoming, that Nature may not yet have set the successful adaptations the species has made over long ages of natural selection. The advantage to an animal of being in an unfinished state can best be demonstrated by noting the fates of those North American animals who were better perfected for existence in their special niches. The bison and the wolf were rapidly vanquished when an agricultural and industrial society reshaped their habitats. The coyote, by contrast, met change with change and survives. Thus, atypical behavior and unique responses, while frustrating to those who, like myself, look for definitive answers, may in fact be the creative side of the evolutionary process.

Bearing this in mind when at last my obsession with the little canines led me to make my own field study, I went in search of prototypes, animals whose exposure to the effects of civilized man had been limited and who, therefore, might not be corrupted by artificial influences. For this reason, after a single fall season I abandoned my first plan to conduct my fieldwork on public lands that are also used by stockmen and moved instead to Yellowstone National Park, where coyotes are not subjected to persecution. There, during two winters, I observed what I regarded to be archetypal coyotes living with other indigenous animals and performing their natural functions in the ecosystem.

But my winter fieldwork here, while it provided me with extraordinary insights into the coyote's food-finding and survival abilities, at the same time confirmed what trappers had predicted—that the wild coyote would permit only fleeting observations of his intimate social behavior. Paradoxically, in the area of social relations more has been learned about the rare wolf than about the relatively prevalent coyote. Yet the very difficulty of obtaining such information acted as an inducement for me to try, for almost anything I might discover about the coyote's social life would very likely turn out to be new knowledge. Although as long ago as the 1930s, a peerless biologist by the name of Adolph Murie made a pioneer field study on wild coyotes, he concentrated primarily on the animal's role in the food chain. The coyote's social life remained shrouded in mystery.

The obvious time and place for acquiring the type of information I sought was in the spring of the year and at a den site, where young pups would require the regular attendance of their mother and where any associated adults (provided adults did associate with one another) might be likely to assemble. But, once again, trappers warned me of the difficulties of undertaking a den study. A mother coyote, I was told, would relocate her pups to a new hideaway at the least indication that her burrow had been discovered. Assuredly she would not tolerate a daily spectator.

Worrying about this, I grew increasingly apprehensive over the approach of spring and the opening of Yellowstone Park to tourists. For even were I to be successful in finding a den that I could watch from afar, the setup could be disturbed by curious hikers. I therefore decided to look elsewhere for a litter of pups and happily found one in western Wyoming, on a restricted section of the National Elk Refuge that is off limits to the casual tourist. There I was able to make long-distance observations of the day-by-day activities of a closely knit group of coyotes I named the "Miller Butte pack." Each member of this fascinating clan, I discovered, exhibited traits as individual and appealing as those found in any assortment of domestic dogs. In fact, their sociability, cooperation, and affection for one another, and the even more remarkable devotion that certain "aunts" and "uncles" displayed toward a litter of pups born to one of their members, so contradicted the prevailing notion of the coyote as a relatively *asocial* animal that I felt it imperative I return the next spring to make a follow-up study and document my findings with pictures. For some mysterious reason, during this second year my pack decided to tolerate a highly conspicuous vehicle I used as a blind. Thus over a seven-week period I was able to live within a few hundred feet of their den, whence I could watch and photograph in intimate detail the social interactions of seven adults and nine pups.

Though I have presented my findings in the form of a personal narrative, I have not always organized my observations in the order in which I obtained them, but according to the coyote's seasonal phases. Thus, I combine two winter seasons in one section and two springs in another. I hope my lack of chronological exactitude will not be disturbing to the reader. For though I have woven my own personal experiences throughout the book, I regard these as of secondary importance to the field studies I have reported.

At the same time, however, I am aware that the presentation of objective facts by themselves seldom has motivated human beings to behave more sanely toward the natural world. Certainly the American public has often been informed about the important biological purposes that the predator-scavenger species serve in healthy ecosystems. Yet this knowledge has not deterred those bent on extirpating the coyote. Nor has it aroused the public sector to halt the massive destruction of wild species by the government to satisfy the demands of special-interest groups. The average citizen often behaves as if resigned to the inevitable destruction, link by link, of biotic communities that are ultimately necessary for his own preservation.

Perhaps something more than the presentation of objective facts is needed to arouse people to action. An even more compelling persuasion than enlightened self-interest might be to evoke in the public consciousness something of that profound feeling for the natural world that Albert Schweitzer called *Ehrfurcht*, reverence for life. An earlier generation of naturalists regarded the experiencing of this emotion as the essence of any study of natural history. Thoreau wrote: "This curious world which we inhabit is more wonderful than it is convenient; more beautiful than it is useful; it is more to be admired than used."

One of my aims in writing this book has been to communicate something of my own unfolding awareness of my subjects as living beings whose suffering and satisfactions are as marvelous and as worthy of attention as any discussion of the usefulness or destructiveness of their food habits. For ultimately my field studies revealed the coyote to be an animal indeed more wonderful, more beautiful, and more to be admired than all the logical reasons I have also tried to set forth to demonstrate why he is so vitally important to whole biotic communities. An older and wiser culture understood all of this when they spoke of him as "God's dog."

Contents

A Scouting Trip

Each night a band of coyotes edged nearer to where I lay stretched out on top of my bedroll high in the Pryor Mountains. It was early fall and though the air was still warm, the little prairie wolves had already begun to howl in earnest, raising their mournful voices to a frenetic pitch until the surrounding peaks pealed with the echoes of their sonorous wails. From higher up the mountains a more remote band of coyotes gave voice to the identical theme, then improvised variations.

I was camped on a mountain meadow along the Wyoming-Montana border, in search of the elusive choristers who were keeping me awake each night. As I lay on my back gazing at the imperceptibly shifting galaxies above, the wild beauty of the coyotes' music filled me with profound emotion. The sound was lusty and primeval. No extraneous noise intruded to muddy the clarity of the canine antiphonal. One of creation's masterworks was being performed by virtuosos, and I was privileged to be the sole human being to hear it.

Suddenly, while in this rapt mood, I was struck on the chest and stomach by two of the three ranch dogs I had borrowed for this field trip. I had taken the dogs with me on the advice of an ex-trapper, Vern Dorn, who suggested they might be an aid in tracking or attracting coyotes. At the very least, he said, they would offer me some protection in the wilderness.

Now two of the dogs, Splinter and Blue, lay quivering against my body, their ears flattened and their spines curled to protect their vulnerable underparts. I shamed the dogs in the hope that my lack of solicitude would restore their self-confidence, but the pair were too busy vying for closer body contact with me to pay any attention to my rebukes. Finally, one settled for a position in the crook of my knees and the other flung her trembling body directly across my neck. I could hear Brownie, the third dog, lurking nearby, making all but inaudible rumbles in his throat.

The dogs' shameless conduct did little to bolster my own 3

flagging courage, and I began to wonder what the coyotes could be communicating that would cause their domestic cousins to behave so. I knew little about coyotes then, and I correctly assumed the dogs were more knowledgeable.

Meanwhile, the coyotes continued to howl. Like phantoms, they shifted position in the dark. Now they sounded at arm's length; a split second later, one hundred yards away. I had not yet heard tell of their ventriloquist powers. Nor did I know that one of the Indian names for the coyote was "trickster"!

There was little doubt in my mind that the dogs had drawn the pack to my camp as Vern had predicted they might. The abject behavior of Splinter and Blue clearly demonstrated that some canine interaction was taking place. But Vern had failed to forewarn me that my decoys might be so fainthearted. Nor had he hinted at the possibility that so many coyotes would turn up in the middle of a moonless night.

Still he could hardly be faulted for the way things were working out. He had generously shared with me field lore gained during his many years as a federal trapper, prior to his public renunciation of the government's indiscriminate killing program. Moreover, he had specifically warned me that finding coyotes would not be easy.

"They are the smartest animals in the world," he flatly declared. "At one time I hated coyotes. You go through a period of learning. I got ulcers dealing with a public that never feels there is adequate control. If one coyote is left, they say, 'Kill the son of a bitch.' They have no compassion, and they're not satisfied until every one is dead. Today I wouldn't kill another coyote for the world. Why not? Because I know coyotes, and I love 'em."

And so, because my purpose was not killing, Dorn had revealed his tracking secrets to me. And I, like the amateur I was, entered into the project with the quixotic notion that I soon would be tripping over my quarry. But during the week that I had searched the broad meadow and explored the wooded peaks that enclosed my campsite, though I found droppings, even an abandoned den, I had not sighted a single coyote!

I had, however, encountered other animals. Surprised cattle, left to summer on the high pasture, had raised their heads and bellowed at the sight of me. They hadn't seen a human being in months. As I climbed the wooded draws, deer spooked out of the brush. And evidence at a half-eaten calf carcass indicated that bears had recently visited the remains.

Lloyd Tillett, the stockman who leased this remote mountain pasture from the Crow Indian tribe, customarily left his cattle to graze here from June until October. In the fall, when he returned to gather his herd, he invariably spotted a coyote or two in their midst. It was on his advice that I decided to begin my search for *Canis latrans* in this place called Dryhead.

"The coyotes have been poisoned about everywhere else around here," Tillett informed me. "Even up there on reservation lands some lessees were in the habit of lacing carcasses with strychnine till the Indians put a stop to it about eight or nine years ago. Funny thing, though, the Dryhead coyotes had already stopped eating carrion as a result of the poisoning. They got educated, I guess. And even today they are too suspicious to feed on any dead critter. Always have to kill their own meat."

I asked if such a change in a predator-scavenger's habits might not be detrimental to a rancher's long-range interests. Normally, carrion makes up the major portion of the coyote's winter diet. If a coyote is conditioned against utilizing dead animals, he will of necessity more often prey on live ones.

"That's the sheepmen's problem," Tillett replied. "Coyotes never bothered my cattle to speak of. Now I have a problem with dead critters. No coyotes around to eat them, and they just lie around for months and stink."

So I wasted little time watching the dead calf I had found. If Tillett was correct, dead meat on the ground would not attract coyotes in this place.

During the week I spent looking for coyotes in Dryhead, I applied every field technique Vern had taught me, plus a few tricks of my own. I was not altogether a novice at tracking animals. I had spent several years studying wild mustangs and, through trial, error, and default, had acquired a certain know-how that I naturally expected would serve me in my search for

Canis latrans. But already I was beginning to realize there was little similarity between finding wild horses and looking for coyotes. Though I had glassed hills with binoculars, blown my predator whistle, climbed rugged slopes, concealed myself in blinds, employed dogs, and searched for tracks, I'd seen no coyotes. Had it not been for their nightly serenades, I might well have decided Tillett was wrong in believing they still existed in this place.

Yet each night when darkness hid them from sight, the little canines turned up and, as if in mockery, surrounded me and began to howl. It occurred to me that these nocturnal serenades might in reality be nothing more than a trick of my imagination. But on this night the dogs' apprehensiveness was sufficient evidence that the invisible creatures making all the noise were indeed there. Since no two seemed content to sustain the same note, the size of the pack could be fairly well estimated. It was a chorus of some ten free spirits.

Then, inexplicably, their vocalization stopped. I did not discern the distant rumble that had silenced the pack and so I drifted off to sleep, held fast to the revolving earth by a gentle force that prevented me from flying into the overhead light show. Sleeping on a mountain can be a mystical experience.

Suddenly I was awakened by the sound of a pickup grinding up the roadless mountain. Then two intrusive beams of light blinded me, as the truck stopped a few feet in front of my bedroll, and to my surprise, the entire Tillett family spilled out. It was nearly two A.M. and the younger children leaped from the back end of the truck and were in their sleeping bags almost as soon as they hit the ground. They had been riding three hours.

Lloyd and Abbie Tillett were friends from my wild-horse days. They had been an incalculable help to me in the beginning, when I needed tips from local ranch people as to the whereabouts of mustangs. Now they were extending themselves in every possible way to assist me, "an Easterner who should have been born in the West," in my new venture.

Lloyd Tillett, who freely admitted being a novice himself at locating coyotes, explained that Vern Dorn had phoned that afternoon to offer a few new suggestions for me and that he and Abbie and the kids, on an impulse, had decided to pile into the pickup and drive up to Dryhead for the weekend to convey the message.

"Besides," he added, "I thought it wouldn't hurt to check on my cows up here."

Such a generous act may still be casually performed by people living anywhere, but I have found that Westerners frequently extend themselves well beyond the ordinary demands of friendship. A three-hour trip in the middle of the night across a roadless mountain range is no perfunctory courtesy. I was touched that anyone would put themselves to so much trouble to deliver a message to me, and I could not bring myself to say that at that moment I was on the verge of giving up my project.

In any case, Lloyd's impatience to move on to the subject of *finding* the coyotes now precluded any discussion of the improbability of ever doing so. He held in his oversized hand a whistle fashioned from a TV antenna, and in an animated voice he explained exactly when and how it should be used. Vern had demonstrated to him how to produce the exact sound made by parent coyotes when they wish to evoke an answer from their half-grown pups, who, by this date in September, would be scattered over many miles of terrain. According to Vern, the young—now approximately five months old—would of necessity be hunting over a wide area to ensure an adequate food supply for all. But though the family unit would have broken up, at frequent intervals the coyote parents would rendezvous with their offspring and they would locate them by vocalizing— producing a predawn call that the pups would unfailingly answer. From the direction of their response, the adults could pinpoint the puppies' whereabouts and would then make the rounds to visit them.

Whether the parents brought supplementary food to their half-grown young or merely joined them was not explained. But since coyote puppies retain their milk teeth until they are five months old, it would seem probable that the parents might help them survive by occasionally contributing to their diet.* Even if parent coyotes do not supply food, long association with their young certainly must have high survival value for the species. In a joint hunt a skilled adult inadvertently serves as a teaching example to an inexperienced adolescent. Thus, Dorn's assertion that coyote families hold regular reunions seemed to make sense.

Now Tillett suggested that we imitate parent coyotes and, before dawn, climb to a high pinnacle some distance from camp, howl, listen for the puppies' response, then hike to the source of their yapping, where he would produce yet another sound Vern had taught him. According to Vern, any naive young coyote could be tricked by this method into believing his parents had arrived and thus be flushed from cover.

I must admit I was skeptical. I had already tried the best professional predator-call whistles on the market and had not fooled a single coyote into thinking I was a rabbit in distress. How, then, with a piece of TV antenna could we deceive half-grown coyotes into thinking we were their own parents? But Lloyd was so enthusiastic I did not have the heart to tell him what I thought of the plan. I agreed to try it.

At four A.M. Abbie woke me, and in the dark Lloyd and I climbed the steep north slope until, once day broke, our view of the meadow below and the surrounding draws that fed into it would be unobscured. Lloyd sat himself on a rock, and for a few moments while we caught our breath, he stared at the homemade whistle he held in his massive hands. Then he made a tentative move as if to blow, but stopped himself and said, "If I mess up on this, we don't get a second chance, you know. You

---

* At a later date, I became convinced that food is indeed brought to the young by solicitous parents throughout summer and well into fall. David Mech in *The Wolf* mentioned that adult wolves bring offerings to their growing offspring and continue to use the rendezvous site for this purpose at least until September. I believe adult coyotes rendezvous with their young for exactly the same natural purpose. In support of my opinion, I have seen adult coyotes regurgitating food for other adult coyotes. Food regurgitation can, therefore, be elicited by a full-grown animal as well as by small puppies. Moreover, observing half-grown pups at rendezvous sites convinced me that they anticipated the appearance of a parent bringing food.

don't fool a coyote twice." Then he grinned and added, "And there's no guarantee what kind of sound is gonna come out of this danged thing."

Squeezing his eyes shut, he cupped his hands around the little piece of metal, took a deep breath, and blew.

Even before the shrill sound had died away, we heard the puppies. Like a pack of yelping hounds in hot pursuit, their frenzied response told us not only their location, but much more. They were as excited as boarded dogs who have just overheard the voice of their returning master outside the kennel door. Lloyd looked completely dumbfounded at the commotion he had precipitated, and I could not refrain from laughing. Then he, too, began to guffaw, and for the next few minutes we laughed for no explicable reason except that we were so surprised. Neither of us had actually expected the trick would work.

It was a long hike to the point where the pups had so guilelessly betrayed their presence, and en route I frequently checked my light meter. As we made our way through the gray dawn, an eagle soared overhead, riding the cold-air drafts that flowed like a river between the two mountain ranges banking the long valley. High on some rimrocks three stags posed so perfectly they appeared to be bronze statues dimly backlit by the predawn sky. And a cow, startled by our sudden appearance in the dim light, leaped to her feet and for one agonizing moment deliberated whether or not to take after us. The world of Dryhead was coming awake.

By the time we neared the willow brush where we judged the coyote puppies to be concealed, the sun was up and the day was a bright one. Lloyd now directed me to hide behind a knoll while he moved farther up the mountain to make his second call. Should a coyote respond and appear, I was in a good position to photograph it.

But a problem immediately developed. That morning, unknown to us, the dog Brownie had followed and now he was making a nuisance of himself. Dogs can be useful in drawing out coyotes and for that reson we had not sent him back while still within a reasonable distance from camp. Now, however, we were having second thoughts about Brownie's value as a decoy. But we were stuck with him.

The problem was simply this: We couldn't call aloud to him without betraying our presence, and Brownie was nosing all over the place. When Lloyd and I separated, the mongrel shepherd first elected to go with Lloyd, but no sooner had I positioned myself in the brush than he returned and sniffed out my hiding place. He apparently thought we were playing a game with him, for he greeted me as effusively as if we had been separated for days. Then he dashed off to find Lloyd again. I hoped Lloyd would restrain him, but a moment later he returned, his tail waving and a big dog smile spread across his face. I grabbed him by a hind leg and while I was trying to make him settle down, I heard the ululation of the whistle.

Almost instantly the young coyote appeared. He was a blue one and as pretty as any candidate for membership in the American Kennel Club. His long, pointed nose was as aristocratic as a borzoi's and his thick mantle was as rich as a husky's. He wore the smart expression of a terrier, and his tail was as bushy as a fox's. In no way did he resemble the mangy critter described by his enemies—who no doubt rely on the fact that few people are likely to check out their stories firsthand.

Though I got a good look at the blue coyote, it was a brief one, for he was heading directly for Lloyd's hiding place at a brisk trot and was out of view before I had a chance to shoot a single picture, a fact that left me in a quandary. Should I move after him and risk spooking him? Or should I wait to see if he might pass by my hiding place again on his return?

My decision was formed not by my mind but by my emotions. After so many days of unrewarded search, now, at last, when a real live coyote was within a few yards of me, I could no more restrain my impulse to see him than I could control Brownie, who suddenly jerked free of me and scampered up the rise. I scrambled after him and topped the hill just as the coyote turned and looked my way. But my brain barely registered his image before he shot off in a curved trajectory and was gone. I had managed to take only one out-of-focus picture of him. And though I gave chase briefly, I was acting out a futile ritual and I knew it. The blue coyote had vanished.

Meanwhile, Brownie was pretending he hadn't seen a thing. Most intelligent dogs avoid tangling with coyotes. In a fight usually the dog will be the loser, sometimes will even be killed.* Now, to save face, the tan shepherd, who had been witness to the whole episode, became engrossed in smelling a blade of grass. He seemed to be taking no chance that I might send him in pursuit of this formidable enemy.

I wished I had had such a face-saving device. I had clearly sabotaged my chance to observe and photograph the first wild coyote I had managed to turn up. In view of the time and energy I had spent locating him, the setback seemed catastrophic. I did not feel simply discouraged; I felt defeated. How could I ever succeed in making observations of such an uncooperative subject?

The answer must have been waiting for my intellect to stop working, for it seeped into my consciousness like something I had always known but didn't know I knew. It was this: My whole approach to finding coyotes was based on a faulty premise. Whereas the whistle, or for that matter any other trapper method I had tried, no doubt would be effective for someone who wanted only the briefest opportunity to kill every coyote piped out of the brush, such tricks would not serve my purpose, which was to observe the animal over a long period of time in an undisturbed context. I recalled Lloyd's words earlier that morning: "You don't fool a coyote twice!" Certainly, the blue coyote would never again be tricked by a whistle. And if I were to continue to employ trapper methods, such as whistles and dogs, not only would I have to be satisfied with the briefest sightings and these always of different coyotes, but worse, I would see only one aspect of behavior, the investigatory impulse, over and over again. I was interested in knowing more than that about coyotes!

Curiously, now that the difficulties of my situation were be-

---

* With the exception of those dogs that have been specifically bred and trained to hunt and kill coyotes.

coming even more evident, my spirits lifted. The morning's lesson had been invaluable. I would start from the beginning again.

The vivid glimpse of the blue coyote, brief though it had been, now returned to my mind. Never again would the night song-sters seem mere phantoms to me; I had seen this member of their chorus clearly and he was real. Never again would my intellect, which concerns itself with such ideas as the place of each animal in the ecosystem, be entirely able to abstract this living subject who had looked me straight in the eye. Something deep within me, something elemental that hungers for contact with wildness, had been touched by the encounter. Coyotes were beings, and the mountain itself seemed permeated with the unseen presence of the little North American natives.

That was the morning I made up my mind. Come what may, I would pursue this project.

I did not immediately abandon the use of the whistle Vern had fashioned. On this initial field trip, while I was only surveying potential areas in which I might later work, the whistle was a handy device for evoking a response and determining the presence or absence of coyotes in a general way. I was also interested in experimenting with the whistle a bit more for another reason. I was curious to learn if our success in calling up the blue coyote in Dryhead had been a fluke, or if parent coyotes actually do locate their dispersed pups in the fall of the year through vocalization. One way to obtain a degree of substantiation for the theory was to repeat the trick in many different places and then seek to locate the respondents. If my call invariably produced a response from half-grown pups, I would have some evidence to support Vern's contention.

Though I had satisfied myself that coyotes existed in Dryhead, I had reservations about the place as a future study site. The fact that coyotes there ignored carrion made them less than desirable subjects. It seemed likely that intensive predator control over many years had selected for a more predatory, wily coyote. I decided to look elsewhere.

Lloyd Tillett was now as enthusiastic as I on the subject of wild canines, and he and Abbie invited me to return with them, remain at their ranch, and work in the vicinity as long as I wished. Though coyotes were scarce in the Bighorn Basin, I decided to accept their invitation. Local children had reported seeing a red male regularly hunting along the school-bus route, and I hoped to find him. The place they described was some eighteen miles from the Tillett ranch, in the lower foothills of the Bighorn Mountains. It, too, was not a place I would select to make long-range observations. There were too many baited coyote-getters in the vicinity. But for purposes of testing out the whistle, the location was fine.

So once again, before daybreak, Tillett and I were on the road   **13** searching for coyotes. We had no difficulty locating the spot described by the children, a stretch of creek bed that ran parallel to the highway for a few yards, where mice and gophers were in plentiful supply. But after searching, whistling, and glassing for two hours, we concluded that the children, perhaps to gain attention, had exaggerated the frequency of their sightings. Reluctantly we got into the pickup and left. A few miles down the highway, however, Lloyd pointed to a small flock of magpies hovering above a similar stretch of brushy bottomland.

"You want to watch magpies when you're out looking for coyotes," he remarked. "I've often noticed they travel together, the coyote and the magpie. I guess each thinks the other is on the inside track of something good to eat—and there he is!"

Lloyd swerved the pickup to the far side of the road, and even before he had stopped, I began shooting pictures of the big red coyote, who with superb dignity regarded us from not more than thirty feet away.

The magpies, angry at the interruption in this cooperative hunt, were making a terrible racket, but the coyote seemed not in the least perturbed. I began to wonder about the stories I had heard of his uncanny ability to sense whether or not a person is armed. He appeared to be in no hurry to be off and even seemed able to gauge how long it would be before I would climb out of the pickup and try for a closer picture. At that instant, and not before, he departed. In the meantime, he allowed me a satisfyingly long look.

He was a handsome animal, rufous red like a chow. His small eyes were glassy yellow, and his long face looked as if it belonged to a fox. I could see why the Indians believed the coyote to be a cross between the fox and the wolf. This particular animal, in fact, more nearly resembled a fox than he did his closest relative, the timber wolf, whose muzzle, like the dog's, is not so long and pointed.

Actually, the coyote and the wolf, though they belong to the same genus, are separate species. Separate species can sometimes interbreed, but ordinarily offspring of such unions are infertile. For example, the mule, which is a cross between a horse and a burro, is almost invariably sterile. Not so the wolf-coyote cross. The fertility of this hybrid has aroused speculation by many as to what factor other than size might have precluded coyotes and wolves from spontaneously interbreeding in the wild over long ages, with the consequent loss of identity of both types. It is generally presumed that differences in courtship and behavior have prevented this from happening. As will be seen, however, even behavioral barriers may break down when the population of either wolves or coyotes falls to an extreme low. In such instances, an occasional individual, deprived of a mate, has been suspected of consorting with a member of the opposite population who does not behave according to prescribed ritual. One subspecies of the red wolf, and the mystery canid of New Hampshire (to be discussed later), are suspected by some biologists to be examples of this type of cross.

Between wolves and foxes, on the other hand, there is little likelihood that such a mating, could it even occur, would result in conception. These two animals have different chromosomal counts, and though it is just barely conceivable that, under rare conditions, a wolf and a fox might produce hybrid young, the offspring would be sterile and could not perpetuate themselves. Therefore, the Indians' notion that the coyote is half-wolf, half-fox cannot be true. Yet, paradoxically, in behavior as well as in appearance, the coyote oftentimes seems more fox-like than wolf-like.

What now delighted me was the difference between the two coyotes I had encountered. If this species normally showed such variation I would have little difficulty identifying individuals and would not have to trap, band, and release the animals again—a technique practiced by many wildlife observers, but one I personally find objectionable.

The red coyote's behavior, too, was distinctly different from that of the blue coyote. He did not seem in the least timid. It was my first lesson in the wide range of individuality displayed by the adaptable coyote. As I disembarked from the truck, the insouciant creature trotted off in as unconcerned a manner as a small-town dog going about some important canine business on a Saturday morning. But though he appeared unhurried, I soon realized he was moving at a deceptively fast pace. At a dead run I could not close the gap, though twice the impertinent animal stopped and looked around to see if I was still following. When he circled back and crossed the highway, I decided to give up the footrace and work my way into a position where I could use the whistle. It would not fool this old male, but I hoped he might have some young scattered about. Perhaps they could be tricked into responding.

Vern had advised me to look for puppies in brushy areas alongside streambeds, and so Lloyd and I headed toward the thick tamarisk stand that bordered the Bighorn River. On this second test of the whistle, I was somewhat more confident of the outcome. This time it was Lloyd who was skeptical.

Coyotes make skillful use of vegetative cover. One peers from brush to try to locate the source of a predator-call whistle.

"I think it's too late in the morning for calling up coyotes," he said. "Besides, the old dog saw us."

But I urged him to try. My own performance on the piece of bent TV antenna was not yet very convincing. I could not risk blowing it myself. Lloyd, on the other hand, was becoming a master, as he proved a moment later by the response he evoked when he rendered a flawless coyote ululation. A high-pitched yipping of puppies pierced the air, resonating from a section of thick willows a half-mile downriver. We wasted no time getting there.

It was considerably easier to conceal ourselves on this occasion without an over-friendly dog along to give away our hiding places. We got behind some brush a few yards from the edge of the willow stand, and Lloyd piped the second call.

We waited in silence, staring at the thicket that rose like a fairytale wall before us. Suddenly a dog-like head poked out of the tangled brush and peered around. It belonged to a gray coyote, and, judging by his small muzzle, I concluded he was considerably younger than either of the two animals we had previously seen. His face wore an expression of expectation, which gave him a somewhat ludicrous look and made me think of the fox target one throws balls at in a carnival sideshow. After a short while, the head withdrew.

I glanced at Lloyd to see if he had seen the puppy and discovered him frantically waving his arms to attract my attention. A second half-grown coyote had fully emerged from the thicket at a point even nearer to the spot where we were hiding, and he, too, appeared to be watching and waiting for something, although he cautiously hung back against the cover, ready to dive into the brush at the first sign of anything strange. Had our coyote call fooled him? Was he looking for a red Papa to appear?

We held very still and watched the buffy creature with the oversized ears survey the landscape. Then, to my delight, he licked his chops and sat down on his haunches, looking for the world like a good little German-shepherd puppy waiting for dinner.

At this point I could no longer restrain myself, and I raised my camera to take his picture. I was seventy-five feet away and well concealed, but the click of the shutter alerted him to danger, and he disappeared into the brush. To our amazement, a moment later he emerged again, this time even closer to where he had heard Lloyd's call. While his tentative movements revealed extreme wariness, his urge to investigate must have been overpowering, for he hung back with his body and at the same time stretched forth his head and neck in a comical effort to peer at whatever was concealed in the bushes. Suddenly he must have seen us, for he vanished with a flick of his tail, which seemed to act as a rudder, spinning him around.

While our attention had been focused on this coyote, the first puppy, who had poked his head out only briefly, had evidently emerged again and, squirming along on his belly, had managed to crawl across open ground to a bush halfway between the thicket and our hiding places. Like a trained soldier, he had kept so close to the ground we had not seen him until now. Spooked by the second coyote, he revealed his presence by his hasty retreat.

Later we wondered if this creeping coyote had actually been the carnival head, or if yet a third pup had been in the area. Whatever their number, it was a fair assumption that the pale-gray adolescents were litter mates. And I suspect, since coyotes are known to be territorial,* they had been sired by or at least were closely related to the red male I had photographed in the vicinity that morning.

Before departing from the Tillett ranch, I spent a number of hours practicing on the whistle, until Lloyd declared my performance satisfactory. As I headed for Jackson Hole, Wyoming, where coyotes were reported to be more abundant, I was fairly confident of my ability to instigate coyote dialogue. My primary objective was to evaluate the National Elk Refuge as a possible place to work, and since I did not plan to return for five months it hardly mattered that my method would probably "wise up" any coyotes I succeeded in calling from cover. When I returned

* Ranchers should take note of this territoriality and think twice before exterminating coyotes that give no indication of being marauders. New coyote tenants—and these will surely arrive when the vacancy signs are out—may not be so circumspect.

I would not be using this device, though I had not yet figured out how else I would find coyotes.

I drove to the National Elk Refuge headquarters, introduced myself to the Department of Wildlife Service officials in charge, and explained my purpose. Manager Donald Redfearn, after approving my plans, permitted me special access to areas of the vast 23,860-acre sanctuary that are off limits to the casual visitor.

"Do coyotes bother the elk?" I asked.

Refuge biologist Buzz Robbins spoke up. "I've only seen one elk killed during eight years working here," he said. "That was a newborn calf. Pair of coyotes brought him down by working together. While one distracted the mother, the other ran in and made the kill. When they saw me they ran away, so I got a chance to weigh the intact carcass. It was exactly half the weight it should have been at birth. Only eighteen pounds. I guess something was wrong with it and probably the coyotes sensed it. That's the only time I've seen coyotes attack any elk here."

The sanctuary is the winter range of a large herd of some 7500 elk that annually funnel in from summer pastures in such places as Big Game Ridge in the Teton Wilderness and the southern section of Yellowstone National Park. It is a peaceful, improbably beautiful valley, bordered by the magnificent jagged-toothed Tetons on the northwest and the older, more roundly voluptuous Gros Ventre Range on the east. On the particular fall day I entered this setting, small bands of elk had already begun to arrive, tentatively picking their way through an aspen wood that fringed the Gros Ventre River on the northern edge of the refuge. Each band was led by at least one bull balancing a top-heavy rack upon his head. While I watched, they panicked and slipped back among the trees. Hunting season had started a few days earlier, while the elk were in migration, and no doubt these animals had faced much peril during their journey between sanctuaries. Though I was high on a butte a long way from them, the vigilant creatures seemed to sense my presence, and they did not emerge from cover again that day.

If elk could detect me at such a distance, I wondered what success I could expect to have with coyotes. I walked along the backbone of the butte and glassed in two directions, looking for signs of movement. But all was still. Then, on an impulse, I half-slid down the embankment to a midway point, where I climbed into a small spruce tree. Acting as if by preordained plan, I proceeded to organize my cameras for a photographic session. Then I reached for the whistle.

Below me was a willow stand surrounded by a network of streams that sprawled across the flats and converted many acres of the grassy plateau into a paradise for waterfowl. Canadian geese, mallards, redheads, and blue-winged teals honked and swept into the air at regular intervals. Then, after much cater-wauling, they would gradually flutter back to earth again like so many colored leaves. Beyond this marsh was a broad meadow neatly tufted with sagebrush, evenly spaced as if planted by a farmer. From where I sat, the willow stand was the only cover adequate to conceal an animal as large as a coyote, and it was only seventy-five feet below me. I was acting on a hunch. If I were a coyote, I would spend this hot and windy afternoon in that willow stand. I raised the whistle to my lips and blew.

As if on cue, a light-colored female with a black-tipped tail emerged from the brush, took several steps forward, and sat down. I noticed at once that her right front leg was useless, and I wondered if she had at some time been caught in a trap and worked herself free. I further wondered how she could hunt with such a handicap. Perhaps she hid in the thicket and de-pended on her mate to bring her food! I had heard, and later confirmed myself through observation, that a male coyote will bring food to his mate during the time she is occupied with the care and nursing of young pups. In time, I would even be witness to a male coyote regurgitating food for a mate too shy to feed on a road-killed deer. But at this early stage of my research, I could only wonder if the coyote was capable of such solicitous behavior.

It was obvious that the tip-tailed female had responded to the whistle in the same anticipatory manner as the half-grown pup-pies Lloyd Tillett and I had called up. She looked about inces-santly, fixing her gaze from time to time on various points that may have been her usual travel routes. She seemed to be expecting something to appear. Luckily, however, she did not look into the tree where I was precariously perched.

Suddenly, from behind her, a clumsy puppy waggled out of the brush and squirmed toward her on his belly. His ears were laid flat, his tongue was making rapid licking motions, and his tail was pumping so hard it seemed to be propelling him along. His affectionate display was not returned by "Tip Tail," however, whom I assumed to be his mother. She gave him a nip that sent him instantly back into cover. Then, after furtively surveying the scene once again, she limped back into the willows herself.

I had managed to take a half-dozen pictures without being seen, and I wondered what to do next. From the tree I had an aerial view of the willow clump, which I now knew contained at least two coyotes. Neither could leave without my seeing them. Moreover, if I waited long enough, perhaps the female's mate, or whomever she seemed to be anticipating, would appear. I sat in the tree for an hour. Then another hour passed. At last I decided to try to call her out again. Once again I blew the whistle. This time the female emerged more boldly and came all the way down to the base of the butte, where gushed a stream. The sound of the water fortunately muffled the noise of my camera, which was clicking like an angry chickadee.

But Tip Tail did not pose for me. Instead, with purposeful movements, she headed for a broken willow branch suspended across the stream by wind, flood, or perhaps the labor of a marten. Even with a limp paw, she seemed able to maneuver about without much difficulty, and to my amazement managed to walk tightrope across this makeshift bridge on three legs. The upside-down reflection of this stunt in the water looked so unreal through my lens I could not be sure I had actually witnessed it until later when my photographs were developed.

Then she scrambled up and began sniffing the ground directly beneath my tree. Here, of course, she picked up the scent of my track, and like a detonated Roman candle, off she shot; up over the butte she sprinted and was gone.

I sat in my tree for another hour before I blew the whistle again. Now that Mama (?) was gone, I hoped to lure the puppy out. But though I played my tune as well as before, the whistle failed to conjure up any more coyotes. Since I knew the young pup could not have left without my seeing him, I wondered if Tip Tail had communicated instructions to him to stay under cover. I remained in the tree until nightfall. Then I left. Predictably, I never saw those coyotes again.

In a few days I moved base to another part of the refuge, called Flat Creek. At this time of year Flat Creek was only an empty, boulder-clogged crack in the earth, but it was edged with giant cottonwoods and the shade was pleasant. When I played my game of "If I were a coyote where would I . . ." I decided that Flat Creek would be a good place to set up operations.

I was right. While lugging my equipment from the station wagon, which I had parked on a jeep road some distance back, I spotted a little grizzled fellow hunting in the dry streambed. Instantly, I dropped to the ground in a most unpropitious spot, whence I had to wriggle and squirm to a nearby rise, very low and without vegetation, but the only cover available. To further shield myself from the coyote's view, I proceeded to pile up what stones were within reach, and somehow I managed to build a low fortress. But the effort was tiring. For several minutes I lay on my stomach dragging on the mountain air and watched the young coyote (who was probably no older than six months) as he hunted mice.

Like a champion pointer, a coyote takes a sighting on a potential victim and remains immobile. The author clocked one such "freeze" at eleven minutes.

Like a dog intrigued by a squeaky toy, he focused his attention on a particular patch of ground and cocked his head from side to side. All at once he leaned forward and froze, one paw lifted, in as graceful a pose as any trained pointer ever assumed. I knew he had his quarry pinpointed and, like a Zen devotee, would in good time direct a blow, suddenly and expertly, neither too soon nor too late, but at precisely the right instant. Even at his tender age, this pup would have the poise to await that moment, however long it might be in coming. For five and a half minutes by my watch, he stood like a stone. Then he leaped. In midair he jackknifed, and when he landed, all four feet were neatly planted together and his victim was pinned to the ground.

The thought occurred to me that if I had the patience to remain as still as this baby coyote, perhaps I might succeed in my venture. The trouble was that every time I tried to remain quiet, an insect buzzed in my ear, a stone bruised my kneecap, or my scalp itched. I was not the equal of the little wild canid, who seemed to have his nervous system completely under control.

He quickly swallowed his mouse dinner without much chewing, and I decided it was time to take out my whistle to see how this hunter would respond. I piped.

Like a well-behaved dog summoned by his owner, the young coyote sprinted toward me, totally unmindful of hidden danger. Until he was within fifteen feet of me he failed to suspect the

A flying leap secures the quarry.

trick, but when he did, he whirled in midair and, without losing momentum, shifted direction and departed in leaps that looked to be eight feet long. I had managed to focus one shot while he was at the nearest point.

Though I was now more than ever intrigued by the question—Do dispersed coyote families give vocal signals to arrange meetings?—I found it hard to believe my imitation howl was convincing enough to be confused with the voice of a known parent. The thought occurred to me that unsuspecting, hungry pups might not be too discriminating. By contrast, the adult Tip Tail had shown great caution and had not responded vocally to my whistle.

Nevertheless, as I was obviously getting a puppy response, something was being communicated. Or would the young spontaneously answer any siren or ululation? Although they had not responded to my "dying rabbit" whistles, I suspected they might reply to any approximation of a coyote vocalization. John Theberge, who studied wolf communication, found that pack members transferred information regarding their location, identity, and emotional state by means of frequency and duration of sound. He also found two types of communication were employed, which he designated "universal" and "individual." Universal communication (such as a growl) seemed to be automatically understood by every member within the species. By contrast, individual communication evolved among wolves who had learned to recognize the individual traits of the animals with whom they associated.

Perhaps the pups were responding to some universal frequency of sound that Vern Dorn had succeeded in building into the TV-antenna whistle. More likely, though, the expectation of the pups that their parents would signal them explained their readiness to respond. Either way, my limited experimentation with the whistle lent support to Vern's contention that half-grown pups and parent coyotes are still communicating with one another as late as October.

Although coyotes seemed abundant on the National Elk Refuge and, more important, were not persecuted by the refuge managers, I was not convinced that it was an ideal setting in

which to make long-range observations. Conditions were somewhat abnormal. Elk were winter fed and, as a result of living
on a dole, enjoyed high survival success, while other competing
herbivores were largely absent. More serious was the lack of
other predator-scavengers. Erratic waves of explorers, exploiters, settlers, and, finally, the tourist industry had pressured the
last bear back into the Tetons not long after the last wolf was
extirpated. It was important to me, or at least I thought it was, to
see the coyote in a more normal setting in order to know who he
is. For today, wherever the tenacious coyote has become the only
viable meat-eater, he may, also by default, have edged into an
ecological niche belonging to the bear, the badger, the weasel,
the wolf, or any other vanished predator. Nature will be served,
and when the coyote alone must bear the burden (or is granted
the privilege) of carrying out her functions, it is not surprising
that he sometimes wears a strange disguise.

But it was not this disguise I wanted to see. I wanted to know
the coyote as he behaved within a normal hierarchy of animals.
In such a condition, his activities would certainly be influenced
by the needs and strengths of other species. For example, where
a variety of predators abounded, he might be the last animal
permitted to feed on a carcass, instead of the only one. Moreover, his range and movements would very likely be restricted
by the territories of more powerful competitors, and thus his
population might be curbed for want of appropriate den sites.
Or, conversely, perhaps he would benefit from the presence of
wolves or bears in his habitat. The leftover scraps of a grizzly or
wolf kill would provide the little scavenger with food he might
otherwise not obtain.

But where in America would I find him in a balanced context?
Surely not where ranching interests have exterminated even
predatory birds, alleging them capable of killing lambs.
Nor in those places where state wildlife agencies, acting exclusively on behalf of hunters, have augmented target herds to
unnatural proportions by reducing populations of competing
species and natural enemies. In such locales, it is understand-
able that the coyote has transformed himself into a marauder or
a dump raider, and even succeeded in overcoming his normal

scavenger impulses in favor of feeding exclusively on fresh-killed meat.

I could think of only two national parks—Yellowstone and Glacier—where efforts have been made in recent years to restore the task of balancing nature to Nature herself. Ironically, in these two places, park managers have endured severe criticism for their "revolutionary practices." Not only have sportsmen expressed dissatisfaction over being denied hunting privileges within Yellowstone Park boundaries, but even a non-exploitative segment of the public has had difficulty comprehending why the park managers should refuse to intervene when a natural calamity befalls a group of animals. Many people fail to see that so-called acts of kindness, such as dropping hay to oversized elk herds or rescuing stranded animals by helicopter, give rise to new problems. Ultimately, a herd that has been artificially maintained must be artificially culled, and when such a time arrives, the selection of individual animals to be killed will be done in a most arbitrary manner. Unlike Nature, man is unable to discriminate which individuals are unhealthy, unfit, and stupid. He shoots either at random or perhaps selects for antler size. As a result he removes prime animals from the gene pool.

Though in times past Yellowstone wildlife had been subjected to artificial regulation, the park still contained a dozen predator species, albeit half of these were rarely sighted. I decided to research further.

When what is now Yellowstone National Park was the summer camp of the Crow Indians, the coyote had little to fear from man. His place in the Indian's heart, as well as on his hunting ground, was secure. When the white man began to explore the West, most wildlife, the coyote included, displayed hardly more fear of him than of any other alien species in their midst. Flight distance, or the nearest point to which a man might approach before an animal would flee, was not very great. The Indian's mode of hunting had not instilled in the creatures of forest and plain the terrible panic reactions they now exhibit at the mere sight of a human silhouette on a far horizon. The Indian's weapons could be flung but a limited distance, the range of which was perfectly understood by the target animals. Moreover, the Indian's view of wildlife was of a different order than the white man's, and this difference no doubt was reflected in his very demeanor. It would have been inconceivable to an Indian to slaughter an animal merely "because it was there." Animals were not regarded as objects but as embodied spirits animated by the same life force that sustains man himself, and when of necessity one had to be killed for food, shelter, or religious ceremony, forgiveness often was asked of the victim-to-be. The rest of the time Indians remained at peace with their quarry and at times could pass among game herds without creating a disturbance. In this respect they were like the well-fed wolves that can lie down beside the caribou herd they trail and sometimes prey upon, for the prey species seemed to have little difficulty assessing both the capabilities and the intention of their natural enemies and they took their cues to run away or remain quiet accordingly. Bullets had not yet eliminated from the population all but the most edgy individuals.

The white man changed all this. Predators, as well as ungulates, quickly learned his treacherous ways and began to vanish at the first inkling of a human being. In 1843, Lansford Warren **27**

Hasting, while traveling through California, noted that the prairie wolves (coyotes) were numerous and passed "within a few yards of you." But before the century ended, no coyote or any other creature lingered for a backward look. The white man, bent on exploiting whatever resource he chanced upon, fired on everything that moved.

Often this wanton slaying was carried out as much to relieve boredom as to supply need or gain profit, as demonstrated by the wanton killing of buffalo by men like Buffalo Bill Cody, who did not even bother to dress the carcasses he left rotting in his wake. The soldier-of-fortune types who set out to find adventure in the West often were ill-equipped spiritually for the solitude that actually confronted them when they reached their destination, and many sought to create excitement with their Colt pistols. Moreover, nothing in the white man's experience had prepared him for such easy targets as the naive creatures that grazed only a short distance beyond the range of arrows. These animals seemed to be "asking to be killed." And since in the white man's view the West was inexhaustible anyway, it hardly mattered to him how many were pointlessly slaughtered.

Animals in the American West were not alone in feeling the pressure of rapid expansionism during the nineteenth century. Wherever the white man roamed, whether in Africa, India, or North America, he carried his guns, and wild animals began to disappear. During the one hundred years between 1800 and 1900, every eighteen months an average of one species of animal was brought to extinction.* It is not surprising therefore that the lengthening of flight distance became a worldwide phenomenon.**

* It is tempting to overlook present-day carnage and focus on the obvious misdeeds of the past. But facts indicate that today one species of animal disappears from this earth forever every *twelve* months.
** In a few isolated places animals escaped contact with man until the present century. In 1956 members of an expedition to Antarctica encountered some naive penguins that waddled toward them in a friendly investigatory manner. Obviously, these flocks had never before seen members of the human race. The trustful birds were clubbed to death.

The Indians were the first to notice this change, and they protested to the white man that his method of killing was leaving the surviving animals "deranged" and impossible to approach and hunt on horseback using bows and arrows. Furthermore, they claimed that many animals were changing not only their habits, but their habitats as well. Elk were no longer found on the plains. Antelope could not be lured to a fluttering object, but had become the most flighty of creatures. And even the trickster coyote had transformed himself into a skulking fugitive. In North America wildlife had had a taste of civilized man and was seeking hiding places.

But wilderness areas were also being conquered, and so the hiding places failed to provide safety for long. Even in Yellowstone National Park, a place set aside by Congress in 1872 to be preserved intact for the use and enjoyment of all people, many species of animals were not granted sanctuary. Early managers saw nothing inconsistent in their policy of hunting predators and the mandate given them by Congress to preserve the area in its natural state. In their view, preserving wildlife meant protecting "good" animals from "bad" ones.

Good animals, of course, were those edible creatures that man himself enjoyed hunting and liked to find in abundance. Bad animals, on the other hand, were those creatures that competed with human hunters for game. Good animals were bison, deer, moose, elk, antelope, and bighorn sheep. Bad animals were wolves, pumas, and coyotes.

It should be pointed out that this illogical program of fostering target species and eliminating predators in Yellowstone was carried out despite the fact that hunting of game was not permitted in the park. Nevertheless, so imbued were those in charge with the prevailing attitudes of the day, they saw nothing irrational in their policies.

But even then a few voices cried out on behalf of the wilderness. President Theodore Roosevelt, to name one, sent a letter on White House stationery to Lieutenant General S. B. M. Young, superintendent of Yellowstone National Park, dated January 22, 1908. It read:

Dear General Young:

I do not think any more cougars (mountain lions) should be killed in the park. Game is abundant. We want to profit by what has happened in the English preserves, where it proved to be bad for the grouse itself to kill off all the peregrine falcons and all the other birds of prey. It may be advisable, in case the ranks of the deer and antelope right around the Springs should be too heavily killed out, to kill some of the cougars there, but in the rest of the park I certainly would not kill any of them. On the contrary, they ought to be let alone.

Sincerely yours,
Theodore Roosevelt

But the President's advice was ignored, and as a result cougars continued to be run down with trained dogs, and wolves to be poisoned.

Park managers compounded the problem they were creating by applying a ranching concept to the management of large ungulates. Attempts were made to offset mortality from disease, inclement weather, and hunger. Hay was fed to the elk, the mule deer, and the bighorn sheep that inhabited the northwest section of the park. And in the Lamar Valley, bison were managed intensively for a period of nearly forty years. Unlike ranch-raised livestock, however, where the yield of husbandry is sent to market, this artificial support of a high population of park animals made no sense.

One early superintendent, U.S. Army Captain F. A. Boutelle, complained in 1889 that "the whole country of the Park seems stocked to its capacity for feeding." Yet that same year Boutelle recommended stepping up predator control, stating that "the herds of buffalo and elk do not seem to have enough calves." Unlimited expansion of select animals still seemed to him to be an index of good wildlife management.

Naturally, this viewpoint was supported by many local people who liked to hunt in areas adjacent to the park. A part of one elk herd in particular, which migrated across the northern Yellowstone boundary, provided seasonal sport. When these animals abandoned their summer range and headed for winter pasture outside the protection of their sanctuary, hunters waited along what came to be known as "the firing line" to greet them with volleys of gunfire. As a result, a substantial number of this migratory portion of the herd no longer leaves the park. Yellowstone biologists speculate that many of the old lead bulls and cows with knowledge of the migration pattern might have been gunned down, and a large percentage of the present herd may no longer have any memory of the way. Some old-timers who live in the border town of Gardiner have quite another explanation for the phenomenon. They say that between 1955 and 1965 elk numbers were too severely thinned, not by hunters but by the park managers themselves.

"We used to see thousands of hunters here in the winter," one man complained to me. "The town of Gardiner just came alive in elk season. Now if those dumb college-bred experts in the park would just leave the elk alone and get rid of all those coyotes in there, maybe we'd have good hunting around here again."

Though this man's attitude is hardly representative of the attitude of the inhabitants of Gardiner, widespread public protest was raised over the culling of elk by Yellowstone rangers, a program that was terminated in the winter of 1967–68. Before that time it was believed that such measures were necessary, in part because of the reluctance of animals to migrate out of park boundaries during the winter months. Too many elk, it was thought, might eat up the winter range.

But the storm generated by this policy grew so heated that in March 1967 public hearings were scheduled. Present at these were animal-lovers who expressed horror at the idea of rangers slaughtering semitame animals within the park borders. Sportsmen, on the other hand, disapproved for other reasons. They resented the fact that rangers, instead of themselves, were having the pleasure of gunning down the so-called surplus. They wanted the park opened to public hunting.

That such activity might result in avoidance behavior toward human beings on the part of Yellowstone wildlife either escaped these individuals or was deemed by them to be of no consequence. Despite the fact that the primary purpose of the park is to give visitors an opportunity to see native animal and plant life in a natural and undisturbed setting, some people believed the fauna had become too accustomed to tourists and, as a consequence, unnaturally docile. Hunting, they said, would reinstill normal fear reactions in them.

Fortunately, a large number of professional biologists and wildlife enthusiasts also voiced their opinions. And though even among these individuals there was disagreement, at least their concern was disinterested. Yet no one seemed to possess a ready solution to the apparent problems created by nearly a century of human manipulation. Should some predator specimens—e.g., wolves or cougars—be introduced to elevate their population levels? Should prey species continue to be culled? Or should man keep his meddlesome hands off and accept the existing animals in their present situation?

Some thought that damage to habitat would inevitably occur unless man continued to regulate herbivore numbers. Habitat, of course, would recover in time, but perhaps not time as man understands it. Others believed the present condition of the vegetation to be similar to historic trends. Where wild animals exist, vegetation can hardly conform to the standards imposed by range managers.

But if man's knowledge of the park biosystems was lacking, at least that might be remedied. Four on-site biologists studying natural population regulation and related questions succeeded in generating a moratorium on elk culling and on the artificial control of bison, deer, and pronghorn antelope for at least as long as their work was in progress. Their data on bison and elk have already produced convincing evidence that wild animals, even in the absence of predators, are self-regulatory. Though herd numbers do fluctuate, periodic drops seem to correlate with the severity of winter. Harsh weather, it appears, may predispose numbers of animals to weaken and die of a variety of secondary causes, including malnutrition, disease, stress, accident, and increased predation. While social-behavior factors may determine which animals survive during such stressful times, the secondary causes of mortality are largely compensatory. Should one fail to operate, another will take the toll. If, then, periodically severe weather is indeed the primary controlling factor, predators should be regarded only as an adjunct to the system, and man, therefore, need not substitute his bullets for their fangs and claws. Nature's backup systems will prevent the elk population from increasing to the point where habitat would be irreparably destroyed.

Park biologists say that this research, while seeming to be revolutionary, is in agreement with studies on population intercompensation made by the esteemed biologist P. L. Errington and, moreover, has added nothing new even to Charles Darwin's insight into the nature of animals' relationship with their environment. No species can be capable of progressively reducing its own food sources or it would become extinct. Since fossil records indicate that elk may have inhabited the Yellowstone area for at least 30,000 years before the arrival of modern man, it seems a fair assumption that the animal's fate and that of its winter range do not rest wholly upon the shoulders of park managers.

The battle for and against artificial regulation of Yellowstone elk was reminiscent of an even more dramatic fight waged some thirty years earlier over the question of coyote-control operations. By the 1930s wolves and cougars were rarely sighted and so no longer persecuted. But records show that between 1907 and 1935 an average of 150 coyotes were killed annually; yet during those same years Yellowstone personnel often complained of having difficulty keeping *Canis latrans* numbers down! Perhaps the coyote, who previously had filled only a secondary consumer niche in the ecosystem, had actually benefited from a predator-control program that had had a more devastating effect on a stronger predator, the wolf, leaving its food sources to him. Or perhaps, more simply, the control program was not intensive enough to affect the breeding population of the clever coyote. In those years such poisons as 1080 had not yet been developed, nor were animals hunted from the air. Whatever the reason, Yellowstone coyotes withstood the assault on themselves so impressively that in 1935, when predator control was finally terminated, local livestock growers expressed apprehension that the park population might serve as a breeding reservoir and spread to surrounding areas.

An early, unforeseen result of the discontinuation of predator control only served to confuse the issue. Coyotes, when no longer persecuted, grew less wary and as a consequence more visible. Flight distance had apparently begun to shorten again. Many people, a few park officials included, misinterpreted this to mean numbers were growing.

Most park officials, however, had slowly come around to the opinion that in the case of the coyote, all previous control efforts had been an utter waste of time and money anyway and had had little or no effect on population size. None of the methods had been potent enough to reach down into the breeding members of the population; only surplus, expendable animals had ever really been affected. The removal of these left survivors more food, and as a consequence they produced healthier and larger litters, which immediately compensated for the coyotes that had been eliminated. Control had not put a dent in their population.

Some local ranchers, however, were unable to accept this view and wanted predator control to be reinstated in the park. Then, in 1937, a young biologist by the name of Adolph Murie came on the scene and began his peerless study of the coyote in Yellowstone. Though at the time Murie's report was made, in 1941, some park officials were reluctant to accept his findings, today his book stands as the authoritative study on the relationship of the coyote to prey species. It clearly acquits *Canis latrans* of playing a villain's role in nature. Moreover, more than any single work, *Ecology of the Coyote in the Yellowstone* by Adolph Murie confirms the correctness of the park's decision to terminate its fifty-year campaign against the coyote. Today the species has nothing to fear from Yellowstone rangers. It is highly regarded as a valuable component of the park's ecosystem.

I was eager to meet the man who had played such a part in bringing about this change of attitude, and so on my way to Yellowstone I made a detour to Moose, Wyoming, where Adolph Murie and his wife, Louise, were among the handful of people living within the borders of the Grand Teton National Park.

Some thirty-five years after completing his field study on *Canis latrans*, Adolph Murie met me at the door of his lodgepole-pine cabin and ushered me in, eager to talk about coyotes. Murie is probably best known to the general public for his pioneer study on wolves. It was he who first observed the sociable nature of the wolf and the astonishing cooperation of pack members in the care and rearing of cubs. And it was he who first dispelled the myth that the wolf is a bloodthirsty beast hungering for a taste of human flesh. For two years during the 1940s he lived in Alaska within close range of a group of Arctic wolves. During this period he succeeded in identifying and noting the behavior of every member of the pack. Their friendliness toward one another especially impressed him. Whenever two wolves met, he observed that they greeted by wagging their tails and licking one another, much as a dog will respond to his owner. Murie began to have serious doubts that an animal with such a gregarious nature could be the vicious beast men had supposed. Later, when he tried to approach and discovered the pack did nothing more hostile than bark, the ancient lie had to be put to rest. On one occasion he even crawled into a den to get a look at some newborn cubs, yet no adult wolf made a move against him.

Since the publication of *The Wolves of Mount McKinley* in 1944, many wolf-watchers have followed Murie's leads and all have confirmed what no white man had previously been able to see—that the wolf is a highly social animal who manifests his attachment to members of his own pack in a manner similar to that of his domestic counterpart, the dog, toward man.

Murie's lesser-known study, *Ecology of the Coyote in the Yellowstone*, was published by the Government Printing Office as part of the Fauna Series, and serious biologists immediately recognized the importance of the work. Today the book has become difficult to find, for after it went out of print, library copies

frequently disappeared into the hands of students and interested wildlife buffs. To obtain the work, I had to write to the
head of the National Park Service in Washington, D.C., who
granted me the privilege of borrowing it for the limited period
of one month.

From the fall of 1936 until the spring of 1939, Murie combed
the Yellowstone River basin, Mount Everts, and the Lamar
Valley, collecting scraps of evidence in the form of bones,
feathers, and teeth, performing autopsies on every carcass he
came upon, sifting through thousands of coyote scats to learn
what they contained, and, most important, observing the interactions of coyotes with other species. Gradually, from his mass
of notes, he came to the conclusion that coyote predation on
game animals is minimal, highly selective, and very likely beneficial to the prey species.

As we talked, Adolph Murie recalled that even while his work
was in progress many people seemed worried by the conclusions
he seemed to be reaching, and they went out of their way to show
him carcasses of game animals supposedly killed by coyotes. Yet,
time after time, when he followed up these reports of a half-
eaten deer or an antelope "lying in a hollow where coyotes had
probably cornered it," he found that the dead animal had died
of other causes. Some were heavily infested with lungworms,
botfly larvae, and other deadly parasites. A great many showed
evidence of necrosis of the bones and teeth. And still others had
succumbed to injuries inflicted on them at an earlier time by
careless human beings, hit-and-run drivers or hunters along the
park border who were poor shots. When a coyote lucked onto
such a windfall he naturally fed on the remains, leaving his
telltale tracks behind to indict him falsely.

Opposite: An ambi-
tious coyote? Not
really. In winter,
coyotes linger
near herds of
large ungulates,
feeding on those
animals that
inevitably
succumb to old
age and disease.

"I was never eyewitness to coyote predation on the so-called
game animals. Incidentally, I dislike that term for wild ungulates," he told me. "And even in those instances where circumstantial evidence pointed to the possibility that coyote predation
may have occurred, the victims were so frequently in poor
condition, I would ascribe their death to other causes. Predation
may have hastened the inevitable, but the animals were already
doomed."

Healthy elk need
only raise their
hackle hairs to
cause coyotes to
scurry for cover.
Here an angry elk
cow puts to flight
an individual who
failed to heed her
warning.

It would appear that coyotes in Yellowstone could easily avail themselves of a plentiful supply of already doomed animals. Perhaps, by helping even the poorest specimens to survive, park managers may have inadvertently lowered the overall vitality of the herds. The coyote, on the other hand, by selectively culling the unfit, was a positive influence, his effect on wildlife salutary.

Murie revealed that he paid particular attention to the possibility that coyotes might be responsible for taking a heavy toll of newborn animals, healthy but defenseless. To his surprise, however, evidence pointed to the fact that weak calves and fawns born to undernourished mothers were the ones susceptible to attack. When both mother and offspring were strong, the coyote had little chance of making a kill, maternal protectiveness being too highly developed in the ungulates. "A healthy doe or cow elk need only raise her back hairs to make a coyote scurry for cover!" he said.

His evidence also contradicted the notion that because coyotes are without natural enemies their population, if unchecked by man, will inevitably explode. He found disease their constant adversary, encountering some animals so weak they could even be run down on foot. Starvation turned out to be a major cause of mortality among coyotes.* During hard winters, when the herd animals grew thin and died by the score, the little scavengers were able to find a sufficient number of carcasses to keep themselves alive. But conversely, when winters were relatively mild and the elk and deer fared well, the coyotes themselves grew emaciated and succumbed to starvation. Even snow

---

* Thus, the ideas of population intercompensation propounded by Errington apply to predators as well as to prey species. Just as available food will limit the size of a herd of elk and not the other way around, so it is the availability of food animals that places a limit on the number of predators which can be sustained in a given habitat; it is not, as has been presumed for so long, the predator who restricts the size of the prey population! Moving up the food chain, life becomes more tenuous and dependent upon an ever larger number of natural factors. Whereas prey are dependent upon forage, predators are dependent upon prey who are dependent upon forage. Under natural conditions, therefore, there can never exist as many predators as prey, for it is the predator species that hang in precarious balance. And it is the predator animals that, out of ignorance and greed, we have most pressured until now they are absent from large sections of North America.

conditions played a decisive role in whether or not the coyotes made it through the winter. If the snow crusted over so that the lightweight canines could walk on top, they managed to maneuver about and find food; if the snow was too soft and powdery to support them, the coyotes became exhausted floundering in deep drifts, and many died.

As for Yellowstone becoming a prolific breeding ground for coyotes who would then spread into the neighboring communities, he dismissed the notion. The forested region adjacent to the park already carried a permanent coyote population. A few emigrants might penetrate the home ranges of entrenched animals, but most of these would be harvested by trappers who worked the area.

During the period that Murie was researching the coyote in Yellowstone, predator control was suspended in the park. After his work was completed, he recommended that park officials not reinstitute their former policy but allow the natural interaction of flora and fauna to become reestablished. As he saw it, such a condition not only would be more interesting to man, but would be beneficial to all species of animals living there, including ungulates, who for uncounted ages had coexisted with coyotes and even wolves without being driven into extinction. Surely, he concluded, Nature must have endowed these creatures with the ability to take care of themselves.

Fortunately, park officials heeded Murie's advice.* Predator control was terminated. Today in Yellowstone the coyote is a common sight and one that delights visitors nearly as much as the appearance of bears. For that matter, even the once-maligned wolf would engender nothing but excitement should he become more visible today.

In the past, many mistakes were made by well-meaning people who lacked an understanding of the interdependency of coexisting life systems. Present-day park managers have a difficult task trying to rectify these errors while at the same time not creating new imbalances. For the most part, animal populations

---

* While this book was in preparation, I was saddened to learn of the death of Dr. Adolph Murie, whom I had come to regard as a friend.

are now allowed to regulate themselves. As one park official put it, "We have stopped playing God."

Before surveying Yellowstone as a possible site for a field study, I drove to headquarters at Mammoth to talk with park officials.

"Come in winter," I was advised. "The best time to look for coyotes is in February and March, during their mating season. They tend to be more visible against a snow background, and you'll more or less have the park to yourself then, too."

I asked advice in the event of an encounter with Bruin. Though bears hibernate, the first grizzlies emerge before the end of March.

"Don't use any predator-call whistles. Don't run, but move away and, if possible, climb a tree."

"Wearing snowshoes?" I asked.

"If worse comes to worst, play dead," I was told.

As I set off to reconnoiter the Lamar Valley, a part of my mind had already made a decision. Yellowstone has been far less disturbed than most wilderness areas, and present managers are doing their best to ensure that Nature retain her rightful sovereignty there. The park would be a good place to observe the coyote, and especially to witness his struggle for survival, not against man but against almighty Nature when she is doing her worst.

Though it was only October, a few wet snowflakes were beginning to fall as I climbed a rocky ridge above Pebble Creek for a better view of the Lamar Valley. An enormous meadow covered with sagebrush and grass rolled below me. It appeared empty, but it was undoubtedly rife with life. Surrounding this vast valley and encasing it were gentle slopes. On one distant bulge, I began to make out moving specks. It took me some time to determine that these were elk. From such a distance they appeared to be insects, their ungainly antlers resembling antennae. Behind the elk stretched a long moraine covered with aspen groves, which probably sheltered moose and some antelope.

Quiet had begun to settle on the park. Only an occasional car hummed along the ugly gray scar that was a highway below. It was the end of the season and soon the last of the season's tourists would leave and Yellowstone would essentially revert to the animals. As I drank in the space and the silence, a coyote barked twice, throwing his voice in such a way that I hadn't a clue where he stood.

"Hello, yourself," I shouted to the ridge behind me. Now that my mind was made up to return, anticipation was rising in me like the wind that had suddenly come up and carried away my voice.

"Have a good look at me then," I called to the phantom creature, "because I'm coming baaaaaaack!"

The coyote barked again, as if to say, "Go back! Go *back!* You're on my domain!"

I could not go back now, though. I was committed and waiting for winter, when I would enjoy a white park by myself.

A
Sea
of
Snow

In February, when I returned to Yellowstone, weather conditions did not favor my endeavors. The snow was deep and soft. Winter had been unusually mild, and much of the base was in a state of thaw. In many places the thin, hard crust that formed each night on top of the year's accumulation did not support my weight, and when this fragile icing broke, the slush sucked me down, snowshoes and all. I was better off not wearing my Bear Paws, for the effort required to pull them out of the drifts was more than I could sustain. I switched instead to high rubber boots but these, too, failed to answer. With each step I plunged in so deep I could not swing my legs out of my own tracks.

For a time I was stymied, until I gradually learned to read the snow patterns and discovered that in certain places furrows created by wind action over the course of the winter revealed shallow snow, often but a foot or two deep. Though it was tiring to plow along these in high boots, it was nevertheless not impossible. I also discovered that I could maneuver about on slopes where shade prevented the snow from softening. There a firm crust often supported me, and I walked on snowshoes as easily as if on bare ground.

The coyotes, too, were having difficulty, but to a lesser degree. Their lack of appreciable weight made it possible for them to tread on thin ice, so to speak, and they managed to maneuver about wherever they pleased. When crossing a particularly weak surface, however, they moved with the utmost caution, neither running nor trotting but tentatively placing one foot in front of the other. Should a testing front paw break through the eggshell-thin crust, the wary animal was usually quick enough to avoid disaster by shifting direction. But on those occasions when a hapless creature did break through, he often had difficulty regaining a foothold. His very struggle to extricate himself defeated him, for the fragile icing would support only his most **47** delicate tread. Once mired, his best hope was to leap and lunge toward some windswept island of rock or oasis of ice, where he could climb out of his predicament.

At the end of winter, with food scarce and every calorie of energy needed to battle cold and avoid starvation, the depleted coyotes could ill afford to spend themselves in this way. The punishing effort of literally swimming across a quarter of a mile of snow would render even the most fit animal incapable of further activity. And while recuperating from the stress, a languishing coyote would necessarily fast, thus reducing further his ability and inclination ever again to find food.

During winter, coyotes, like all wildlife, function on low reserves, and any extraordinary effort not only incapacitates them but sets up the chain reaction described above. The popular winter pastime of chasing animals by snowmobile is not the innocuous sport its adherents claim. Though no shots may be fired, the act of driving an animal to exhaustion in freezing weather is tantamount to killing it, for a broken-winded coyote or a deer left panting will not afterward seek food. During this most precarious time of year, when stored energy is low and must be conserved or quickly replenished, a single day of fast may spell the difference between survival or death. Recognition of the dire effects of snowmobiling on wildlife has led legislators to draw up measures to halt some of the abuses. Montana has passed a law that forbids "driving, rallying or harassing any of the game animals, game birds or fur bearing animals of the state with snowmobiles." This law, however, does not protect the coyote. Obviously, in Montana only exploitable game and fur-bearing animals are granted humane consideration.

Though unplowed roads in Yellowstone Park are open to snowmobilers, chasing of animals is strictly forbidden and, it is hoped, does not occur. A similar regulation in nearby Grand Teton National Park has been disgracefully flouted by the public. There in 1971 two men were caught in the act of running over exhausted coyotes with their machines. In court they explained they meant to transport the bodies of the victims to a sheep-rearing area where bounties would be paid for them.

(More coyote migration occurs after death than while the coyotes are still on four legs.) Park rangers, although they are often called out to investigate reports of such incidents, told me that they are seldom successful in apprehending the culprits in the act.

Not surprisingly, outside the federal park system, chasing coyotes in deep snow is not only lawful, but regarded as clean family fun.* Near Jackson Hole, Wyoming, several youngsters boasted to me that they enjoyed running over coyotes with their machines because they liked to see them get buried in snow. My ill-concealed horror elicited the following explanation from one of the youngsters: "The coyotes don't get hurt 'cause the snow is soft, and when they come up again they sure look funny running with their tongues hanging so far out of their mouths."

I asked the boy what he did after spending a day in this manner, and he replied that he went home to eat his dinner. When I asked him what he thought became of the coyotes he had driven to exhaustion, he was at a loss to know. I daresay most snowmobilers do not reflect on the consequences of their activities, and I am sure many would be surprised to learn they have signed death warrants for the animals they only meant to pursue for a lark.

In the northernmost part of the 2.2-million-acre park, where I tracked coyotes, snowmobiling is at no time permitted, and for that matter, by the time I arrived in February, the season elsewhere in Yellowstone was over. As a result the park was virtually deserted. Even ranger Larry Hays, who in 1972 was manning the only year-round station in the interior of the park, had chosen this slow month to take his annual vacation.

Since I had not planned to camp out-of-doors, I looked for a place to live. In Gardiner, some five miles beyond the northwest entrance, I found a comfortable cook-in cabin that suited my purposes very well. But it was thirty miles from the Lamar Valley, where Yellowstone biologists had promised coyotes would be visible, so each morning I set out before dawn, driving along the only plowed road in the park, which was kept open to

* Even in New York State, where *Canis latrans* has appeared, there is now talk of the new winter sport of "bush wolfing."

link remote Cooke City, at the northeast corner of Yellowstone, with the outside world.

Though the mass of snow that blanketed the Rockies was trying to melt, flurries continued at night, and as I usually traveled ahead of the snowplow, I frequently drove without a track to guide me. What's more, by evening, when I made the return trip, the effects of the daily scrape often had been obliterated. Hence, I carried a sleeping bag, extra clothing, matches, kerosene, and food in the event I became stranded.

I had been well advised. The coyotes were indeed visible on the glistening bed of snow that rolled like a timeless glacier down the immense Lamar Valley. Seen from the road, they looked like tiny dogs inching their way back and forth across the brilliant whiteness. I was reminded of huskies I had once filmed on an Alaskan tundra.

The coyote's large ears are well adapted to picking up faint sounds of rodents moving about beneath the snow.

The Lamar coyotes, I quickly discoverd, were active animals.

When not feasting on carcasses, singing, or hunting mice, they moved about with at least the appearance of purposefulness. Many had paired, and mates were traveling together, one usually trailing the other, sometimes by one hundred yards or more. At times the female took the lead, at other times the male did; and often after traveling a certain distance in one sequence, the pair exchanged places. During this season I did not discover one sex to be dominant over the other, nor either to be consistently the leader.

But regardless of which temporarily assumed leadership, at frequent intervals he or she would stop and look back to check on the progress of the other—and with good reason. Coyotes easily become sidetracked. The sound of a mouse tunneling under snow, or the urine mark of a precursor, will naturally arouse the interest of a normal canid. And while such fascinating business is being investigated, a too-preoccupied lead coyote might outstrip his mate and miss all the fun.

But this seldom happened, for every dozen or so steps the coyote up front would look back to see if his companion was still coming along. If not, he might sit down and wait while the loiterer satisfied her curiosity about something in particular. Having already covered the same ground, the leader seldom backtracked to investigate the matter except when it appeared that the other had discovered a snowbound mouse. Then the coyote up front would eagerly bound to the side of his mate to assist in the delicate task of excavation.

For minutes the two might stand at attention, heads cocked, listening for sounds of the mouse's movements under the snow, neither making a move until sufficient information regarding the creature's subniveous maze had been picked up by ear. Then their tails would begin to wave excitedly and one or the other of the pair would leap high in the air, jackknife, and dive headfirst through the snow crust until only the top of a plumy tail was visible. A minute or two later, when the acrobat backed out, the only clue as to whether or not he had hit the mark was often a hardly discernible but highly significant lick of the chops.

During this season of courtship and mating, each member of a coyote couple never failed to add a splash of urine to his mate's.

Urine, it would seem, is a coyote's signature; it can be used to stake out what he regards as his, whether territory, food cache, or mate. By depositing his scent over the scent of his mate, a coyote may be informing any competitors in the vicinity of his proprietary rights.

Although all female coyotes come into oestrus at approximately the same time, fighting among males is not often seen. During the few days when copulation is possible, those animals that have paired protect their own interests by staying close beside their chosen mates. Nevertheless, a yearling male, still bonded to his mother, may begin to exhibit more than usual interest in her and thus arouse the ire of her chosen mate. Though these short-yearlings usually are too immature both physiologically and behaviorally actually to mate, during this season their ubiquitous presence can incite a fight. *National Geographic* photographer David Hiser watched one old male walk over to a sleeping yearling and make a perfunctory attack

As a prelude to mating, coyotes nuzzle, lick, paw, and even harmonize in "love duets."

upon him before mounting his mate. After copulation, the male
repeated the attack on the bewildered juvenile.

I myself saw two coyotes mate repeatedly over a period of
several days. They were never disturbed by other males in the
vicinity. Their ritual was beautifully simple. A short but most
lyrical duet preceded the female's presentation. After mounting, which lasted but a short time, the male slipped both forelegs
to the ground on the same side of the female and gingerly made
a 180-degree turn so that the pair was standing "in tie," tail to
tail. During the next twenty or so minutes, while the animals
were unable to separate, they accepted being locked together
with equanimity. When release occurred, the female circled
around and playfully tapped the male with her forepaw and
gave his face a lick. Then the two would curl up for another long
rest. At the end of a week's time, however, when the male made
overtures, he was rewarded with a gaping mouth full of fangs.
Oestrus was over.

After successful
copulation, a pair
may remain "in
tie" for several
minutes, during
which time they
are physically
unable to separate
and extremely
vulnerable to
attack.

Oestrus over for
another year, a
female rejects the
advances of her
dumbfounded
mate.

Only by observing the posture of urination was I able to
determine with some certainty which animals were males and
which females, for anatomical differences were difficult to distinguish at a distance and were often entirely obscured by thick
winter coats. This method of sexing certainly led to some
confusion in the beginning. I was not aware that the male coyote sometimes squats to relieve himself and the female just as
frequently lifts her leg. Until I discovered this fact, I made

notations on the strange behavior of a presumably homosexual
pair.

Later, when my observations became more discriminating, I
discovered that though the male may squat upon occasion he
does so in a different manner from the female. He pulls himself
forward so that his bent hind legs extend in a line behind his
hips, much like a stallion's. The female, on the other hand,
sits directly over her haunches. And when the female lifts her

Resigned to his change of status, the male will
remain in close association with his
mate and help her raise their offspring.

leg, invariably she brings that leg forward, whereas the male stretches his raised leg behind him or lifts it at right angles to his body.

I was too late to observe the early stages of courtship. In fact, I was late for many things. Or perhaps the spring thaw, arriving prematurely, had accelerated many of the animals' behavioral patterns. Long before my arrival, the greater part of the elk herd had abandoned the valley and climbed to surrounding elevations, where wind had swept the snow off the spiny ridges and uncovered patches of cured grass. Only a few old bulls, still wearing their antlers, had remained below in the soggy snow. But among these laggards coyotes were in evidence, trotting about as complacently as domestic dogs moving among cattle. Through my binoculars, I watched one pair work back and forth through a half dozen of the giant ungulates at rest on the snow. Neither the elk nor the coyotes paid the slightest attention to one another. Obviously, at that moment neither species was emitting aggressive signals, and so each found the other's proximity tolerable.

I watched for a long time hoping to see some action. I expected to see the bull elk charge the little coyotes and drive them off. In fact, it seemed strange that the wild canines should crowd these magnificent specimens in such a vast open space, and I began to suspect there might be a purpose behind their brashness. Yet I knew that two little coyotes could not and would not attack a full-grown, healthy bull elk.

Then I discovered their real motive. Each time one of the bulls roused himself to move a few steps, one of the coyotes dived swiftly into his freshly made hoofprint and bounced back again as rapidly as a paddleball on a rubber string. And sometimes on a return spring one of the coyotes would clench a mouse in his or her teeth, which tidbit was not swallowed until the clever hunter had retreated to a safe distance. On their part, the elk did not appreciate what was happening underfoot and occasionally one did make a short charge at the artful coyotes, who always managed to dodge the formidable hoofs.

I marveled at the coyotes' ingenuity. On this overcast afternoon the snow crust was particularly hard, and the lightweight

coyotes, unable to penetrate it by their usual high-dive maneuver, had hit on this unique method of reaching the semi-
dormant mice that wintered in a wedge of air between the earth
and the snowpack. By exploiting the elk and making use of their
powerful, tool-like hoofs, the opportunistic creatures were able
to gain their objective: mouse dinner.

As the sun's long rays filtered through the wintry sky, the
snow took on a golden cast, and the coyotes, their hunger
appeased, moved thirty yards from the bulls and curled up.
When not in movement, they appeared indistinguishable from
the tops of the giant sage that tufted the snowy field. Even the
reclining elk with their branched antlers resembled the upper
portion of protruding vegetation. I wondered how many creatures that I failed to see actually studded the vast panorama! I
learned to look and look again. Usually, at first glance the valley
seemed to be devoid of animal life. Yet after careful scanning, I
often discovered as many as a half-dozen coyotes, some lying
under sage tops, others walking in the snow trenches that had
been created by the recently departed herd animals.

On this open field, where visibility was unimpeded, there
seemed to be no way to sneak up on these wary creatures. To
compound the problem, snow here in the valley was extremely
deep, in contrast to the surrounding slopes, where the action of
wind and gravity had swept the ground of some of its heavy
load. And here no giant conifers shaded and preserved the snow
in crisp condition, so when I tried to cross the valley, not only
was I absurdly conspicuous, but I broke through the shallow
crust. While I foundered in neck-high slush, naturally my subjects fled. I soon gave up all attempts and confined my photographic ambushes to hilltops and ridges, where the ground was
less treacherous and where rock piles and trees helped to conceal me.

Nevertheless, the slushy Lamar Valley still seemed to suit a
number of coyotes, and it proved an excellent stage upon which
I witnessed many moving dramas from afar.

Courtship

One of the most fascinating incidents that took place in the Lamar Valley involved a female coyote, her mate, and another coyote of undetermined sex.

I had spent the morning glassing the area with my high-powered spotscope and had located a buffalo carcass half buried in the snow.* It was a fortunate discovery. A procession of scavengers filed to the half-eaten beast to pick and gnaw on its remains. Coyotes and ravens feasted together without incident, sometimes only inches apart. Magpies, on the other hand, often became alarmed at the sudden tugging action of a coyote intent on separating a bone from the worked-over carcass, and would suddenly flutter into the air like so much tossed confetti. Yet when the long-tailed birds settled once again on a horn or protruding rib, the coyotes took no notice of them.

Coyotes seemed to behave with less forbearance toward one another than toward their feathered competitors. Usually no more than four tried to feed together on the ample carcass at one time. They seemed to understand that crowding could lead to trouble, although curiously they did not seem to mind serial sharing, and often several coyotes would lie in the snow at discreet distances, patiently awaiting their turns.

I thought it likely that those who fed together were members of the same family, or at least animals who had settled the major question of rank at an earlier date. Yet even among these, skirmishes would occasionally erupt over a choice bit of meat that had broken off the frozen beast, or over a better position on the carcass.

Most incidents were settled quickly and, I might add, somewhat mysteriously. I never was perceptive enough to catch sight of the coup de grace that determined the victor. It always ap-

---

60 * Although the "buffalo" is not a true buffalo but a bison, popular usage seems to demand perpetuation of the misnomer.

peared to me that the combatants were equally matched, yet suddenly the snapping and snarling would cease and one animal would give way to the other.

Actually the battles were more sham than real, though the antagonists always managed to put on a convincing show. Each would hunch his back like a spitting cat, tuck his tail between his legs, and, with jaws wide open like a gaping alligator, dash at the other. Then, after circling and charging for a few rounds, unaccountably one coyote would acknowledge defeat and withdraw. Time and time again I strained to see if the loser had stopped the fight from escalating by communicating submission through a change in posture, but never was I able to see this interaction, which has been so well described in wolves. Both combatants seemed to me to maintain exactly the same stance throughout an encounter. These displays of aggression were unique to winter and different from conflicts I saw later in the spring, when one coyote might attack unless the other clearly ritualized defeat in advance of actual battle.

For that matter, only in winter did I observe the strangely ambivalent hunched-up, gaping, tail-tucked posture, which seemed to signal aggression and submission simultaneously. Once I noticed a coyote evacuating his bowels while maintaining the exaggerated hunch before an enemy, and I was struck by the fact that this stance and the posture of defecation are one and the same. I began to suspect that a repellent scent was being released from the coyote's anal glands.

But why should the stance be evident only in wintertime? And why do two confronting animals assume identical postures? One explanation may lie in the fact that during the cold months coyotes, of necessity, probably range beyond their normal territorial boundaries to look for fallen game. Thus, many strangers meet for the first time on ground that is alien to both. According to Konrad Lorenz in his book *On Aggression*, an animal on foreign turf is generally fearful and reluctant to fight. Upon encountering a resident animal he will make every effort to ritualize himself out of his difficulties, for lack of familiarity with the surroundings will have undermined his self-confidence. By contrast, the same animal when on home ground

Friendly coyotes partake of a carcass together in relative harmony. A minor altercation is settled by means of a well-directed hip lash.

might be quick to make an attack. Perhaps, then, when two coyotes meet and neither is a resident, both may unwittingly betray insecurity by hunching.

There is much to be learned about this strange behavior. Since one coyote inevitably does give way to the other, some placating gesture, however imperceptible, must finally be employed by the loser to signal his willingness to withdraw peaceably. Only briefly were hostilities expressed; in general, the animals' orderly behavior in the presence of scarce food seemed truly remarkable. When a small group of feeding coyotes had eaten their fill, they would depart to a short distance, wipe their faces in the snow by pushing their noses along the ground, and lie down to sun, whereupon animals waiting on the sidelines would take a turn at transforming carrion into living energy.

It occasionally happened, however, that a highly aggressive animal came along who would jump the queue and force a feeding coyote to yield up his place. As I watched, one such animal arrived on the scene. I was not able to determine with certainty the sex of this creature, but because it was large and aggressive, I guessed it to be a male.

Not only did this Johnny-come-lately immediately usurp another animal's place on the carcass, he also refused to toler-

ate any other coyote dining alongside him and, with much snarling, hunching, and dashing about, managed to disperse all the feeders. He even bullied a puppy (a short-yearling) who had dragged the stripped remains of a rib bone some distance to one side, and he forced the young animal to drop his pitiful treasure. Then, like the dog in the manger that he was, the bigger coyote lost all interest in the bone and returned to the carcass. In short order all the coyotes departed, including many who had been lying about waiting their turn, and the contentious fellow, whom I decided to call "Fang," had the whole buffalo to himself.

Fang feasted until glutted, then left at a trot, crossing the frozen valley with his tail held straight out like a wolf's, a position that clearly denoted his healthy high regard for himself. I followed his movements with waning interest. As he had been so eminently successful at intimidating every coyote in the area, I did not expect to see any more social interaction.

Suddenly, however, Fang stiffened, and with an intensity peculiar to predatory animals he streaked across the snow toward a clump of sage. I did not have to wait long to see what had aroused his hostility. A small buff-colored female leaped from the vegetation and, with her mouth open wide like a

Exhibiting conflicting emotions of fear and aggression in an ambivalent display that has been dubbed the "threat bow," a stranger approaches the feeding coyotes.

hungry fledgling and her back arched high like a Halloween cat, dashed forth to meet him.

Fang immediately assumed an identical posture, and for several minutes the two animals circled belligerently, each giving the other a show of dentition. I could not help but admire the spirited female, who was no physical match for the formidable Fang. No other coyote had dared to make such a stand against him. Yet I questioned her judgment. There was little doubt in my mind that the big coyote could make short shrift of her.

As the tension mounted, I expected to see Fang go for Buff's throat, which she seemed to be trying to shield with her dropped jaw. I recalled hearing descriptions of coyotes finishing off hunting dogs with one savage lunge. Yet in this showdown both animals appeared reluctant to make an actual assault. By the same token, neither showed any sign of backing down either.

All at once, and for no apparent reason, Fang dropped his agonistic posture, turned, and allowed himself to be driven away by the tiny female, who followed him for a short distance before she headed back to her bush at a mincing trot, looking for all the world like a smug little terrier who has just routed a Great Dane. I could not make sense out of what I had seen: the weaker-appearing animal had intimidated the stronger.

As Buff neared her lying-up place, her posture again altered; her tail dropped and began to wag, her ears flattened against her head, and across her face there spread what could only be described as a grin. I wondered if this new body attitude was the outward manifestation of some euphoric state of her coyote mentality. Could she be experiencing something equivalent to what human beings call "gloating"?

But anthropomorphism aside, Buff was not bowing to her own inner audience, but to a very real admirer. There in the brush stood another coyote, a male, who I soon concluded was her mate.

Now I was truly puzzled. Why had this sturdy-looking animal remained passive while tiny Buff was driving off Fang? It occurred to me that the mighty Fang might not be a male after all,

Opposite: Mated coyotes keep in touch by howling.

but a large and aggressive female. Male coyotes, like male wolves and dogs, perhaps are reluctant to assault a member of the opposite sex.* (In time, during my spring studies around den areas, I was to see females expel intruding females in the presence of their unconcerned mates, and males drive off interlopers of the male sex while the females remained indifferent.)

One final question baffled me most of all. How did it happen that Buff had not been intimidated by Fang but had unhesitatingly met her head-on? Even hunger had not elicited such defiance among coyotes feeding at the buffalo carcass. Had Buff regarded Fang as her rival? Was possessiveness of a mate so strong?

While speculating on these questions, I watched the greeting ceremony of the pair. Buff scrunched down and waggled back and forth under the male's chin, puppy fashion. Each time she turned, she licked his muzzle and coquettishly brushed his chest with her hip. Then she seated herself squarely in front of him, raised her right front foot, and pawed him entreatingly. She reminded me of a self-satisfied little dog who, certain that her behavior merits reward, actively solicits a response from her master.

And she got it. Suddenly the male broke into the most lyrical coyote song I had yet heard. For a few seconds Buff seemed rapt. Then she tilted her long nose in the air and joined in. Without repeating a phrase, they improvised a duet in which the two never sounded the same note. When the male inadvertently slid onto a pitch Buff was holding, she instantly dropped two whole tones. And when she opted for the note he was sustaining, the male broke into a falsetto.

Although the two animals were so distant from me that when I was not viewing them through my spotscope they were barely discernible, their music filled the valley, bouncing back from so many directions that, had I not known where to look, I could not have located its source. If this magnificent duet had a natural purpose other than the pleasure it obviously gave its impro-

---

* In studies of confined coyotes the male will sometimes threaten the female but rarely will attack her.

visers, it perhaps served to announce to Fang or any other potential rivals within earshot that a bond existed between these two animals.

Coyote-watchers believe that in many cases the pair bond in coyotes persists throughout life. It does appear that coyotes are at least seasonally monogamous, and a male and female will remain together until their offspring are old enough to forage for themselves. But do they seek a different mate the following year?

Government trappers from widely divergent areas of the West reported to me they often observed the same two coyotes denning together year after year. Two predator-control agents even confessed they sometimes would designate one such familiar pair as their "breeding coyotes" and were careful not to destroy them. They explained that a shrewd predator-control agent does not annihilate all the coyotes in a given area. One of the men elaborated: "That would be like killing the goose that lays the golden eggs. You always want to leave a breeding pair out there to raise litters and keep the sheepmen thinking coyotes will drive them into bankruptcy if predator control is ever halted."

In recent years such exploitative individuals have been replaced by federal poison programs that indiscriminately kill not only every coyote, but badgers, eagles, kit foxes, skunks, opossums, and many other animals as well. As a result, large areas of the public lands in the West are devoid of wildlife. Even where coyotes persist, it is unusual to find any that have survived to age five. And since coyotes usually do not breed until they are two years old, finding a mated pair that has lived to celebrate an anniversary is difficult. However, in the spring of 1972 I spent several weeks watching a male and female raise three puppies on the National Elk Refuge; the following year, I returned and located the same two coyotes in the process of rearing another family—of nine! In this instance at least, the two animals proved to have remained faithful to one another.

Perhaps it is because Nature intends their relationship to be long-lasting that coyotes are so choosy in selecting their mates in the first place. Biologists who attempt to study them in captivity often report having difficulty getting two to mate. Arranged matches apparently do not appeal to coyotes.

In a study of coyote habits and pelage changes conducted by Eldon E. Whitman, it was assumed that proximity and lack of options would inspire a match between two confined animals of the opposite sex. But when the female came into heat, the male showed no interest in her. The pair were separated, each animal housed in a cage by itself. The following year, when the female was again in oestrus the two were placed together for a few hours each day. Still the male behaved in an apathetic manner toward the female. At last, he made a desultory attempt to mount her, which she resisted violently. Finally a brief and perfunctory mating did take place, but the lack of a true bond between these two incompatible animals was obvious and manifested itself in several results, some behavioral and one physical. After copulation, the male uncharacteristically lost all interest in his "mate," and the untended female bore only a single puppy!

In his need to form a compatible liaison before mating, the coyote differs radically from his domestic cousin the dog, who is ready for the sex act with any willing bitch and who afterward does not "acknowledge" his puppies.* By contrast, the coyote, like the wolf, carries on a protracted courtship, sometimes even bringing food offerings to his intended. Lois Crisler, in drawing a comparison between the prenuptial behavior of dogs and her captive wolves, speaks scornfully of the "terse, business-like rump orientation" of man's best friend. Her wolves, on the other hand, developed clear mate preferences while still yearlings, although physiologically wolves are incapable of copulation before the females are two years old and the males three.

As suitors, coyotes may even outshine wolves. At least, pair bonding appears more visible in coyotes, but perhaps this is only because intense pack affiliation does not obscure it. For though the coyote does exhibit allegiance to a few pack members, he is by no means no group oriented as the wolf. On the contrary, the

---

* Frank Beach has found that some beagles show mate preference. Huskies, too, seem to have retained the monogamous tendency of their wolf ancestors, and sometimes males will even try to assist in the rearing of puppies. All other breeds seem to be promiscuous.

coyote's primary social unit seems to be the pair, not the pack. Consequently, his devotion to his mate may be the more compelling. Moreover, coyote couples, unlike most wolf pairs, are not restrained from consummating the match. In a typical wolf hierarchy, animals below the status of second-in-rank male or top-ranking female who attempt copulation with their chosen mates often incur the wrath of the entire pack. David Mech saw several such incidents in the wild wolf pack he studied on Isle Royale. He writes: "Each time mounting occurred the nearby wolves rushed to the pair in an apparent free-for-all."

It is little wonder, therefore, that a whole population of wolves may produce only a single litter annually, and that these puppies are well tended by numerous solicitous "aunts" and "uncles" as well as by their own parents. This strange method of birth control—policed abstinence—seems to serve a dual purpose. Not only does it limit population growth, it also minimizes the possibility that several sets of parents will fall into conflict over available food for their respective litters. Pack solidarity is thus ensured among animals to whom cooperative behavior is of prime importance in bringing down large game.

Since pack affiliation has no great survival value in the smaller coyote, who feeds primarily on small rodents and carrion, his first allegiance is to his mate. Perhaps to reinforce this intrinsic loyalty, Nature has made the male coyote as cyclical as the female. Both come into season in late winter and are uninterested in sex at all other times of year. A U.S. Department of Agriculture study of the reproductive tracts of eight hundred animals and records of three thousand litters from thirteen states showed males to be sterile during eight months of the year and females unproductive during ten months. Obviously, this factor, besides conserving the animals' energies, tends to retard promiscuity and thus ensure paternal care for what offspring are conceived.

Months before either sex is in season the pair bond is formed. Thus compatibility rather than hormones would seem to be its basis. That such should be the case makes good sense. If the male's interest in his mate were to wane with a seasonal decline in his testosterone, his participation in the rearing of the young might not be guaranteed. Neither would he help the female dig her den, nor would he bring her food while she is nursing.

Perhaps the most revealing material on coyote breeding behavior came to light inadvertently in a study in New Hampshire sponsored by the National Science Foundation, which attempted to compare the physiognomy and the behavior of the Eastern coyote with the Western coyote and various canid hybrids. To produce the desired number of each type of animal under comparison, Helenette and Walter Silver of Concord, New Hampshire, bred and crossbred some eighty wild canids over a period of six years. I visited Mrs. Silver and asked her to describe the difficulties she had encountered in bringing about successful matings in each control group. She laughed at my question and said that I had hit on one of the most interesting problems of their study.

"We, of course, needed a certain number of crosses, but the coyotes had different ideas about this. They were especially reluctant to breed with dogs. We presented one of our Eastern coyote bitches who had been kept isolated from her own species since birth with a number of breeds before she finally became friendly with a collie type that closely resembled herself. Even then, she wouldn't stand for him until they had known each other two seasons. I guess coyotes believe in long engagements!"

I asked Mrs. Silver to describe the way pair bonds normally would form between animals who were allowed to select their own mates.

"Ours chose their mates at a very young age," she said. "You might say that they began going steady when only about six months old, though none actually reared pups before the age of two years."

"During that long courtship did you ever see a pair split up?" I asked, curious to know if the long engagements served any useful purpose.

"Occasionally, during the early stages," she replied. "Sometimes one animal's first choice would reject him and prefer another animal."

"In that case who would win out, the male or the female?"

Mrs. Silver smiled. "Why, the female, invariably," she replied.

"One of our New Hampshire males, Borris, from the time he was a little puppy, was very attached to a particular low-ranking female. Every time he saw her, he wagged his tail and even allowed her to eat from his dish. But in the same pen was a high-ranking female who had set her sights on Borris, and whenever he paid attention to the female of his choice the dominant bitch would knock him down and stand on him." He finally submitted and became her mate.

"What then happened to the low-ranking female?" I asked.

"We had to move her to another pen to prevent Borris's mate from killing her. Sometimes when he caught sight of her in the far pen, he would stand by the wire and wag his tail. If his mate happened to notice what he was doing, however, she would knock him down and stand on him."

I asked Mrs. Silver if she thought that Western coyote females dominated their mates under wild conditions. She told me she didn't know, but in confinement the males were the dominant animals and sometimes so much so that they inflicted injury on their mates.

"But in matters of the heart, the female is extremely tenacious," she added. "Of course, not all females are strong enough to drive away competition. The low-ranking bitch I described, for example, was unable to compete for Borris. Yet had the two not been restrained in a pen, I believe they might have gotten together." Then, after a pause, Mrs. Silver added a little ruefully, "Though I suspect wherever they might have gone that dominant female would have found them."

Somehow this conversation added weight to my suspicions that Fang might indeed have been a female and that the confrontation I had witnessed was just one of many showdowns between the two females over Buff's mate.

Clannish Behavior at a Carcass

During the two winters I spent watching coyotes in Yellowstone National Park, I had many opportunities to watch the interaction of high-ranking and low-ranking animals vying for choice positions at carcasses. In general, smaller animals gave way to larger ones; females surrendered choice parts to males but continued to feed alongside them; and low-ranking yearlings stayed at a distance until mature animals had fed and left. Once I saw a mated pair defend their claim of an almost completely submerged elk carcass and prevent all strange coyotes from approaching it.

When first I came upon the bogged elk, it was still alive and an eagle was perched on its branched antlers. There was no hope that the creature could extricate itself from the streambed it had entered to nibble on the sedge that was already beginning to green along snowy banks. The hapless animal had lingered too long, and its great weight, some one thousand pounds, had caused it to become mired. Struggling had only wearied the old bull, and by the time I found him only the top of his back and his head were above water.

With a mixture of pity and anxiety I watched him fight for life. He took too long to die, and I, who had bemoaned the fact that there were too few carcasses for the coyotes to feed upon, now found myself hoping that this elk's struggle for survival would somehow succeed. If not, I wished for him a speedy death.

But the animal refused to yield to his fate. More than eight hours passed before he drowned in the muck that engulfed him. Too weary to hold up his antler-laden head any longer, he finally lowered it into the water and his struggles ceased.*

---

* Objectively speaking, his death might be regarded as being caused by old age. A younger, fitter animal could have extricated himself from the bog before sinking in so deep.

For the coyotes, the old bull's death was a boon. It occurred during my second winter of observation, when scavenger animals were suffering gravely from the fact that the deer, elk, and bison populations were faring so well. Unusually light snow permitted these ungulates to paw and nose through the shallow drifts and feed on cured grass, and as a consequence few were dying.

By contrast, the coyotes, deprived of their normal winter fare of carrion, were in distress. On one day I found the body of a male coyote, probably dead of starvation, and encountered a female so famished I could have run her down on foot. A few individuals, very likely the more resourceful ones, had even begun to beg for food along the road—behavior certain to bring

An aged elk sinks into a bog. His death is a boon to hungry scavengers, who depend on such attrition to sustain them through the winter.

them to grief. The distended bellies and frightened eyes of one of these coyotes haunted me; thus, I experienced mixed emotions. While feeling a deep sense of pity for the mired elk, I realized he would now provide much-needed food for other suffering animals.

To my surprise, however, the coyotes were slow to discover this windfall. I watched one oblivious old dog trot within fifty yards of the drowned creature without seeing it. Nor did any scavenger birds arrive until twenty-four hours after the elk's demise. Then suddenly, late on the second day, a raven dipped down, cawed, and, after making several low passes over the half-sunken carcass, flew off, croaking noisily to telegraph the news of his discovery to his flock. Soon I counted twenty-two of the big black birds circling, lighting on the ground, hopping, pecking, and attacking the hide of the elk. And shortly thereafter, coyotes also began to appear from various directions, each approaching at a trot, head tilted skyward, eyes taking a fix on the noisy birds.

The first to arrive was the old mated pair. They cautiously noted my parked vehicle and did not at once push their way in among the black ravens, who with their strong beaks had already opened the elk's tough hide and were beginning to devour the pink flesh.

The day was overcast, sleet falling steadily, a condition that worked in my favor. The streambed was only fifty yards from the road where I parked, and the drizzle helped conceal from the coyotes the fact that my car was occupied. I hoped the animals would grow accustomed to a stationary vehicle and allow me to use it as a blind. But the nervous pair paced the ridge and would not come down to feed. The dead elk was too close to the road for their liking, and despite the hard times they were enduring they dared not approach it.

Before long, however, less prudent coyotes arrived on the scene. One unmindful fellow even trotted within five feet of my vehicle and failed to notice me inside, so intent was he on obtaining something to eat. But to my surprise, before he reached the carcass he stopped dead in his tracks. The old male from the ridge above, his eyes blazing and his mane ruffled, was taking stiffly deliberate steps downhill. At any moment, I expected his stealthy pace to turn into a rush. But actual attack, it turned out, was unnecessary. The intruder, who had been so oblivious to an occupied car, clearly read this more serious threat to his safety and spun around and fled, never to return. The old male thereupon lay down beside his mate and, resting his head between outstretched paws, continued to guard his as yet untouched provisions.

During the previous winter I had often seen coyotes lying about patiently awaiting a turn to dine on an already claimed carcass, but never had I seen animals who were not themselves feeding chase off all comers. This winter, because of the scarcity of food, the act of hoarding was perhaps necessary. What was most remarkable, however, was the restraint displayed by these two hungry animals, who were able to postpone eating until nightfall would provide them cover from the road.

Their extreme caution suggested to me that the two had attained some age. I was reminded of a study made by Robert Chesness in Minnesota, in which 113 coyote carcasses were collected from trappers from January through early April. Most of the coyotes were young; 45 percent were less than one year old, and 35 percent were under two years old. Obviously, young coyotes are eliminated from the population at a disproportionate rate, and those few who make it to adulthood must be the most canny individuals.*

The old pair on the hill bore many other marks of maturity. For example, the stocky appearance of the female hinted that she had borne litters of puppies. By contrast, the less discreet coyotes I had been seeing all day appeared correspond-

---

* Another study, made by H. T. Gier, demonstrates the cyclical pattern of age distribution within the coyote population in Kansas. Gier found that a breeding population of 100 coyotes will annually produce an average of 250 offspring. But by the following spring, all but 50 of these young will be dead. And of the 50 surviving yearlings, 40 percent will succumb to a variety of causes before attaining breeding age themselves.

ingly less well developed. Had these not been in a protected sanctuary, they might well have become easy targets for somebody's bullets.

Then a yearling female arrived, who like the others hardly bothered to inspect the car but headed in single-minded fashion for the carcass. Unlike the others, however, she was not routed by the testy old pair on the hill. In fact, they seemed to take little notice of her. Even when she made a spectacular leap from the bank onto the back of the drowned elk and began tearing at the flesh, they did not challenge her.

She was then below my eye level in the creek bed, though I could still see the tip of her tail wave as she tugged and jerked on the tough hide. From its position I was able to determine that she faced away from the road, more evidence of her lack of caution.

Since the two old coyotes made no move to dispatch the young animal, I surmised they were acquainted, and I wondered if she were their offspring, a conjecture that gained support a half-hour later when, glutted, she ran uphill to join them. The old female seemed overjoyed to see the yearling. The two coyotes wagged their tails, licked one another's muzzles, and pranced back and forth along the ridge like two happy dogs playing in new-fallen snow.

Then, tiring of this, they made a mock attack on the more reserved male, bussing him with their noses until at last he got up and moved a short distance away in what appeared to be an attempt on his part to preserve some dignity. Then all three lay down side by side and rested.

Within a short time another coyote, attracted by the ravens' noisy announcement, came upon the scene. This newcomer was by no means tolerated. The old female instantly leaped to her feet, raced halfway downhill, stopped, and, with back arched and mouth gaping, quickly convinced the stranger of the wisdom of making a hasty retreat.

And so the day progressed. By five o'clock, seven coyotes had been turned back by the two animals on the hill. Then one young female arrived whose left front foot was missing. It seemed unlikely that she could have lost it in a trap as she was deep within the sanctuary of the park. Yet it was cut off as neatly as if sliced by steel. Though the stump had healed, the coyote was in poor coat, indicating she was having difficulty feeding herself.

I wondered how she had even managed to keep herself alive. Hunting for carcasses requires much traveling across weak snow, a difficult enough task for a coyote with four legs. And pouncing through deep drifts for mice would be no easier a task for an animal with such a handicap. Nevertheless, this three-legged coyote looked better off than many whole-bodied coyotes I had seen begging along the road. And to her credit, she, at least, seemed to be making efforts to obtain her natural food.

As she neared the carcass, I focused my attention on the old pair on the hill, fully expecting they would drive her away as well. But to my surprise, they remained at ease and made no move against her. The three-legged coyote, on the other hand, noting the guardians, assumed an agonistic pose herself, and with back hunched, mouth wide open, and tail curved between her legs,* waddled forward toward the food. This fierce display was also ignored. Not one of the three coyotes on the hill even raised head from paws as the newcomer, whom I dubbed Stump, advanced.

After making what must have been an impressive three-point landing onto the back of the carcass, Stump was out of my line of vision and remained so for a half-hour until she scaled the bank, wiped her face in the snow to clean off the blood, and, to my amazement, began hobbling slowly uphill toward the three resting coyotes.

But even this bold move failed to arouse them. Once again it was Stump who demonstrated an unfriendly attitude. As she drew near them, she began to posture, hunch, and show her teeth. Though the three coyotes got to their feet, they remained

---

*R. Schenkel, in a 1947 study of the modes of expression used by wolves, describes the tail-tuck as connoting "strong restraint." In conjunction with the back-hunch and the mouth-gape, it becomes more complex. Schenkel defined all behavior related to social competition as "agonistic," a term that students of animal behavior have found to be extremely useful.

Above and opposite;
In a fawning
display, a
subordinate
coyote rotates in a
complete circle. Her
obsequious
behavior gains for
this three-legged
female the
goodwill of her
two superiors.

impassive. Finally, when but five feet from the threesome, Stump relaxed, flopped down on the ground, and, after beating her tail on the snow a few times, rested.

She was marked exactly like the first yearling, although by no means in such fine coat, and I wondered if the two were siblings. It seemed a likely possibility inasmuch as the old pair had raised no objection to either young female partaking of their provisions. Moreover, had there been no preexisting bond among these animals, I doubt that Stump would have tried, much less succeeded in, joining them.

Yet if she were an offspring, why had she not received the same effusive greeting shown the first yearling? I wondered if her sheared leg could have been the reason. Only human beings favor underdogs; animals usually reject them. Many domestic dogs kill malformed puppies at birth. Coyote mothers may do the same. And offspring who acquire their deformities at a later age, after social bonds have been established, seem to lose rank and may even become "whipping boys" upon whom the others vent their aggressions.*

---

* At the same time, it should be noted that altruism has also been observed in animals. Wolves and coyotes have been seen bringing food to trapped or injured fellows.

It is therefore possible that in times past Stump's friendly overtures may have been met with attack; thus, she may have learned to make a cautious and defensive approach whenever she felt the urge to socialize with familiar coyotes. On this occasion, when the others gave no indication they would move against her, her relief and pleasure were obvious—expressed by a brief but significant wag of her tail.

For an hour the four coyotes lay peacefully together. (The coyote is diurnal as well as nocturnal, sleeping some during day and night.) Then the old pair and their favored daughter became intrigued by the activities of an eagle far across the plateau, and they headed in that direction. Stump made a vain attempt to follow, but, finding she could not keep up, wandered off alone.

By then it was almost dark and all around me coyotes were tuning up for their nightly howl. I did not stay to hear their vesper songs, however, as I was unbearably cold, having remained immobile beside an open window throughout this raw day. Now that the coyotes were at last out of sight, I could hardly wait to start up the motor, turn on the heater, and leave.

The next morning before sunup, I was again in position. Even before the snow began to reflect the yellow glow of a new and brighter day, I could make out the rough shapes of the old pair lying atop the ridge. From their lazy manner, I was certain they had spent a good part of the night feeding. But sated or not, they were as possessive as ever of their larder. Again, only their favored daughter and Stump were granted access to the body of the bogged elk. All other hopefuls who appeared on the scene were promptly driven off. Again Stump, after making several trips to the carcass, joined the clannish trio on the top of the hill. And again the old pair were too wary to feed during daylight hours.

All day I waited, hoping they would eventually become adapted to the presence of my car. Finally, as the light began to fade, my long vigil was rewarded. While eyeing my vehicle suspiciously, the old male began to pick his way downhill. But en route he lost courage and retreated to the ridge top, where his mate was nervously pacing. A second approach, however, brought him all the way to the carcass, and a sudden leap, onto the elk's spine. As he dropped from my sight the air exploded with black ravens, who, resentful of the intrusion, protested noisily and incited the old dog to chase them. Back up on the bank he leaped, snapping and jumping at flapping plumage until he had dispersed all but two of the birds. These refused to be intimidated and soon settled down again to feed quietly by his side.

The raven, like the magpie, has a very special relationship with the coyote. Though a coyote may on occasion chase these birds in play or in an attempt to drive them off a carcass, he does not prey on them. The symbiotic relationship of ravens, magpies, and coyotes has been noted by even casual observers who have given little thought to the mutual benefits each bestows on the other. In summer, when the coyote hunts brushy cover in search of rabbits, gophers, and other rodents, magpies and ravens often hover about or perch in nearby trees, where they watch for a chance to pick up leftover scraps. But in winter, when traveling is difficult for the coyote, it is the airborne raven or magpie who is likely to discover food, and the ensuing circling and squawking of these excited birds alert the coyote to the exact location of their find. Thus, the coyote is spared having to make a random search through deep snow, which could leave him footsore and weary.

The benefits of this three-way partnership extend even beyond the area of food-finding. For example, a raven flock invariably includes a few members who act as sentinels. An
experienced coyote learns the significance of the alarm cries of
these alert birds and will abandon a carcass at their first warning.
More than once my blind has been discovered by a passing raven
and reported to coyotes I had hoped to observe.

Now as the old male bolted food, he tolerated the two per-
sistent ravens and made no more passes at them. He behaved
somewhat like a nervous bird himself. After every bite his head
popped up so he could keep my car under surveillance; thus,
only his chewing face bobbed in and out of my line of vision until
he finished feeding. Then he swiftly climbed the hill without
performing the usual coyote ritual of wiping his face in the
snow.

Meanwhile, on the ridge above, the female had paced con-
tinously. When at last she saw her mate returning, down the
slope she bounded and greeted him at the halfway point with
such enthusiasm one would have thought the two had been
separated for days rather than minutes. At first I assumed her
behavior was merely a manifestation of relief from the anxiety
she had experienced during her mate's brief exposure to danger. Such behavior is fairly common in canines. I once had a dog
who became extremely agitated whenever I entered water to
swim. She would pace the bank in a frenzy until I emerged
safely, at which point she would express her relief with an
exaggerated display of affection that all but drove me to take
refuge in the water again. The female coyote was cavorting
about in a similar fashion, crouching and waggling, leaping and
licking her mate's face.

But there was more to her behavior than first appeared.
Suddenly the male began to regurgitate the load of food he had
consumed, and while the female quickly devoured it he stood by
placidly and watched. What a vixen! Too timid to venture near
the carcass herself, she had managed to have it catered.

Such behavior in wild canids is not so extraordinary as it may
seem. Both wolf and coyote adults regurgitate food for their
young. The puppies are thought to elicit this response in their

parents by licking the adults' lips. But this behaviorist explanation—that food offerings are but a conditioned response reinforced by the rewarding behavior of the puppies (in this case, muzzle-licking)—fails to take into account that the adult receives his so-called reward (muzzle-licking) *before* he regurgitates. Likewise, the physiologists' explanation that parental regurgitation is but an autonomic reflex induced by lip stimulation raises other questions. If such were the case, coyotes would inadvertently bring up their dinners on those many occasions when they lick one another's muzzles in greeting and in play.

In my opinion, the action of offering partially digested food to puppies stems from the parents' care-giving nature. Perhaps muzzle-licking in some instances facilitates the adult's *ability* to regurgitate, but the etiological basis for the behavior seems to me to be rooted in a simple, but real, *intention* on the part of the donor.

This care-giving behavior obviously may be extended by one adult to another, as witnessed between the old pair on the hill. Perhaps the female, by simulating a puppy-like demeanor and by licking her mate's muzzle, made the suggestion to him to feed her. However, had he not been amenable to the idea, he would have had little difficulty denying her "request."

Canids are endowed with an amazing capacity for attachment to one another, a quality that enabled man to domesticate the dog and bind this innate devotion to himself. In so doing, however, he acquired a companion who is also innately gifted at begging. Upon reflection, no dog owner who has ever been cajoled into sharing food with his pet should be particularly surprised at the old female's success in gaining some of her mate's dinner!

During my first winter in the park I learned a lot about snow, but I learned the hard way. My harsh lesson in winter survival occurred just at the conclusion of what I regard to be the most extraordinary display of wild-animal behavior I have ever observed in nature. The entire event spanned three days. It started, as usual, with ravens.

One dark afternoon I drove to the Lamar Valley to check on the condition of a feeble moose I had noticed on the previous day, which was also being closely observed by a pair of coyotes. I found that the weary old cow had revived after an afternoon in the dazzling valley sun and had tottered back into the aspen grove to the south. Apparently she had decided she was not yet ready to be turned into coyote food.*

But across the mountains in the opposite direction I suddenly became aware that another drama was taking place, for the sky was teeming with flapping ravens.

Immediately I began to look for an ascent route to some point where I could see what was going on. Snow was relatively shallow along many of the southern faces of the long mountain chain. On these sunny exposures, only the draws feeding into the Lamar Valley were still choked with impassable drifts. And the top of the long ridge was nearly windswept. I knew that by taking care to ascend alongside a particularly high line of sage whose protruding twigs disclosed that the row of brush was set in a mere foot and a half of snow, I could make it to that barren height.

---

*Coyotes, like vultures, often hang about animals that are about to die. Frank Calkins, writer and former game warden for the state of Utah, observed that sometimes the mere proximity of scavenger animals is sufficient incentive to cause a sick animal to revive. Elk with stomatitis, for example, will die if they stop moving. Calkins told me of watching an afflicted elk that was so disturbed by the ubiquitous presence of two hopeful coyotes that it could not rest, kept moving, and eventually recovered its health.

83

I pulled on my high boots, loaded my backpack with camera gear, and began fording snow. It was hard work. The angle of ascent was extremely steep, and plunging in and out of even eighteen-inch drifts is exhausting labor.

As I slowly worked my way uphill, I noticed something strange about the ravens' behavior. They seemed to be maintaining a holding pattern above one particular spot just behind the ridge. Usually one or two birds will remain airborne or perch in a lookout tree while the rest of the flock feeds. But in this case some thirty ravens were continuously circling. It occurred to me that the object of their scrutiny might not yet be dead.

It was four o'clock and I realized that unless I hurried, shortly after reaching my destination I would have to begin my descent. I struggled onward, resting only to get my breath. Then, three-quarters of the way up, the inevitable happened. A sharp-eyed

A ten-month-old elk calf guards the body of a former companion while a hungry coyote looks on.

raven spotted me, swooped down to investigate, and, croaking
noisily, led the entire flock away.

I wondered—was it worthwhile going on? Surely, I would not
see any coyotes up there after ravens had sounded alarm. But
having already invested so much effort in the endeavor, I decided to continue climbing and at least satisfy my curiosity about
what had been the object of the birds' attention.

As I neared the summit, the angle of the slope rounded and
the snow became sparse. I could now have walked with ease were
it not for the new necessity of bowing low so as not to be seen by
whatever might be over the ridge. I ended by crawling Indian-
fashion up to a large rock, collapsing on my stomach, and there
lying prostrate until my heavy breathing subsided. Presently, I
raised my head and peered at a small mountain plateau slightly
below me. Standing in a feeding crater of cropped dried grass
was a half-grown elk calf about nine to ten months of age.
Directly in back of this barren ground, which had obviously
been cleared of snow by a recently departed herd of elk, were
two coyotes. Beside the calf there lay a dead elk whose hindquarters had been partially eaten.

It was clear that the coyotes were intent on obtaining more of
the fresh meat. But the elk calf was equally intent on protecting
the dead animal. As I watched, the calf suddenly sprang at the
pair of coyotes, who artfully dodged his redoubtable front hoofs
and circled uphill. But the calf did not pursue them far before
he returned and once again straddled the dead animal defiantly.

I had never before seen or heard of one wild animal so
attached to another that he would defend its dead body.* This
remarkable behavior explained, of course, why the ravens I had
seen earlier had not landed. This bellicose calf not only dispersed coyotes, but also held ravens at bay.

I was curious to know what prevented the two coyotes from
attempting to kill the young creature who stood between them
and scarce food. Certainly a herbivore that is separated from its
herd is at a distinct disadvantage and extremely vulnerable to

* At a later date I saw a mother elk defend her dead offspring from coyotes who
were trying to feed upon it.

While his mate assumes an air of nonchalance, a male coyote tries to steal a bite of carrion . . .

attack. Moreover, this particular animal, being both immature and small, would, in the opinion of most knowledgeable people, be an easy mark. But the coyotes seemed fearful of the short-yearling* who so ably demonstrated his high degree of viability. As he milled about the grassy circle, he reminded me of a self-confident rodeo bull who is aware of his own charisma.

Though the actual encounters between the two species seemed more like posturing than violent attack, the drama being enacted on the mountain that day was a life-and-death confrontation, in which I suspected the coyotes were merely biding their time until they would surprise the plucky calf in an off-guard moment and possibly kill him.

I had long wanted to satisfy myself firsthand that predation by

* It is correct to refer to this animal as a calf. However, an elk of his size is sometimes called a short-yearling, meaning he is not quite one year old.

coyotes on wild animals larger than themselves did sometimes occur, but now that such an attack seemed imminent, I became almost sick at heart over the prospect of witnessing it. Suddenly I could better understand the impulsive act of a road-maintenance man who once told me how he, upon seeing coyotes closing in on a deer, had thrown stones at them to allow the deer a chance to escape. His deed I regarded as highly misguided. Although he believed he had prevented suffering, he very likely caused more of it. Afterward not only would the coyotes go hungry, but the deer itself, already sufficiently weak to be earmarked for attack, would probably die a slower and more agonizing death. The quick blow inflicted by a predator is sometimes merciful.

Nevertheless, now that I myself was about to view a killing, I could at least sympathize with the man's feelings. His very naiveté provided him with a degree of justification that I find totally lacking in some supposedly enlightened scientists, who, in order to obtain a scrap of data, have been known to shoot baby monkeys out of their mother's arms. In the mind of the maintenance man, it would have been a devastating experience to stand by and watch a creature be killed. At the same time, to make a judgment favoring the survival of one member of creation over that of another is to play at being God. I steeled myself to remain an onlooker.

I speculated about the animal lying dead on the ground. It was too small to have been the calf's mother. Yet what other bond between two animals is sufficiently strong to endure beyond life itself? Perhaps the two had been siblings. Twinning, though rare, does occur in *Cervus canadensis*. Months later I was to return and collect the jawbone of this animal, and a park biologist was able to answer my questions. By studying the molars, he determined that at the time of death the animal had been approximately ten months old, the same age as the live calf I watched.*

I could see evidence all about me that a rather large elk herd had recently pastured and bedded in the area. A freshly made trail ran directly across the feeding crater where the dead animal lay. Had it died before or after the herd had departed? And why had the live calf not followed when the others felt the urge to move on? Now, left alone, the audacious fellow stood slim chance of survival. Perhaps that, in part, explained why he so tenaciously defended his lone companion, who lay partially eaten at his side. There is no creature more pathetic than a herd animal who has lost his herd.

Twice the calf walked over to its former companion(?), stretched out his head, and nudged the face of the carcass, as if trying to rouse it to life. How little we know what animals feel! How fatuous is man to assume that he alone among all creatures that walk the earth is capable of experiencing the pain of loss.

Discreetly, I fired my camera whenever I felt the wind would muffle the sound of the shutter release. But the mood that prevailed cried out for the touch of a painter, not a photog-

* The central incisors and third molars had not erupted.

rapher. I recalled Charles Russell's famous work *Waiting for a Chinook*, which depicts an emaciated steer standing knee-deep in snow while coyotes in the background look on and await its demise. That picture took on new meaning for me now. The two coyotes I was watching looked every bit as dejected and cold as the ones in the painting. And though, outwardly at least, the elk calf appeared more viable than the dying steer, it was actually vulnerable in the extreme. Yet the coyotes hung back, seemingly reluctant to make an attack.

By now nearly two hours had elapsed, and during this time the persevering coyotes had made repeated forays into the calf's arena which the "heroic" calf had just as doggedly repelled. Only twice, by employing a ruse, had they succeeded in snatching portions of meat. Both times the female decoyed the calf while the male dashed in, pulled out entrails, and promptly carried them across the feeding crater, where he consumed them by himself very near to where I was hiding.

He ate as if starved, bolting the coil of intestines as if it were some kind of serpent that required subduing. I dared not photograph him gorging himself for fear of betraying my presence. Nor could I leave until he had finished and returned to his mate's side. The moment he did, however, I started down the mountain, for light was rapidly fading and by the time I reached the road I was groping in darkness. Neither moonlight nor starshine penetrated the dense cloud mass that had been steadily unfurling across the Rockies throughout that day.

At night the park seemed remote from the hustle of the twentieth century, silent and awesome. And the mountains that separated me from my warm cabin and creature comforts loomed like the megalithic shadows of some preternatural presence. Amid such antiquity, my own existence seemed as tenuous and fleeting as the flash of lightning that momentarily illuminated the improbable scenery. Oh, tutelary spirit of the Rockies, I thought, self-renewing provider to countless generations of animals, small wonder that the Indians venerated your sacred ground! I recalled Henry Beston's description of man's need to revere Nature:

Nature is part of our humanity, and without some awareness and experience of that divine mystery man ceases to be man. When the Pleiades, and the wind in the grass, are no longer a part of the human spirit, a part of very flesh and bone, man becomes, as it were, a kind of cosmic outlaw, having neither the completeness and integrity of the animal nor the birthright of a true humanity.*

Perhaps it is too late for us, a profane people who tear at the earth for raw materials, energy, and amusement, to experience the divine in Nature. In a few months, a million cars would encumber these arcane heights, their radios playing. Above the din, how could the timeless mystery be felt?

As I drove, my thoughts returned to the calf's ordeal, which, in the dark of this cold night, was certain to be still unfolding, the coyote being a nocturnal as well as diurnal seeker of food. What awesome tests are faced by wild animals. And Nature shows no partiality, caring not who among her offspring emerges victorious. In hunted and hunter alike she has instilled the will to live, though in the course of time she will deliver death to both. I recalled Loren Eiseley's description of how wild things die "without question, without knowledge of mercy in the universe, knowing only themselves and their own pathway to the end."

* *The Outermost House*, Viking, 1962.

The next morning I was eager to ascend the mountain again to see what had developed while I slept. During the night the temperature had dropped and hardened my tracks of the previous day into boot molds, which I had to step into with some precision. As I neared the summit, I repeated my Indian crawl to the same fortuitously placed rock, which once again served as a blind.

With some trepidation, I peered over the top, half-expecting to find that the living calf of the previous day had met the same fate as his companion. To my relief I discovered he was still alive. His grave face stared in my direction and his large ears were cocked forward, leading me to suspect he had caught some sounds I had carelessly made while settling into my hiding place. I dropped my head and waited, and when I looked again he was grazing.

Then I caught sight of the greatly reduced body of his former companion. It had been dragged some twenty yards downhill into a snowbank, where three coyotes were hungrily devouring it, using their strong front legs to brace themselves as they tugged and yanked at its hide. A short distance away another coyote lay in the snow, apparently awaiting his turn.

I had not expected to see normal feeding activity in the presence of the fighting calf. Something had changed. I studied the three coyotes on the carcass. They appeared to be a pair and a juvenile. For several minutes they ate in peace. Then the female decided to better her position on the meat, and with her hip she slammed her mate, knocking him away from the part she coveted. Taken by surprise, he looked dismayed, like a dog being teased, who doesn't know the appropriate response to make. Finally he resignedly walked around to the opposite side and accepted the inferior place for himself.

Meanwhile, the young coyote on the sidelines summoned courage to join the party. Hunching his back, he (or she) dashed in. But the mated female quickly sent this young one packing, and with no inhibited display either, but with actual snaps and snarls. Not until she had satisfied her hunger and moved away did the juvenile dare to make another attempt to dine, at which time the remaining two coyotes permitted the intruder to join them.

The calf, when he wasn't grazing, watched the above proceedings passively. Mercifully, I thought, he has forgotten. But I wished he would move away. In the distance I could see two more coyotes approaching from an adjacent mountain, obviously bound for the carcass. Their arrival would bring the coyote count to six, and with meat on the ground rapidly disappearing I could think of no reason why, when it was gone, six hungry coyotes would not act in unison to obtain more food.

The impact the two newcomers had on the disadvantaged calf, however, was to rouse him to action again. Not only did he block their passage to the carcass, but, emboldened by this success, he followed up by charging the animals who were already feeding, and drove them away. Then he lowered his head and regarded the pathetic remnant of what had once been a creature similar to himself. Only the upper portions of its body

On the second day, the calf regards the now-unrecognizable remains of his former companion.

were still intact; the hindquarters were gone, and the ribs had been stripped and looked like the red frame of a wrecked boat. I wondered how much longer the calf would be able to make any association between this ravaged skeleton and the live animal to which he presumably had once been closely bonded.

Meanwhile the coyotes had distributed themselves in an imperfect circle around him and were lying about in various (calculated?) postures of repose. Two more had shown up from behind a little rise where, unnoticed by me, they had been sleeping all along, and these, too, spaced themselves in the ring so that the living calf was now surrounded by eight predators. The suspense was terrible. With so many pairs of ears in a state of alert, I hardly dared to breath. With great care, I readied my camera for the showdown.

Looking through a viewfinder is not a satisfactory method of following events. Until my rapidly fired pictures later verified my quick impressions, I could not be certain that in the melee that followed the calf held the advantage at all times. I did know, however, that it was he who initiated the action. First he dashed to the right and dispersed four coyotes in one wild scramble. Then he turned his attention to the opposite front and began to move with stealthy, measured steps toward the coyotes lying there, until they ran off, their tails straight out as if to give them lift. After making three or four sprints after them, the calf returned to dead center, where he fixed a baleful gaze upon a sole remaining coyote, who assessed his situation quite correctly, assumed a blasé pose, and, taking care to avoid eye contact with the elk calf, high-stepped it to the safety zone. The calf had won the round.

But as time passed, the coyotes once again began to edge in and some even attempted to approach the carcass. I was fascinated to see them hunch up and gape as they tried to bluff past this hoofed dragon who guarded such a rich lode of meat. I had previously thought of the hunch display as an agonistic posture reserved exclusively for testing dominance among fellow coyotes. But no. Twisting their heads upward to allow the elk the full impact of their terrible weapons and rounding their spines until they walked as if hobbled, they tried to waddle past. Two in

At one point, the elk calf succeeds in dispersing
eight coyotes who have encircled him.

fact succeeded, and once these were actually feeding, the elk calf ignored them.

By then, four more coyotes had shown up on a ridge some two hundred yards away. But these did not appear inclined to approach. Instead they viewed the spectacle from afar, like city dogs who sit all day at windows, content to remain nonparticipants in the life below. Were these animals members of another pack?

I now realized how lucky I had been to land in the precise spot where I was hiding. It was the single route to the carcass not being traveled by coyotes. Apparently, the snow-clogged swale that banked three sides of the rock was intentionally avoided by the animals in favor of more windswept approaches.

Below and opposite: Using coyote body language, an enterprising individual passes the hostile elk calf, gaping fiercely, and attempts to bluff his way onto the carcass.

As the hours passed, events tended to repeat themselves. From time to time, a coyote would break through the elk's defense and succeed in reaching the carcass. Once there he would be allowed to stay, until the calf, aroused by the approach of still another would-be feeder, would drive them all off.

Nevertheless, little by little the carcass was being consumed.

In the distance a coyote howled, and the male of the pair I had observed early in the day threw back his head and responded. I wondered if his vocalization would attract still more animals to the scene.

It did. Within half an hour, coyote number thirteen arrived at a trot, stopping first on the brow of the plateau before proceeding in a hunched dash for the meat. Something about the animal struck me as familiar. Was it Fang? With the exception of one juvenile who was totally preoccupied with feeding, all the coyotes began to shift uneasily, and one pair even departed, led by the male. Judging from the newcomer's deportment, and taking into consideration that I was no farther than three miles from where I had once observed Fang's churlish behavior at the buffalo remains, I decided it was not improbable that I was indeed viewing a repeat performance by one and the same animal. I decided in any case to label this one Fang 2.

To my surprise, the feeding juvenile alone refused to be

intimidated by Fang 2's boorishness. Responding evasively to the larger animal's snaps and snarls, he boomeranged repeatedly to the carcass, sometimes grabbing mouthfuls of food before being driven off again. I was frankly impressed by his boldness and concluded he was destined to become a dominant animal in some future coyote hierarchy.

With the arrival of Fang 2 on the scene, the possibility that the calf might be attacked seemed even less likely, for this aggressive coyote had a divisive effect on the others. Some departed, and those that remained behaved in a restive manner, keeping a wary eye on Fang 2's movements. It seemed highly improbable that they would now act in unison. Certainly some concerted effort on their part would be required if they were to bring down this vital calf, who at a conservative estimate outweighed any coyote present by twelve times.

Still, despite the coyotes' lack of esprit de corps, the calf's predicament remained desperate. Had he made the slightest move to run off, I am convinced that every wild canine present would have come to life and been after him, like excited dogs who compulsively chase speeding cars. Happily for him, however, he was endowed with a calm temperament, and neither panicked nor bolted; all of his movements were deliberate and assured, and the coyotes, reading his demeanor as a sign of superior strength, made no attack.

By nightfall, when I once again punched my way downhill, my fears over the ultimate fate of the beleaguered elk were greatly relieved, and I looked forward to enjoying a good night's sleep.

But I was too excited by all that I had witnessed to sink into easy slumber. I had seen and photographed a very young hoofed animal, one who was disadvantaged by separation from his herd, successfully hold his ground and even defend a dead fellow against numerous coyotes, whom he had no difficulty whatsoever intimidating. This direct observation supported conclusions frequently deduced indirectly from herd counts and autopsies, which show that *healthy* prey animals rarely become victims of predation. The dynamics of this behavior have been most clearly demonstrated in the case of wolves and moose. David Mech, in his study *The Wolves of Isle Royale*, found that predation does not come about simply as a result of random contact between wolves and their natural prey, but is complicated by a process in which the ability of a potential victim to escape is tested. If an individual bull or cow holds its ground and refuses to run away or give up, wolves apparently do not waste their precious energy reserves trying to kill it. The wolf, therefore, has evolved into an opportunistic hunter, taking only what comes easily, while the characteristics of prey animals, their reactions to threatening situations, determine whether or not they will be victimized. What surprised me in the case of the elk calf was that such a young animal could prove invulnerable to attack.

Equally exciting to me was the impression I received that the calf I watched had acted out of an attachment for a dead animal and that he was experiencing something like bereavement.

As day number three dawned, I was as eager as ever to see what had occurred while I slept, and I was back on top of the mountain by sunup. But to my dismay the calf was gone! I scanned the surrounding slopes for a sign of him. Had he been felled during the night, ravens would surely have been attracted to the fresh blood. But no birds were in evidence anywhere under the low-hanging sky. Only a solitary coyote lay on the edge of the feeding crater in front of me, energetically gnawing on what remained of the now unrecognizable carcass.

I waited for him to finish and leave, then moved onto center stage myself. The ground was so mottled with tracks I could find no clue to which direction the young elk might have taken. I felt terribly let down. Somehow I had taken it for granted that I would be present to witness the denouement in this confrontation between *Canis latrans* and *Cervus canadensis*, although what I had expected to see I could not have said. Perhaps a brief glimpse of the calf meandering down the slopes, cured at last of his fixation on the pile of bones for which he had felt compelled to risk his life. Or if fate decreed that he, too, must become coyote food, then just that, the sight of coyotes feeding upon him. But not a blank!

Without making a plan, I intuitively climbed to the spine of the long ridge that guards the northern edge of the Lamar

Valley like a sleeping dinosaur. Along its lofty vertebrae, I could see for miles on two sides of the range, and since walking was easy there I decided to traverse its windswept length and look for the missing calf.

I don't know how long or how far I walked, for isolation and silence can affect one's internal sense of time. At one point I rested, descending a few feet on the lee side of the range, where I settled among lichen-painted rocks and heard the question arise from some startled part of my innermost being: What am I doing here?

But I saw no calf and no ravens in the sky. At last I turned back, convinced that the calf, though he may have dematerialized, had certainly not died. Then I saw two black birds. They floated on a downdraft, dropping out of my line of vision behind a small rise a half-mile below me.

It was slight evidence. Ravens can exist where carcasses do not, although the reverse is seldom true. But feeling compelled to exhaust all leads, I headed downhill across the snow-clogged gap.

The slope I had to cross was a glaze of pristine beauty, which seemed firm enough to support my first tentative steps. Gathering courage, I walked lightly and quickly, imitating the coyotes I had watched tread snow all winter. It worked. The surface had softened to water under the direct rays of noonday sun, then iced over when the late-afternoon temperature-drop occurred. Now it felt as solid as rock. But when I was halfway across, it caved in.

There is one essential difference between being caught beyond one's depth in water and becoming submerged in snow. Neck-deep in a drift, one cannot swim to shore. Nor can one pull oneself out. Any effort to move simply fills one's boots and clothing with snow.

Initially I flailed. Then I tried to think. My one hope was to regain a foothold on unbroken surface and walk away. But my efforts to raise myself put pressure on the surrounding crust, which naturally caused it to crumble. I needed something long or wide to grab on to, like a ski or snowshoe, that would distribute my weight across a greater area. But foolishly I had not packed such gear.

Contrary to the common belief that burrowing into a snow-drift will protect one from freezing, the snowpack drew heat from my body at an alarming rate. Anyone who has developed cold feet from standing on ice or snow will understand this. Unless one is heavily insulated with layers of Arctic-survival apparel, perhaps it is wiser to stay out of drifts.

After some random tunneling in several directions, I again took stock of my situation. I had wasted much effort burrowing first downhill, then up again, without progressing toward anything that might be categorized as a "shore." I was unclear as to what direction I should take. Then, noting some sprigs of vegetation protruding from the snow, I decided to try to reach them in the hope that they would prove to be the uppermost branches of low shrubs. If so, I might find myself in a more manageable depth.

I don't recall when I noticed the ravens. They floated around me in even circles as they had done while surveying the elk calf. I tried to blot them from my mind, but the beat of their wings whined overhead, marring the absolute stillness of the mountain. It was then I realized the seriousness of my situation, and though I was weary beyond description, I made a promise to myself not to rest.

It took all my strength to reach the twigs and to my disappointment I found the brush they capped was five feet tall. By that time I was soaked with perspiration from exertion, my neck, ankles, and wrists were raw from snow burns, and my heart was pumping blood so hard I thought my head would burst. More than anything I longed to rest, but the overhead beat of black plumage, like some kind of terrible clock, acted as a reminder to me that time was running out. Whatever strength I could now muster would have to be directed toward burrowing straight uphill toward a windswept ridge some one hundred yards away, for I no longer had other options. I was too exhausted to waste further energy on the gamble that I might find an easier course closer at hand.

Resolve is probably another name for the survival instinct. I do not know how I managed to push so much snow for such a long time. At one point I won twelve free steps and this gift kept me going. I had chanced upon a submerged log and, using it as a step up, I was able to slide my body onto the crusted surface and take a short walk before breaking through again.

This stroke of fortune caused me to simplify my objective, to bring it down from the faraway ridge to the more attainable next step. With each foot of progress I made, I looked for another submerged log. And though I did not happen upon one, the aim kept me going.

When the ravens coasted away, I knew that I would make it. But when I was at last standing on bare rocks, shaking with fatigue, the sight of the trail I had carved through the snow filled me with horror.

So that is how it is, I thought. It is the same for me as for the animals that die on this mountain. But it was not merely a thought, for I comprehended the realization with my whole being. I, too, am part of the chain of life.

Two days later, while scanning the slopes with my binoculars, I spotted a small and solitary elk wending his way along the rimrocks. I watched until he disappeared from view, and though I could not prove the animal was the same indomitable calf I had seen stand off more than a dozen coyotes, I would have been willing to take a wager that he was.

Elsa

I do not like to see a wild creature beg food from human beings. Such an animal is not only abnormal, but like the flawed character in classical drama it is heading inexorably for tragedy. I witnessed this fact in Yellowstone National Park during my second winter there.

In 1973 unusually balmy weather had attracted fair numbers of Sunday drivers to visit the officially closed park on weekends. The visitors cruised the road between Mammoth and Cooke City, observing and photographing large herds of elk, bison, and bighorn sheep so visible against a backdrop of snow. Standing knee-deep in shallow drifts, the animals created striking pictures.

But an even more unusual photograph could be taken, and many people discovered it. As has been previously noted, during mild winters herd animals fare quite well, thus reducing the amount of food available for scavengers. As a result, a handful of emaciated coyotes, desperate for something to eat, had taken up panhandling along the road.

The Sunday visitors, of course, encouraged the coyotes' aberrant behavior. As cameras clicked, candy and stale bread were tossed to the mendicants. When edibles were gone, the photographers, in a desperate attempt to hold the subject within photographic range, jettisoned anything handy. As a result, starving coyotes filled up on Polaroid paper, bubblegum, and dirty Kleenex.

I could not suppress my indignation over this, and I protested to the guilty parties, pointing out that wild animals quickly become habituated to receiving handouts and give up seeking their natural food. Coyotes have a tendency to take the easiest obtainable meal.

My speech had little effect. Empty beef-jerky packets were produced to demonstrate that some quality food had been tossed. It was difficult to convince these people that any reward, **103** especially an occasional nourishing one, would serve only to reinforce the coyotes' self-destructive habit, and that a single feeding could corrupt an animal irreparably.

Yellowstone officials did their best to correct the situation. Finding it impossible to control *Homo sapiens*, they concentrated on the wayward coyotes. One park biologist concocted a bitter pill for the rangers to toss from their patrol cars in the hope that its disagreeable taste would discourage the animals from ever again accepting tidbits thrown at them through automobile windows.

It didn't work. Once the animals were conditioned, the begging response was almost impossible to eliminate. The coyotes' own nature probably compounded the difficulty. Born with a capacity to learn to solicit food from one another, it was but a small step to direct their entreaties to man.

Admittedly, only a token number of coyotes succumbed to the temptation. But others, possibly mates or family members, looked on from afar, seemingly intrigued by the antics of their more audacious fellows. Park biologists expressed concern that

A male looks on as Elsa solicits food from tourists. *Opposite :* Rangers'fear that Elsa's begging behavior might be imitated by other coyotes is grounded in fact. Observational learning occurs in the coyote, an animal high up on the phylogenetic tree.

these normal, man-fearing coyotes might begin to imitate the beggars. If so, an epidemic of begging could spread through the population to rival the bear problem that had for so many years plagued Yellowstone.

I shared this worry. Imitative behavior is characteristic of the dog-like members of the Canidae family. The tendency to copy has high survival value, especially for young coyotes, who must quickly acquire food-finding skills from their parents. Thus it was not improbable that a few begging coyotes might in the course of time corrupt numbers of their compeers. Yet when I pleaded with people not to feed the soliciting coyotes, I was invariably regarded as some kind of crank.

I must confess I was also irked by the ease with which everybody was suddenly able to obtain close-ups of the hard-to-photograph coyote. Nonetheless, I was anxious to observe and document the phenomenon myself, and I chose as my subject a gray female whose beat was a mile of road in front of the Tower Ranger Station. This animal had grown so bold she literally blocked my car from passing. When I failed to produce food, she ran under the chassis and began to lick axle grease.

While I was waiting for her to emerge, she suddenly caught the sound of another car approaching, and in anticipation of the handout she had failed to receive from me she blithely trotted to meet it. As if staged for my camera, the car stopped, windows were lowered, and bread crusts were tossed to the beggar, whose ragged coat revealed her poor state of nutrition.

I leaped from my car and ran up and down the shoulder of the road, snapping every conceivable angle of the transaction. Paradoxically, the coyote's conduct toward human beings appeared less dog-like than the demeanor of fraternizing coyotes freely responding to one another. Her eyes lacked expression and her body maintained a rigid, cowering attitude as she nervously paced the road in front of the standing car. What attraction this demeaned animal could hold for people, I could not imagine. Yet they tossed bread crusts at her until their supplies were gone, at which point she skulked right up to their vehicle, stood up on her hind legs, and placed her front paws on the driver's open window.

Immediately, the occupants of the car began crooning words of endearment. But the eyes of the wild canine remained impassive—cold yellow slits. The emotional quality of the human voice seemed a subtlety that eluded her. Her single purpose was to obtain food.

Evidently exasperated by her lack of responsiveness, one person exclaimed, "Look at her eyes. They look positively diabolical. No wonder people hate coyotes."

Meanwhile, another car had stopped behind the first, and the ravenous coyote quickly ran to it and repeated her stand-up performance at the driver's window. From the back seat a child's mittened hand reached out to pet her. Anticipating food, the coyote snapped, barely grazing the child's hand. As the window was quickly rolled up, I heard a woman's excited voice ask, "Did he bite you?"

"He tried to," the child whined.

I headed back for my car deeply disturbed. A single report of such an incident would send the rangers out with guns. Though these men would be as distressed as I over the necessity of shooting the coyote, they would have no alternative. Obviously, it was only a matter of time before this brash animal would bite someone.

As I approached my vehicle, the coyote was close at my heels, too close, in fact, for me to obtain a photograph of her. I backed away and stooped to get a coyote's-eye view of her and suddenly, to my horror, she turned and leaped into my car. In my haste to get pictures of her soliciting food, I had failed to shut the door.

To anyone who has ever tried to lure a coyote into a trap, it will seem almost inconceivable that the animal would permit itself to become cornered. But this one did. And, of course, it was then incumbent upon me to free her. I opened all four doors and shouted and clapped. But the coyote merely flattened her ears and jumped from the front seat to the back and then to the front again.

I wondered what would happen if I got in, slammed the doors and drove off. With a wild coyote as my passenger, I could well imagine the stir I would create along the road. Actually, the idea had some merit. Abducting this doomed animal was probably the single means by which she could be saved from execution. Unfortunately, I did not possess sufficient nerve to rustle a park coyote, nor was I wearing a suit of armor.

Meanwhile the coyote busily inspected my camera bags, nosing for food. All at once her purposefulness gave me an idea. My lunch was in a bag on the floor of the back seat. If I could get my hands on it I might be able to entice her outside.

After several abortive grabs, which created pandemonium inside the car, I succeeded in whisking the bag through the door, unwrapped a peanut butter sandwich, and placed it on a snowbank. In a flash the coyote was outside, voraciously eating, and just as quickly I had my car secured against further invasion.

It was ironic that circumstances had forced me to commit the very act I deplored: feeding a wild animal. Should any of the people I had lectured on this subject now happen to pass by, I realized I would have some explaining to do. I decided to make a hasty departure.

As I drove off, I reflected on what had taken place. Not one of the other three mendicant coyotes I had observed in the park matched this one's boldness. Was she indeed wild? Or could she have been raised by human beings, who had then released her in Yellowstone in the hope that she, like the renowned lioness Elsa, would learn to survive on her own?

Few people have the fortitude to cope with a fully grown pet coyote. Though an occasional pup will grow up to be as tractable as a dog, *Canis latrans* lacks the ten-thousand-year history of domestication and selective breeding that has molded *Canis familiaris* into such a dependable companion. Yet because a coyote is so dog-like, so playful and affectionate and intelligent, he is also expected to be the dog's counterpart in qualities of docility and trust. When it becomes apparent that he is not—when his exploratory nature impels him to investigate the sofa stuffing, when his wild temperament rebels against discipline, and when he reacts with what seems to be unreasonable fear or flight to the slightest change in his surroundings—most people begin to have second thoughts about his value as a house pet.

Opposite:
Elsa.

Rare individuals, of course, find life with such a high-strung creature rewarding. One such person, Helenette Silver of Concord, New Hampshire, happily cared for a series of wild canines over a number of years. Yet she is quick to caution others not to assume a like burden unless they are willing to adapt themselves to the animals' life-style. "You don't discipline a coyote," she told me. "You simply learn how to cooperate with him."

Nevertheless, people continue to acquire coyotes, often against their better judgment. A trapper finds a den and agrees not to slaughter a number of puppies previously spoken for by local children. When presented with a cuddly, teddy-bear-like ball of chocolate-colored fluff, few parents have the heart to say no. There is no young animal more appealing than a baby coyote. Besides, what else can be done with the orphan?

As the puppy grows, however, so does his investigative drive, as well as many other hard-to-live-with instincts. No less than his parents before him, the hand-reared coyote is generously endowed by Nature with qualities essential to independent living. Genetically he may be a basic dog, but he is an unmodified breed of dog with heightened sensitivity, instantaneous reactions, and an indomitable spirit.

Upon discovering this, his keepers (I hesitate to use the term "owner" in connection with the coyote) may seek to return their hyperbolic canine to the wild. But turning a tame coyote loose in the West is hardly different from dropping a goat into a tiger pit. He will be killed. Long before he acquires proficiency at relieving his hunger, he will be shot, trapped, or poisoned. Indeed, he will be fortunate if his lack of suspicion does not bring him to a worse fate. It is impossible to exaggerate the intensity of loathing a coyote engenders in some Westerners. Starved animals have been found with their lower jaws sawed off, others with their mouths wired shut.

Bearing this in mind, it seemed a likely possibility that some exasperated guardian of a coyote might have decided to release a loved troublemaker in a protected area such as Yellowstone National Park. In fact, the more I thought about it, the more convinced I became that the gray female, whom I began to call "Elsa," was not a wild coyote at all, but an abandoned one. Like a

lost dog, she haunted the road. Had she not leaped into my car
and made herself at home there?

My heart went out to her, for a half-tame coyote would obviously experience great difficulty competing with truly wild
coyotes for territory and food. She would quite naturally turn
for help to the human beings she encountered on the road.

Though my theory could not be proved, I clung to it, for it
gave me the excuse I needed to rescue her. If it were true that
this particular coyote was not actually a park animal, Yellowstone officials might not object to my removing her. And if it
were true that she had been hand-reared, the right person
might be able to restore her trust in man. I suspected that Lloyd
Tillett would agree to give her a home, and equally important, I
knew that he possessed the rare insight needed to coexist with a
pet coyote.

I was right. After hearing my description of the coyote's
behavior, Tillett said he would take her. But he was nearly four
hundred miles away, via the only route across the Rockies open

Elsa's troubles
are over.

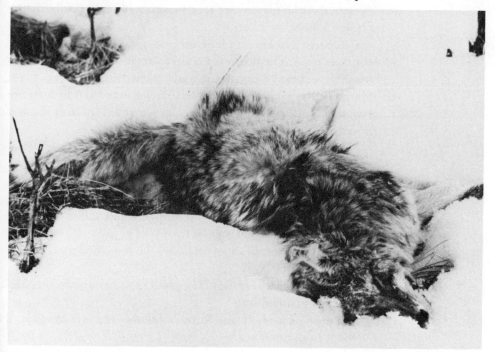

all winter. There was no point in asking him to come until I had made the necessary arrangements with park officials and had actually succeeded in capturing Elsa.

By phone Lloyd offered suggestions on how to snare the coyote, and I enlisted the aid of three brothers, sons of the owners of the cabin I was renting. Their father, Wallace Bent, cleared out his tool shed to serve as a temporary holding pen, and we set out. En route I stopped to speak with a park official and casually broached the subject.

"I know someone who would like to have a female coyote," I began. "What happens to the begging animals I see along the road?"

"Unfortunately, if they become too familiar with the public, we have to shoot them" was the reply. Then he added, "But I'd rather break the arms of the people who make them that way."

"In that case, would you mind if I did a little coyote-removal work?" I queried as nonchalantly as possible.

"If you mean that problem animal at Tower Junction, I guess everybody'd be glad to see that situation happily resolved," he replied somewhat absently.

I departed before he had time to give the matter deeper consideration. The boys were waiting in my car, armed with raw meat, rope, heavy-duty gloves, and a homemade divider to place between the front and back seats. It was our plan to lure the coyote into the trunk, but failing this we would try to entice her into the car.

Sleet was falling when we arrived at the Tower Ranger Station, creating what is known in the West as a "white-out." We could see only a few feet ahead, and Elsa was not visible on the road. I drove back and forth, hoping the sound of a motor would bring her out. Finally I stopped and inquired of the Tower ranger if he had seen her.

"We have orders to shoot that one," he informed me. "She bit somebody yesterday."

I would have to work fast. The child's mother apparently had registered a complaint.

"I know," I said. "I also know someone who will give her a home if I can catch her."

The ranger smiled. "Well, good luck to you," he said.

But by late afternoon, it was obvious that good luck would not favor my project. The day-long drizzle had created a road hazard, and I decided to drive the boys home, despite the fact that on the following morning my helpers would have to attend school and I would be forced to work alone.

That evening I phoned veterinarians for miles around to say that I shortly expected to have a half-starved coyote in my possession and would want rabies and distemper shots for her. All but one turned me down, and he agreed only reluctantly, after forcing me to listen to a lecture on the savage nature of *Canis latrans*. Said he: "They kill anything—deer, cattle—anything . . . and they don't even bother to eat what they kill. Just love to kill. . . ."

I wondered what explanation he could give for the number of famished coyotes visible among abundant game herds in Yellowstone. But I was too relieved to find somebody willing to vaccinate Elsa to argue the point.

The next day was clear, and I set out early to look for her. The first thing I did was to check for fresh tracks along the mile strip that was her haunt. But I could find no evidence that she had been near the road since the previous day's sleet fall.

The snow supported my snowshoes as I tramped across the dazzling field, squinting for signs. Two ravens were courting in a lodgepole pine, and their billing and cooing looked more like a parody of love than the real thing. I watched the male play at feeding the female. She scrunched down, making herself appear small, and opened her beak like a fledgling. Then the two left their perch and soared and dipped in an aerial act that clearly celebrated the joy of being ravens.

Then I saw Elsa. A trickle of blood stained the snow beneath the place where the bullet had entered her body. I turned her over. She was intact, though her lightweight body was hardly more than a ragged pelt. Her frailty made me want to weep. How valiantly this creature had responded to Nature's edict to survive. Truly her only crime had been her refusal to submit meekly to the inevitability of an untimely death. Instead she had tried to stave it off with courage and ingenuity. I held her a long time.

A
Poaching
Incident

I was hoping to witness an instance of coyote predation on one
of the species man has designated as "his" game, namely,
deer, elk, antelope, or bighorn sheep. Local people assured me
that I would see deer being terrorized by packs of coyotes any
morning I cared to drive along a gravel road just outside the
park's northern boundary. I took the tip seriously. During this
season of want, I felt certain a few coyotes would live up to their
bad reputation and hunt the animals man himself so covets.

Snow was patchy at the lower elevations, and no coyotes were
visible against the fissures of cured grass that perfectly matched
their tawny coats and provided them with natural camouflage.
So, instead of searching for coyotes I staked out their purported
prey, the mule deer, and waited for action. After two weeks of
watching these graceful animals from dawn until noon, however, I began to suspect I had been directed to the wrong place.
Though coyotes occasionally trotted past the small bands of five
to twenty deer that stood in clusters along the melting slopes,
neither species took any notice of the other.

I tried to obtain more specific information, but was assured I
was looking in the right place. Moreover, the coyotes, I was told,
chased the mule deer every day.

"How do the coyotes bring them down?" I asked.

"Hamstring them," was the ready reply.

Yet I was unable to locate anyone who had actually been an
eyewitness to an actual kill. Thus, I remained skeptical.*

---

* Through repetition, stories of coyote depredation tend to become increasingly
fictionalized. One Western senator declared to me on his oath that when he was a
boy an entire herd of thirteen fully grown deer had been wiped out by coyotes in
one savage attack. When pressed, he had no explanation why twelve of the
alleged victims did not take flight while the first was being killed. Nevertheless, I
was assured the incident was authentic and was urged to "put that in your book."
The story, it gradually emerged, was thirdhand. As a boy, he had overheard an
old-timer repeat it to his father. And now, forty years later, he seemed somewhat
chagrined by my refusal to accept as prima facie evidence the testimony of such

At the same time I had no reason to doubt that coyotes ambushed deer herds from time to time to determine if they contained any easy prey. But as the deer were wintering exceptionally well in 1973, it is likely the coyotes were not making many prolonged runs after them. Their indifference toward a thriving herd gave support to the view of a park biologist, who summed up current scientific thinking as follows: "Any wild ungulate that falls victim to a coyote must already be predisposed to death. Predation can only be regarded as a secondary cause of mortality."

I recalled Adolph Murie telling me that during the many years he studied coyotes in Yellowstone National Park he had *never* witnessed coyote predation on so-called game animals.

Despite all this, with depressing regularity letters to the editor were being printed in local newspapers, and statements by sportsmen were being quoted over Western radio, that reinforced the endemic assumption that the coyotes were "getting all the game."

I happened to comment on this to Murie and he replied, "The people who make such statements must have fantastic powers of observation. Scientists who have studied coyotes all their lives have not been privileged to witness such behavior."

There could be little question that the barrage of anti-coyote propaganda stemmed from two sources: hunters, who were worried about the decline in game and anxious to blame another predator; and sheepmen, whose problem with coyotes was totally unrelated to game animals, but who hoped to incite hunters into becoming their allies. In addition, a large segment of the Western population, having been nurtured on these fables, was convinced it was in possession of the true facts.

Yet, there were other Westerners who were skeptical. And anybody whose daily work put him into direct contact with coyotes disputed the prevailing view. Almer Nelson, retired supervisor of the National Elk Refuge, reported that during the twenty years he managed a herd of between seven and ten

---

reliable men. My rejection of all but firsthand accounts of coyote predation disappointed many people who had favorite tales to tell.

thousand wintering elk, on only two occasions had he witnessed coyote depredation on the herd. Said he: "From time to time the government predator-control men would approach me to request permission to poison the refuge coyotes. They were introducing trumpeter swans, and they argued that the coyotes would kill them. But I didn't think so, and the coyotes never bothered the birds. I needed those coyotes, in any case, to clean up the normal herd attrition. Can you imagine what the nearby town of Jackson would smell like if coyotes weren't eating up elk carcasses?"

The Yellowstone rangers I spoke with could recall seeing only one attack on a deer, elk, antelope, or bighorn sheep. Ranger Larry Hays described that incident: "It was an elk calf, and a pair of coyotes killed it so quickly I could hardly see what happened. When I examined it later, I saw it had a deformed hoof." (Predisposed to death!)

Yet the myths prevail. Part of the public's conviction obviously stems from the fact that scavenging coyotes, when not actually observed feeding on dead game, leave circumstantial evidence in the form of tracks around half-eaten carcasses. Chief ranger Norman Dodge told me he frequently received reports from park visitors about these so-called kills. But upon investigating them, he invariably found coyotes were scavenging on already dead animals.

Dodge described watching a wounded deer take two days to die, surrounded by a half-dozen coyotes who patiently awaited its demise. "I was wishing the coyotes would hurry things along," he said, "but they were not about to risk getting a kick in the ribs for a prize that would inevitably fall to them anyway."

He then inquired if I had ever seen coyotes feed on an animal immediately after it had died.

"The reason I ask," he said, "is because I don't believe I've ever seen a coyote eat a carcass that wasn't at least twenty-four hours dead."

I recalled waiting near the body of the drowned elk somewhat longer than twenty-four hours before any coyotes appeared, but that being the sole time I had witnessed an animal in the act of dying, I could draw no inferences from the example. All the carcasses I had found had been dead an undetermined length of time, and I was guided to them by animals already in the process of feeding.

"Keep an eye out for fresh road-kills," Dodge suggested. "I can't tell you why it is, but I never saw a coyote feed on a deer or an elk the same day it was hit by a car."

That evening Wallace Bent told me of a road-killed deer he had passed not an hour earlier while driving from Livingston to Gardiner. We hopped into his van and sped to the place. I hoped to find the deer before the highway department carted it away, intending to remove it to some strategic and photogenic location where coyotes were numerous. In one respect I disapproved of my own plan inasmuch as I would be manipulating the environment. But I rationalized that the highway department, by depriving scavenger animals of a chance to feed on wild-animal accident victims, was the real meddler. By preventing this routine interference of man from occurring, I was actually allowing the natural food chain to operate again.

We found the dead deer in a well-concealed ditch, and to our surprise it was more than a little ripe. Evidently the highway department had overlooked it for some days, as had any coyotes or ravens. Undeterred by the stench, we dragged the bloated creature into the van, got in, and drove off with our heads well out the windows.

The location I had in mind was one just beyond the park boundary where coyote tracks were very much in evidence. The site was ideal, as it offered excellent cover for me along the opposite bank of a rushing stream, which incidentally would drown out the noise of my camera. We unloaded our unsavory cargo and left quickly, leaving as few traces as possible.

The next morning at dawn I was in position. But the carcass, which framed so beautifully through my long lens, had not been touched. I wondered—could the coyotes detect the lingering scent of our gloved hands above that stench?

For seven days I made periodic visits to the setup, but during that week not even a bird paid a call. It seemed inconceivable to me that in this season of famine scavengers would pass up a meal of such magnitude. Did the too-propitiously placed bonanza smack of a trap? Or was the carcass simply too putrid for even a starving scavenger to stomach?

Meanwhile, I made frequent stops to check on Elsa's body. Coyote remains have, on occasion, been recorded in coyote droppings, and I fully expected my little friend would be recycled into ongoing life. But she, too, remained untouched. As there was little likelihood of decay at this higher and colder elevation, where snow still blanketed the mountain, she lay day after day in a state of perfect preservation.

It was anybody's guess just what the coyotes were eating. By the hour I watched their dog-like silhouettes moving back and forth across fields of snow, vainly searching for mice. The pattern was very different from what I had observed the previous winter, when a squeaking *Microtus* could be pulled from almost any snowbank. I could only surmise that a rodent population crash had occurred to compound the famine brought on by the carrion shortage. If so, Nature had dealt *Canis latrans* a double blow.

I telephoned my friend Franz Camenzind, who was studying coyotes some hundred and fifty miles to the south, to learn how widespread was the famine.

"I never saw a winter like this one," he told me. "It's so mild here the elk aren't dying and the coyotes are. Today I just found my ninth body. I'm sending the carcass off to the University of Utah for autopsy." *

Ironically, three months later Camenzind and I were to sit through twelve hours of predator-control hearings in Casper, Wyoming, and listen to a roomful of sheepmen testifying before a committee of United States senators that, since the presidential ban on poison had gone into effect in February of the previous year, the coyote population had exploded.

"Since they don't have no natural enemies," one deluded rancher explained, "nothing but poison is gonna get 'em."

---

* The autopsy report cited canine hepatitis as the cause of death. Famine, however, might more rightly be regarded as the primary cause of mortality. Hungry animals rarely die of starvation. Before such an extreme is reached, endemic diseases afflict their poorly nourished bodies, reducing numbers to a supportable level.

On the day following my long-distance phone conversation with Camenzind, an auspicious burst of ravens brought me to a screeching halt on a mountain curve halfway between Gardiner and Mammoth. High on the slope, I spotted two coyotes sitting on their haunches and surveying with keen attention the site abandoned by the panicked birds. I looked more closely at the small patch of snow exciting their interest and saw that it was spattered with blood. Some massive animal had experienced no quiet passing!

I quickly got rid of my car and hiked to a high vantage point from where I could see magpies wheeling and braking above the gory slush. Through my binoculars, I followed the trail of red that stained the mountainside until I spotted the bird-covered remains. Like ants, magpies were swarming over the largess. But the victim had apparently fallen too close to the road to suit the coyotes, who I presumed had inflicted the mortal wound at a point higher up the slope. Four of them were now visible, pacing these loftier reaches.

I could not make out what kind of animal had died. Its shape appeared totally unfamiliar and I wondered if I was viewing a dismembered portion of it. The more I scrutinized the ravaged remains, the more confused I became. For one thing, I could see no hair, nor were there any horns or antlers anywhere about. Curiosity finally got the better of me, and I descended to make a closer inspection. What I saw caused me to run for my car and speed to park headquarters.

"It was the work of a poacher, all right," the ranger agreed, as he examined the gut pile.

"Was it an elk?" I asked.

"A big one."

I pictured the antlered beast, accustomed to having long lenses pointed toward it, as it must have been standing at the moment of death, calmly staring at its killer.

"The park elk are so tame," I lamented. "Who could be so heartless as to gun one down?"

"The same type of people who complain that the 'dirty no-good coyotes' should be destroyed for getting all the deer," came the bitter reply.

Alongside some drag marks and running from the point where the body had fallen to the shoulder of the road (where the guilty parties had apparently experienced difficulty lifting the heavy animal into their pickup) was a double trail of blood-filled bootprints. The poachers could not have left a more symbolic mark of their passing. One pair belonged to a man, the other to a woman. A hasty gutting had lightened their load, and it was this offal—an enormous stomach pouch, a spleen, and a liver—along with a greal deal of blood-drenched snow that was now attracting hungry scavengers to the scene.

Below and opposite: While his companions look on, a wary coyote carefully tests a suspicious gut pile left by a poacher.

I asked permission to move the gut pile from the road back to where the elk had originally fallen, in the hope that some plucky coyote might hazard to feed upon it there. Then I left

to give any such resolute animal an opportunity to approach.

Meanwhile, for the eighth straight day, I returned to make a routine check on my road-killed-deer setup. To my surprise, I found a magpie blithely pecking on its rancid hide. Obviously, then, the decomposed flesh was not entirely unpalatable. Had scavengers simply failed to discover the windfall earlier? Now that a bird had located the bounty, I guessed it would not be long before coyotes, too, would find it.

I then returned to view the gut pile and counted fifteen magpies pecking the membrane surrounding the stomach pouch, trying to release undigested grassy provender. While dragging that organ uphill I had estimated its weight at fifty pounds—a lot of bird food! And a short distance upslope I

spotted three coyotes lurking among the trees, a pair and a female yearling.

After a time the male of the threesome made a reconnaissance trip downhill toward the food. En route the still-fresh scent of my recent track stopped him, and he withdrew to the trees again.

A short time passed and then once again, impelled by hunger, he descended, this time to within a few feet of the offal. But he made no move to feed. Instead he carefully investigated the surrounding area, while from the trees his two female companions watched his every move.

This coyote's behavior intrigued me. He trod the ground in so tentative a manner I got the impression he half-expected it would at any moment open up and swallow him. Several times when contentious magpies broke into dispute, he jumped. But quickly he regained his composure and continued making his tour of inspection. I began to suspect he was testing the man-tainted ground for pitfalls, and that during his lifetime he had had experience with traps. In fact, he finally made a move that convinced me he was actually trying to spring such a device. Craning his neck, he stretched his head forward as far as possible until his nose just touched the stomach pouch, and simultaneously made a spectacular leap backward. When nothing snapped, he trotted back and forth across the slope as if discharging built-up nervous energy. Then he repeated this stratagem three more times.

Finally, his mate decided to join him and, following his example, she, too, avoided the suspicious organs, assuaging her hunger by eating only blood-drenched snow. Then the pair moved uphill together, and the yearling descended, making a ritualistic gesture of submission in passing. Like her parents (?), she, too, would not approach the bait and only licked bloody snow at a safe distance from the organs. At this point I was fully convinced that the canny old male had established this avoidance pattern for the others. Unable to spring what he seemed to have determined to be a trap, he managed by his example to communicate that, famine or not, the organs were for the birds!

At this point an automobile passed, stopped, and after a

moment noisily ground into reverse. As a man emerged and began to follow the bloody trail uphill toward the offal, the three coyotes dashed for the trees. I knew my observations were about to come to an end, so I decided to leave and make one final stop at my deer-carcass setup before the winter light faded.

There I found the lone magpie had been joined by two others, and, with voracious energy, the three birds were excavating a large red crater in the hindquarters of the deer. The gory color, I knew, would soon attract ravens, and these raucous creatures would in turn be conspicuous to any coyotes roaming the area. I began to grow hopeful that after all this time my decoy might still pay off.

It did, but not quite as I had expected. At five the following morning I slipped into my hiding place, and while waiting for the sun to rise and warm my shivering body and, not incidentally, to illuminate the scene across the stream, I strained to see the gray-brown form I had propped on the opposite bank for fullest photographic impact. During the night a light snowfall had dusted the ground with crystal, and each time I shifted slightly, an avalanche of the pretty stuff dropped from the thick brush in which I was concealed into the neck of my sweater. I pulled my cap down over my face and suffered patiently until a faint aura told me that the sun, at last, was making its way up the back of the mountain. Slowly, as a chiaroscuro of brush and snow began to take shape, the stream bank where Wally Bent and I had planted the road-kill emerged. But where was the deer? I scanned the shore with my telephoto lens, then tried binoculars. Finally, I pulled out my spotscope and trained it on the spot where I was certain three magpies had been feeding but twelve hours before. Where was the deer?

I emerged from my cramped blind and began a long hike downstream to a cross point, then followed the opposite shore back to the scene of the mystery. There, a thousand coyote tracks pocked the new-fallen snow. But not a bone was to be seen! No teeth, no skull, no rib cage, no hide, absolutely *nothing* remained of the carcass! Except for a few coarse deer hairs, and no more of these than any live animal might shed on the spot where it had bedded for the night, no clue remained that would

A rare white coyote in Yellowstone Park has survived trappers who make high profits on white fur.

lead the most astute woodsman to suspect that a few hours earlier an intact carcass had lain here.

Only the rapidly melting coyote tracks told the tale. Up the bank and down the bank and across the slope they ran. Some were paralleled by drag marks, which indicated directions taken by the animals who had garnered the largest portions of venison.

How many coyotes had fed? For an instant I had a vision of a score of ravenous creatures dismembering and carting away food at a furious pace, illuminated only by falling snow that frosted their coats and whitened their muzzles. Had they telegraphed the news of their discovery to one another by howling? How else could it happen that after all these days so many coyotes had suddenly gathered so quickly?

As I stood and watched, the sun came up and erased all traces of the nighttime revelry. The earth is a resilient backdrop for Nature's myriad dramas.

Though my well-laid plans for the road-killed deer carcass

had melted like the snow without producing photographs or observations of coyote interactions, the incident had taught me an unexpected lesson about my subject. Any theory I was beginning to formulate about coyotes avoiding extremely putrid meat was forever dispelled. It was now clear to me that a hungry *Canis latrans* relishes anything as long as it does not reek of a trap. But I now suspected he was not so clever at finding food as I had previously assumed. Perhaps this accounted for Dodge's observation that a number of hours usually elapsed before coyotes could be seen feeding on road-killed animals.

Still, before spring and its easier living arrived, with luck, constant traveling, and the helpful guidance of birds, a certain number of the species would manage to survive by performing their duties as Nature's sanitation workers.

In April the coyotes made themselves scarce. My tutor, ex-trapper Vern Dorn, advised me by phone that they were occupied in making cleverly concealed dens for their soon-to-be-born puppies. He added that there would be little point in looking for these burrows in advance of whelping time. Each pair, he said, would excavate several old badger holes, restore their previous year's various dens, and dig perhaps half a dozen or more new burrows across their territory in preparation for the birth of their litter. Any one of these often widely separated dens might serve as a convenient holing-up place for the female whenever she began to feel labor. Afterward the pups might be moved, if the mother chose, or if she were disturbed.

As usual, Vern's information proved to be correct. Through my spotscope I observed pairs of coyotes sporadically engaged in excavation work. And later in the summer, when I returned to some of the places where I had witnessed these digging operations, I found many completed dens that had never been occupied. In fact, most of the coyote dens reported to me by local people turned out to be just such unused homes.

It was difficult to find coyotes at all during this period. By April even a fresh carcass often failed to lure them into open view. With vast stretches of meadow released from snow, small rodents were so easily obtainable that the coyote did not need to venture far afield to satisfy hunger. Perhaps, too, hormonal changes were transforming the winter roamers into recluses in preparation for the time when they would be cautiously catering food to a sequestered family.

During this period in both my first and second years of fieldwork I decided to take advantage of the lull and look into other aspects of coyote life. I journeyed east to investigate the coy-wolf of New England in 1972, and during April 1973 I put the time to good use by viewing a number of coyote pets.

My first contact with a tame coyote had occurred a few years   **129** earlier, long before I ever dreamed of making a study of the animal. The experience had left me with a somewhat distorted idea regarding the domesticability of *Canis latrans*. During a visit to the Paul Maxwells in Grand Junction, Colorado, to obtain information regarding a band of wild horses in the region, I was introduced to Hobo, a male coyote of extraordinary size. Unaware that hand-reared coyotes are defensive toward strangers, I greeted him as if he were a friendly dog, and he reciprocated by making springing leaps at my face, each one culminating in an on-the-mouth kiss. I learned later that even for such a friendly coyote as Hobo, this was unusually demonstrative behavior.

"Hobo took an instant liking to you," Maurine Maxwell recalled when I returned several years after the incident, this time too late to take a second look at him. Hobo, I learned, had died of a kidney infection at the age of eight, shortly before my arrival.

"I always heard you couldn't tame a coyote," Paul Maxwell drawled. "Well, I was a government trapper enough years to know that most of those folks are accomplished liars. So I figured there probably wasn't much to the rumor. I believed I could tame one and I did. Hobo was even housebroke, and he rode in our car and looked right out of the window like a dog."

The backyard of the Maxwell residence contained a number of pens housing numerous wirehaired terriers and two new female coyotes, acquired since my last visit. Before being introduced to three-year-old Kiki and a beauty of unknown age named Amber, Paul Maxwell explained to me why he had given up his job as a government trapper.

"This killing business is out of hand," he said, with a touch of anger. "I grew up on a cow ranch, and as a kid I remember my uncle would no more kill a coyote . . . Now the ranchers, the Fish and Game people, and everybody has gone just plumb insane. All at once they're even saying the coyotes are killing all the deer and antelope. For thousands of years these animals lived together. Now suddenly the coyotes are killing them off? They're just figuring every angle they can think of to keep a bunch of bums on the payroll."

Maxwell leaned back in his chair, and his eyes looked pained as he continued. "I quit trapping about eight years ago. Something happened to me after I found I'd killed two old coyotes that never in their lives bothered a thing. I tell you I'd watched this pair year after year and they were as harmless as could be, fed on mice and minded their own business. I got so I really admired them, and I got real pleasure out of seeing them out there every year. They were a part of the countryside.

"Well, one day I found the old dog of the pair had gotten into one of my traps. I tell you I was sick. And less than two weeks later the bitch done the same thing. Maurine was with me when I found what had happened, and I turned to her and said, 'This is the last steel trap I'm ever going to set.' And it was."

"You sound like Vern Dorn," I told Paul. "He's a 'reformed' trapper from Wyoming. He and you seem to have arrived at the same conclusion. Only difference between you two is he never had your luck rearing coyotes. He told me all the males he tried to tame turned on him in the end, and the females were too nervous and timid to make good pets."

"I think that's usually the case," Paul Maxwell agreed. "Hobo, well, he was kinda unique. It's the individual animal, you know. Sometimes there's an especially gentle one in a litter. The two coyotes we have now, they won't let me get near them, though Kiki used to when she was a pup. She still likes Maurine, though. Anyway, you go on out there and see them. . . ."

"May I go inside their pens?" I asked.

Maurine looked apprehensive.

"Oh, sure, go right on in. They won't mind *you*," Paul Maxwell assured me.

I looked at Maurine.

"Well, coyotes are usually kind of fearful of strangers," she said. "Everything new or even something familiar that is out of its usual place will frighten them."

"Oh, go on in," Paul insisted. Then, turning to his wife, he said, "They'll take to her. You'll see."

Maurine led me outside to make the proper introductions before leaving me alone to get acquainted with the two coyotes, which were housed in separate pens.

"Why don't you put them together?" I asked.

"Oh, once they got into an awful battle over Hobo. Two females, you know. I think they might have killed one another if we hadn't separated them. Now that Hobo's gone, we might try to put them together again."

As we approached Kiki's pen, this smaller coyote caught sight of Maurine and began to pace the fence line excitedly, her tail waving gracefully.

"She hides when she sees Paul," Maurine observed. "It kind of hurts him that she acts that way, 'cause he likes the coyotes so much. We wonder if some man might have come by and scared her."

Kiki eyed me suspiciously, but in her eagerness for Maurine's attention, she managed to resist an impulse evidently at work in her to withdraw from me into her house. As she skittishly danced about, Maurine threw her some meat, which she quickly devoured without taking her eyes off of me.

While the coyote fed, Maurine said, "She was bottle-raised by a sixteen-year-old girl, the daughter of a sheep rancher. When Kiki was six months old this little girl called us, and she was in tears. Her father, she said, would not let her keep the animal another day. Threatened to kill it. She had heard about us having a coyote and, well, she just begged us to take Kiki. What could we do? We took her and it turned out she and Hobo got along real well."

The sheepman's daughter had found asylum for a coyote with an ex-trapper! Perhaps if the world lasts long enough, I thought, the whole human race may come to its senses.

Kiki now looked as if she would allow me to enter her pen, and we slipped in carefully, giving her no chance to make an escape. Immediately she leaped on Maurine and began pulling on her pants leg, enjoying the game of tug-of-war.

"Coyotes like to play rough," Maurine explained. "You can't change them. Anyway, they don't mean any harm. That's just their way."

It was obvious that Maurine's slacks would soon be in shreds unless the attention of the high-spirited coyote could be diverted to some other object.

"You know the coyote is different from a dog," she said. "You can't impose your will on 'em. You have to wheedle them into doing what you want. If you try to force them, you'll spoil your whole plan."

Maurine demonstrated by pulling off her scarf and floating it in front of the coyote's eyes. Instantly, the animal let loose of her slacks and jumped for the scarf, and a game of keep-away developed. The coyote obviously was relishing the fun. Her tail never stopped wagging, and her eyes gleamed with excitement. Maurine handed me the scarf, and I replaced her as Kiki's playmate.

"She doesn't usually let other people inside her pen, but she seems to have sized you up and you've passed muster. Usually they're one-man animals and very, very jealous. One thing I learned about coyotes: They let you know your enemies better than a dog."

The animal bounding about my feet seemed so like a high-spirited dog, I could well understand how people might forget

Kiki plays tug-of-war with the author.

to bear in mind that a hand-raised coyote is not really the docile creature that ten thousand years of selective breeding have made of its first cousin.

After a time, Kiki settled down and presented her back hips to be scratched. An ecstatic expression spread across her face as she waggled hard against Maurine's hand, letting it be known that she enjoyed the relief she was experiencing in this hard-to-reach spot.

After even this short contact with the high-strung Kiki, I was beginning to appreciate what the Maxwells had accomplished with their first coyote.

"How did you manage to housebreak Hobo?" I asked.

"Like we said, Hobo was unique. We could speak sharply to him, but still we couldn't cuff him. Coyotes have too much self-respect to accept being punished. People make a big mistake thinking they can dominate a coyote like a dog. Coyotes regard themselves as no less important than people. They'll try hard to get along with you, but only as long as you treat them as equals."

"How do coyotes feel about dogs, your wirehairs, for example?" I asked.

"They love dogs," Maurine replied. "When our female terrier, Teensy, gave birth to a litter, Hobo began to regurgitate food for the puppies and we couldn't keep Teensy out of his pen. She ate what he regurgitated."

As we talked, my attention was occasionally attracted to the coyote in the nearby pen, who was staring at Kiki and Maurine with what could only be described as a wistful expression.

"Does she want attention?" I asked.

"That coyote never tamed up!" Maurine told me. "She won't play with me or allow me to pet her at all."

"She looks like she wants attention, though," I said.

"Well, you can try, but she hides in her house the moment anyone goes near her."

Amber was far more beautiful than Kiki, and well named. Her golden eyes glowed like jewels and seemed to express such longing I was convinced they were begging for love. But Maurine was right. The moment we approached, she dived for cover.

Opposite: Amber—a coyote who couldn't be "gentled."

"I wish it were possible to turn this one loose," Maurine told me. "But around here she'd be poisoned or shot in a day."

"How did you get her?" I asked.

"Oh, somebody called up and said there was a coyote in their backyard. We drove over to check and, sure enough, there was Amber wearing a dog collar several sizes too small. We had a tough time catching her. She must have been hand-reared and probably dumped by somebody who was disappointed when she didn't turn out like they expected, like an obedient dog. Coyotes never forget. I doubt she'll ever trust a human being again."

After a time Maurine went away, and I tried to make up to Amber. I was deeply moved by this animal whose gaze expressed such hurt. For a long time I talked soothingly to her, telling her how sorry I was that she would never know the freedom enjoyed by the wild coyotes I had been watching in Yellowstone. She listened attentively but would not leave the far corner of her pen, where she perched on top of her doghouse. She brought to mind Elsa, and I now grew more convinced than ever that the ill-fated Yellowstone coyote had been just such a case as Amber, a hand-raised animal who had failed to meet somebody's unrealistic expectations, and been turned loose to fend for herself.

After a time I decided to enter Amber's pen. I had no particular plan in mind, but I wanted to make some kind of contact with this deprived creature. Canines are such social animals, and Amber had no pack with which to go through the greeting ritual, to howl with, or to buss with her long pointy nose.

Carefully I slipped through the chicken-wire door and seated myself on the hard-packed ground. Amber responded to this unusual intrusion by wildly pacing the opposite end of her pen and jumping on and off her doghouse. After a time she calmed down and regarded me with a gaze so unflinching it gave me an eerie feeling. Indeed, her steadfast look projected a kind of mute sorrow so intense that it affected me deeply.

I remained quite still and stayed in the pen for more than an hour, during which time Amber grew more quiet. Occasionally, when her attention was attracted by a pair of battling birds or a car backing down the nearby road, she even managed to shift her fixed stare from me to the outside world. I did not try to approach her, for I was certain that any such attempt would only incite her to resume her pacing. But I did receive the impression that, given time, I could win her trust, for I felt she longed for companionship. The Maxwells seemed surprised that I had made any progress in calming her, small though it was. They were as troubled over her plight as I.

Before leaving for Laramie, Wyoming, to make the acquaintance of still another tame coyote, I met a tame wolf. The Maxwells happened to mention that their neighbor was raising a timber wolf and they drove me over to see it. I was curious to find out how tractable was a hand-reared *Canis lupus*, compared to a hand-reared *Canis latrans*. Bearing in mind that temperament varies radically from one animal to another regardless of species and that it would be impossible to make any realistic comparison on the basis of but three coyotes and a single wolf, I was nevertheless struck by the sharp contrast in temperament these examples presented.

Though the wolf's owners were not at home, making it necessary that we view him through a mesh fence, the one-hundred-pound animal accepted me on sight and wriggled and squirmed against the wire like a puppy, demanding that I, a stranger, reach in and stroke him. Such an intrusive move would have unstrung the two coyotes I had just visited. At a later date, I was able to observe the same instant friendliness in a number of hand-reared wolves I visited near Wilson, Wyoming. Compared to the more nervous coyote, these large canines seemed positively easygoing. Of course, given sufficient time, many coyotes will exhibit similar sociability. Nevertheless, though both species can be tamed, neither a coyote nor a wolf should ever be regarded as domesticated. And only people who understand and appreciate these animals just for their wild traits should ever attempt to rear either one of them.

Mingo
and
Gip

Mingo was another experience. I found him in Laramie, Wyoming, where good fortune had landed him in the home of JoAnn and Gary Spiegelberg. The Spiegelbergs, who have a fine understanding of wild creatures, took him into their menagerie of family dogs and orphaned bobcats.

"From his earliest days Mingo could defend himself better than our bobcat babies," JoAnn told me, as we watched the yearling coyote energetically digging up the Spiegelbergs' backyard. As it was April, Mingo seemed to be responding to some innate drive to create a large number of dens under the lawn, a fact that did not seem to perturb JoAnn. Her concern at that moment was whether or not Mingo would accept me. Out of caution she had put him outside on a long chain prior to my arrival, and we watched him through a large picture window in the kitchen.

"He can clear that four-foot fence without a bit of trouble," she explained. "And after he discovered our neighbor's chickens, we were forced to begin chaining him."

"Could you train him to stay home?" I asked, and immediately felt foolish.

JoAnn laughed. "Well, he understands the meaning of the word 'no,' but if anybody tries to hit him with anything, he growls. And when I scold him, he starts to bite himself."

I was interested to learn more about this behavior, for it sounded like an example of what psychologists call "displacement of hostility." I asked JoAnn to demonstrate and was able to photograph Mingo inflicting bites on his hind leg after a mild reprimand.

"It makes it difficult to train him when he takes things so hard."

"What about using the reward method?" I asked.

"No," JoAnn said. "You can't buy a coyote with food. He is 138 above that sort of thing. But we don't worry about training him.

After all, he's a coyote, and we think we've done awfully well with him as it is. He's very loving and sleeps right on the foot of our bed at night. When we shift around too much, he lets us know with a growl that we're disturbing his rest. But at the same time he is very careful not to lie on our feet and bother us. Before he lies down he walks in a circle and feels with his forepaws to see just where all the feet are. Then he takes whatever space is left."

I asked JoAnn if she thought a coyote is difficult to train because he might not be as intelligent as a dog.

"Not as intelligent! Why, Mingo's smarter than any dog I've ever known," was her response. "He's just independent. He

When provoked, Mingo relieves his aggressive feelings by biting himself.

doesn't miss anything. The slightest change in the room can upset him. If we get a new plant and set it on the TV set, for example, Mingo notices and will pace for hours." This behavior, called "neophobia" by psychologists, is a wild trait, and it is easy to understand its survival value for a species as persecuted as the coyote.

JoAnn continued, "A dog might be able to learn a lot of tricks, but a coyote is much more aware. Anyway, learning tricks takes confidence, and a coyote doesn't trust people that much. For example, nobody ever steps over Mingo. He knows where everyone and everything is at all times. He even looks up to locate airplanes and birds flying overhead. A dog never tries to find those sounds. And Mingo always knew about the fish in our aquarium. Our dog Rocky has never noticed them."

I told JoAnn about how coyotes locate carcasses by looking up and following the flight of ravens. Much of Mingo's behavior, as observed by JoAnn, seemed related to purposeful drives I had observed in the wild.

"How is he like a dog?" I asked.

"Well, in every way, really, only more so. [This statement corroborated my own thought that the coyote is a kind of super-dog.] He wags his tail and licks us and he is playful and likes to be scratched and loved. He, of course, thinks he *is* a dog. He idolizes our Labrador, Rocky. When he was a baby, he often made Rocky mad by biting his jaws all the time. I guess that is how coyote puppies beg food from their mothers."

I had some difficulty convincing JoAnn that I was willing to accept the risk of more intimate contact with her coyote than was possible through a pane of glass. Her reluctance to expose the animal to strangers was realistic. When the still-young coyote was but a baby, he had ingenuously accepted everybody as his friend, but as he began to mature, he developed fear responses toward all strangers. The presence of a guest might produce in him such symptoms as crouching, urination, tail-tucking, trembling, and pacing, and might cause him to try a variety of escape maneuvers.

A study of the socialization process in wolf packs by J. H. Woolpy and B. E. Ginsburg indicates that wolves develop fear responses toward strangers beginning in the second month and continuing throughout the animal's first year. During this period of the animal's life, the mechanism of fear of the unfamiliar makes it difficult for him to form new social relationships, and benefits the species by guaranteeing the exclusivity of the wolf pack. A review of pet-coyote behavior (both observed and reported) leads me to believe that coyotes are similar to wolves in this respect. In other words, no matter how much love had been lavished on Mingo or how careful were the Spiegelbergs in making him feel secure, during his first year of life he would spontaneously begin to manifest fear of strangers.

JoAnn, sensitive to Mingo's complexes, made it a policy not to expose the nervous animal to casual callers. But I declared myself no casual caller, having driven several hundred miles to observe this coyote. JoAnn relented, suggesting as a precaution that I make Mingo's acquaintance in stages. First, accompanied by the dog Rocky, we visited him in the backyard.

At the sight of the big Labrador, the little coyote could not resist getting up a game. While fixing a wary eye on me at the far end of his yard, he grabbed a rag and shook it vigorously in an attempt to seduce Rocky into playing with him. When Rocky accepted the challenge, I was able to move closer and photograph the two canines engaged in wild play.

Mingo was a handsome fellow. His coat was more colorful than those of the coyotes I had seen in Yellowstone, perhaps because he was a different subspecies, *Canis latrans mearnsi*.* As he charged about the yard, JoAnn mentioned that Mingo would never play rough with their female poodle, who could completely dominate the coyote and even make him whine.

"How do all the animals behave at feeding time?" I asked.

"The dogs and the coyote eat together without incident, but the coyote doesn't risk being shortchanged. He takes huge mouthfuls. He can hold six chops in his mouth at once. Six!"

I looked at Mingo's wide mouth and recalled a story told me

---

* Yellowstone coyotes belong to the genus, species, and subspecies *Canis latrans lestes*.

by ranger Larry Hays. One day he watched a male coyote trying to carry off a cache of pack rats. Time and time again the animal would scoop up the nine dead rodents, but always, when ready to trot off with his great prize, one would spill out. And in retrieving it, he inevitably lost others. After many unsuccessful attempts to juggle the load, the coyote stopped and studied the pile of bodies. Then inspiration seemed to strike. Larry said it almost appeared that a light bulb went on over the animal's head. Methodically, the coyote proceeded to eat four of the pack rats, then picked up the remaining five and trotted off.

After a time JoAnn suggested that I precede her into the house while she remained outside to try to calm Mingo. I was eager to see how the animal would behave in the tastefully furnished living room. As a precaution, I decided to keep on my parka, which would provide some extra padding should Mingo resent my presence there. Through the window I watched the forty-pound coyote resist JoAnn's patient attempts to coax him toward the door. Several times he stopped and bit himself. But she firmly guided him forward and into the living room, where the animal began pacing the floor. A wild look in his eye put me

Below and opposite: Gip extinguishes a small fire, proving that Smokey the Bear could be replaced.

off, and despite Jo Ann's remark that you can't buy a coyote with food. I instinctively reached for a package of beef jerky that was lying on a counter. Thus armed, I tried to make myself as inconspicuous as possible.

"I hate to do this to him," JoAnn said in a sweet voice. I could only agree. Nevertheless, in the interest of knowledge, it seemed important that I observe all aspects of behavior in hand-reared coyotes, including this display of fear. I promised her I would make a quick exit if it appeared Mingo was not going to relax in my presence.

JoAnn suggested we sit down at the table and have coffee and try to ignore the pacing animal. It seemed a good idea. But Mingo shifted his route to the small space between the wall and my back. The fact that his nails, unlike those of a dog, made no ticking noise as he glided silently behind me did not make it any easier for me to forget his presence. At last, deciding to make an overture, I turned around and offered the nervous animal a bite of beef jerky. Instantly two paws touched my knee and the coyote swiftly and gently withdrew the tidbit from my hand.

This was progress! But Mingo was no slow savorer of food.

The jerky disappeared instantaneously and two paws were again on my knee as the coyote importuned me for more jerky. I quickly appeased him. But as I fed him another piece and then another, his inscrutable expression did not soften and I could not help but be impressed by the speed with which his formidable teeth were churning the tough dried beef into hamburger. In no time I was out of jerky. But the coyote, eyes blazing, did not believe it. He leaped up and demanded more and when I held open my hands to show they were empty, he clamped his wide mouth around my arm. Before thinking better of it, I shouted "No!" whereupon the coyote loosened his hold and scurried to the opposite side of the room, where he reverted to pacing.

JoAnn regarded me with a poorly concealed look of reproach. "You shouldn't have yelled at him," she said quietly. "I could have handled it."

"Yes, but you weren't the one being bitten," I responded.

But my face was burning, for I realized that I wasn't actually being bitten. Had I known then what I know now, I would have understood that Mingo's grip was but his way of offering friendship. And I blew it by yelling at him! So primed was I for an attack that I overreacted to his gentle clamp as if I were about to be eaten alive.

I now interpret Mingo's "mouthing" as a variation of the muzzle grip, which in wolves is a kind of caress by means of which existing friendships are reinforced. Sometimes, too, a low-ranking wolf will use the gesture to appease a more aggressive member of the pack. I was not then familiar with the coyote version of this behavior, for coyote literature is less than replete with behavioral studies. Since the Mingo incident occurred, however, I have questioned many people who have raised *Canis latrans* and all have spoken of the strange habit of their pets of gently grasping people they like with their mouths. Marty Murie, sister-in-law of the late biologist Adolph Murie, told me that her pet coyote gripped her in such a fashion on many occasions.

When I met Gip I redeemed myself.

Gip was a female coyote in Cowley, Wyoming, who had taken

a black Labrador dog as her until-death-do-us-part mate. At
first sight, I was appalled by Gip's lack of tail. She looked positively unbalanced without the plumy ballast that a coyote tosses
about as artfully as a scarf when making turns or pounces.

"We bobbed it in case she ever gets loose, so nobody would
think she is wild and shoot her," Everett McConahay explained
to me, after taking a deep drag on his cigarette. Then he asked
me, "Did you know coyotes put out fires?"

I admitted I didn't.

Everett proceeded to take an envelope from his pocket and
with what remained of his cigarette he set it on fire. Then he
tossed the flaming paper at the coyote, who, quick as a hare,
pounced on it and began drumming the flames with her forefeet
while bouncing on and off the blaze until only the edges of

Straining her
leash to its limit,
Gip manages to
reach and nuzzle
her only pup,
fathered by a
Labrador
retriever.

the envelope were gilded with dying sparks. But the coyote still was not satisfied. With her shoulder she pushed the charred scrap against the hard ground. Then, after examining it, she repeated the action with her opposite shoulder until the paper disintegrated.

My astonishment pleased Everett.

"How did you ever teach her to do that?" I asked.

"Didn't. All coyotes put out fires," he said, laconically.

Such an incredible observation, if true, probably would never be made by an unsuspecting scientist working under controlled conditions. The very idea of testing for such behavior wouldn't occur to anyone. I asked Everett to repeat the experiment so I could photograph it and I witnessed the same lightning response by Gip. Stomping and rubbing the blaze, she extinguished the flames in a matter of seconds.

Some months later, at a predator symposium, I met Dr. Michael Fox, whose studies on canid behavior have won him wide acclaim. I asked him to perform a fire experiment on his laboratory coyotes and write me of the results. To Dr. Fox's surprise, he found that his coyotes did respond to fire by rolling and/or stomping on it. In a letter to me he said that their reaction to flaming paper was similar to their reaction to other "novel stimuli" and, therefore, he interpreted their behavior as "a series of stereotyped 'fixed actions' which leads to putting out a small fire." He did not, however, believe the animals were motivated by any intention.

I agree that coyotes are probably unaware of the consequences of this behavior, but I find the fact that they extinguish flame no less fascinating for that. Most species panic at the sight or smell of fire, and I suspect that the coyote's fearless response has had some survival value for this longtime inhabitant of the prairie, where grass fires are so apt to erupt from July to November.

Between Gip and myself there arose an instant rapport. I was openhearted when I met her and obviously projected this attitude of goodwill, for she no sooner saw me than what would have been her tail began to wag her back end. The McConahays seemed surprised, since this coyote usually avoided contact with strangers.

After a long greeting, Gip brought me her ball and I tossed it for her. She obviously needed an outlet for her natural exuberance, which was severely crimped by the long chain to which she was fastened. Then we howled together. According to her owners, Gip had quite a range and would take any pitch offered, be it soprano, tenor, or bass, harmonizing accordingly. I made a recording of our duet and afterward discovered how poorly I imitated the coyote song. But Gip overlooked my lack of musicality. When I gave the pitch, she would throw back her head and join in.

Her real obsession, however, was her only puppy, a coy-dog, sired by Butch, her Labrador mate. Incredibly, the bobtailed coyote had whelped a tailless pup, a coincidence sufficiently strange to revive the old battle between Darwin and Lamarck as to whether or not acquired characteristics can ever be transmitted by heredity.

The four-week-old pup was a constant worry to Gip, for he ran free while his mother was restrained. Most of the time the baby seemed to have wandered just beyond the range of the coyote's long chain, and Gip, who was so frightened of the unfamiliar, was powerless to protect him from the terrifying world of man. Even a dog mother, whose nerves are far steadier than a coyote's, might revolt under such stress. And four days after my visit, my heart sank when I picked up a local newspaper and read that Gip had bitten the McConahays' granddaughter Cheryl. As a result the coyote had been sent away to undergo observation for rabies. The story went on to say that the coyote would not be welcomed back when the incubation period was over.

"It all goes to prove what we knew all along," Everett McConahay was quoted as saying. "You can't trust a coyote."

Gip, like most hand-reared wild animals, had come to grief.

On the Track of an Unknown Animal

During another April, due again to low visibility of my subjects in that month, I decided to make a trip east to check on reports of a coyote-like creature in New Hampshire.

Canis latrans is native to the western two-thirds of the continent only, and recent sightings of him in New England have stirred up much controversy. In other Eastern states, too, the species has been reported. In Florida, fox hunters imported it by mistake, but none survived. In West Virginia, the presence of a solitary coyote incited citizens to form posses and hunt the animal relentlessly by foxhound and airplane, until it was finally killed eighteen months later at a reputed cost of $75,000. In New York State coyotes have been documented since 1912. And in Pennsylvania, too, the species is thought to have successfully colonized.

It is highly probable that most coyotes sighted in alien places are in actuality descendants of escapees from zoos or released pets. Just such speculation was offered by J. Frank Dobie in *The Voice of the Coyote*, when he observed in 1947 that during the preceding quarter of a century *Canis latrans* had been noted in every state of the Union except Delaware. It is also possible, however, that unrelenting pressure on the coyote in his natural range in the West may have driven some animals to migrate eastward into regions where the virtual extinction of stronger predators—bears, wolves, and cougars—opened up good habitat and food sources previously unavailable to the small coyote.

Regardless of how the animals in question reached the East Coast, in the late 1950s in Vermont rumors began to circulate of a strange wild creature that was larger than a coyote but smaller than a wolf. Shortly thereafter, New Hampshire reported the same phenomenon. And in 1960, when a den containing five pups of the unidentified species was discovered near Croydon,

New Hampshire, serious studies were undertaken to determine just what this creature might be.

My initial opinion was that the mystery animal was a coy-dog, the hybrid offspring of a wild coyote and a domestic dog. It was not until I learned it was breeding true—bearing offspring that were consistently uniform in appearance—that I began to wonder. Second-generation hybrids predictably exhibit great variability, some resembling each grandparent in a kind of "throwback" phenomenon. Moreover, these wild canids were producing offspring in the spring of the year, when, studies show, the coy-dog hybrid does not whelp.

I first stopped in Concord, New Hampshire, to see biologist Helenette Silver, senior author of a behavioral study of the animal that had been funded by the National Science Foundation. She mentioned that her project had been opposed by many sportsmen in her state, who incorrectly assumed that money was being diverted from the New Hampshire State Fish and Game Department to investigate a nontarget species. The public, too, had been stirred up against the creature by journalists, who could not resist playing up the story and elaborating on the possibilities of allowing a weird race of wild dogs to breed. Some even suggested that the New England woodlands were haunted by werewolves! Free-roaming domestic dogs were known to be killing deer in the state,* and the prospect of yet another competitor for the New Hampshire game animals did not sit well with the hunting public. Many people took the position that the mysterious canids were nothing but domestic dogs gone feral, and the sooner the scourge could be eliminated, the better. As a result, in 1961 the New Hampshire Legislature was persuaded to add the "timber wolf" and the "prairie wolf" to the state's bounty list, for lack of a better definition of the species. But when people began to shoot their neighbors' dogs and to present the bodies for money, the law was again amended, in 1965, and the "prairie wolf" and the "timber wolf" were dropped.

While New Hampshire was agonizing over the unidentified

*Pet dogs were reputed to have killed 550 deer in New Hampshire between 1969 and 1971.

beast, no proof existed that it had caused anybody any harm. There was not even any hard evidence that it had ever preyed upon the coveted deer herd, although tracks around half-eaten carcasses excited many stories. But since carrion happens to be the major winter food item of the Western coyote, a strong likelihood existed that the New Hampshire canids had not actually killed any of the animals they had evidently been feeding upon. At a later date a study of the stomach contents of twenty-seven of the wild canids shot over a two-year period showed that the presence of deer meat was related to the start of each hunting season, when wounded game escape hunters but die anyway. At least four stomachs contained maggots and in three were found carrion beetles, proof that the wild canid was to some extent a scavenger.

In any case, the New England deer herd, in the view of many knowledgeable people, could only be benefited by the return to the region of an effective wild predator. Unlike pet dogs, who can afford to wear themselves out chasing healthy specimens, and unlike human hunters, who try to select prime animals as their targets, wild canines are opportunistic hunters who pursue only those creatures that exhibit signs of becoming easy prey. Thus, they eliminate from the gene pool the weak, the diseased, and the genetically abnormal.

This predator-prey interaction was well understood by the New Hampshire State Fish and Game officials I talked to, many of whom confided that they would welcome the return of even wolves or mountain lions to the region. But since the rank-and-file hunters they served held more simplistic views and resented the loss of even a single game animal, the agency was remaining noncommittal on the subject of the mystery canid. One field officer told me that the deer herds were at a low point and had been for two or three years.

"It's a cyclical phenomenon, probably weather-related," he explained, "but you can bet the new animal is going to be blamed when the hunters don't find a deer behind every tree."

The new creature was not entirely without friends. Conservationists were delighted at the prospect of a predatory animal coming back to the region and hoped that the event would signal a return to a better balance of nature. But a correct identification of the animal was central to the issue of whether or not it would be tolerated. If hunters were right in their assertion that it was nothing but the domestic dog gone feral, the wild canids would soon become the object of an all-out extermination campaign. Even a coy-dog hybrid would not likely be granted wildlife status in New England. Only a pure coyote or a coyote-wolf cross stood a chance of gaining public acceptance.

As mentioned earlier, the coyote, unlike almost every other known species, is capable of interspecific breeding; it can mate with either the dog or the wolf and produce offspring that are not sterile. Behavioral differences between coyotes and wolves have probably been the sole barrier preventing one of these two species from being absorbed by the other eons ago. Observations of interactions between coyotes and wolves support the view that the two species are highly antagonistic. Records are not difficult to find of coyotes that have been killed by wolves. In recent times, when *Canis lupus* migrated onto Isle Royale, Michigan, the indigenous coyote quickly vanished. Since members of a wolf pack will not tolerate a strange wolf on their hunting range, it is to be expected that an intruding coyote, which closely resembles a small wolf, likewise raises the hackles of *Canis lupus*. The coyote, after all, is to some extent a competitor for the wolf's food, and it is to space out these carnivores and guarantee each pack member an adequate diet that Nature has made the wolf so clannish. In the face of such solidarity and hostility, *Canis latrans* would not be likely either to seek or to win a mate from the ranks of a wolf pack.

Coyotes do not readily mate with dogs for different reasons. As I had already observed in the West, the female coyote is highly selective in her choice of mate, for he plays a role in the rearing of his young.

Nevertheless, dogs have been known to crossbreed spontaneously with wild coyotes in areas where *Canis latrans* is indigenous. I have firsthand knowledge of one such match, which occurred in the Grand Teton Mountains near Wilson, Wyoming. When the male dog trotted home after a two-day honeymoon, he was trailed by a wild female coyote. The dog's owners told me that for the next few weeks the pregnant coyote could be seen lurking near their house trailer, waiting for their pet to be let out. It would appear she was making every attempt to sustain the crucial bond with her dog mate, for without the help of a male, the odds of her successfully raising pups would be greatly lessened.

Even if a litter of coy-dog pups is successfully reared by the mother alone, these hybrids must later face still-greater obstacles when seeking mates for themselves. Coyotes, both male and female, can breed only in late winter. Male dogs, of course, are ready to mate throughout the year; thus, no barrier exists

A New Hampshire "coy-wolf."

WALTER T. SILVER

to a first-time coyote-dog match. But the offspring of such a union, the coy-dog, inherits an annual breeding pattern from its wild parent with one hitch. Both male and female coy-dogs come into heat in the fall, three to four months earlier than do pureblood coyotes.* Thus, they can never mate back to the wild side of their family, a fact that prevents mongrelization of the species *Canis latrans*.

The mongrel generation does, of course, have the option of finding mates from among other coy-dogs or of pairing back to domestic dogs. But given the untimeliness of its period of oestrus, any issue born to it must meet life during the harshest time of year, in midwinter, and the prospects of such an unfortunate litter surviving under wild conditions are poor indeed. To compound the handicap, studies show that coy-dog males take after the domestic-dog side of their family in that they do not assist in the rearing of their young. It is doubtful, therefore, that a coy-dog female can, by herself, find sufficient food during the winter months to nurse and feed a litter. For these reasons, it is unlikely that a race of wild coy-dogs has arisen or ever will arise to plague worried citizens who claim this has already happened.

Nevertheless, the myth persisted that the coyote-like creatures sighted in New England were coy-dogs. The first scientific investigation of the animal (which henceforth I shall refer to as the New Hampshire wild canid) was not launched until April 1960, when Helenette Silver and her biologist husband Walter finally obtained that litter of five pups near Croydon.

From this stock the Silvers bred seven litters numbering fifty-five specimens. For purposes of comparison, they imported six Colorado coyotes and two Wisconsin coyotes and obtained two litters from them. Then, after a few initial failures, they succeeded in obtaining two crosses between one of the New Hampshire coyote-like females and two different domestic dogs.**

---

* H. T. Gier in *Coyotes in Kansas* states that, out of 22 litters of laboratory-bred coyote-dog crosses, no animals were in breeding condition during the coyote period of oestrus.
** Further attempts to breed crossed animals either to known coyotes or back to the New Hampshire canids failed because of the disparity in their breeding seasons.

The offspring of these two unions were then mated to one another to produce two second-generation families of hybrid stock. All told, then, the Silvers succeeded in breeding some eighty assorted wild canines over a six-year period, an accomplishment I believe to be unparalleled.

Using as their criteria the nine patterns of behavior classified by John Paul Scott and John L. Fuller in their well-known study of hereditary differences in various breeds of domestic dogs (investigation, care-giving, care-soliciting, group activity, conflict, reproductive activity, elimination, ingestion, and comfort-seeking), comparisons were made between the New Hampshire wild canids, Western coyotes, and the dog hybrids. Additional factors, such as general appearance, age of tooth eruption, onset of sexual maturity, and others, were monitored. Ultimately, the analysis of this data showed the New Hampshire canids to be unlike the domestic-dog hybrids and favored the acceptance of predominantly coyote ancestry.

For example, whereas in appearance the dog hybrids were highly variable and indistinguishable from an assortment of full-blooded dogs, the New Hampshire litters were uniform and resembled their wild parents. This suggested that had the animals in question resulted from past hybridization with dogs, they would have had to be around a good deal longer than anyone had noticed for their genetic structure to have become so stabilized. Hybridization with dogs, therefore, seemed improbable.

A more plausible theory was that the animals were simply oversized coyotes, who had experienced what evolutionists call *adaptive radiation*, a term used for the changes that occur when a whole new population arises from a few variable individuals. Yet the New Hampshire canid did not look much like even an atypical coyote. Its nose pad was too broad, resembling that of a wolf, its paws were ungainly, as opposed to the neat little feet of the Colorado specimens, and its coat was considerably darker and more variable than the archetypical coyote. Moreover, it dwarfed the imported coyotes, the males by 50 percent and the females by 70 percent. H. T. Gier documents forty-three pounds as the outside weight of a male coyote in Kansas. Some of the New Hampshire canids weighed in at sixty pounds!

On the other hand, behaviorally the mysterious animal very closely approximated the coyote, while further deviating from the control group of dog hybrids. Like coyotes, the New Hampshire litters established a dominance hierarchy at an early age, and in the process the pups exhibited much aggressivity among themselves. The dog-hybrid puppies, by contrast, could hardly be induced to compete over a bone, so amiable were they toward one another.

Perhaps the most significant difference noted was in the manifestations of male parents toward young. The New Hampshire male, like the Western coyote and the wolf, was extremely solicitous concerning his puppies. Not only did he clean and care for them, he also deferred to their mother during the period she nursed. The hybrid male, on the other hand, behaved like the domestic-dog side of his family and remained totally oblivious of his offspring.

And finally there was the matter of breeding season. Like coyotes and wolves, the New Hampshire canids were programmed to whelp in the spring of the year. Not so the dog hybrids. Nature had doomed their offspring to be born in winter.

After compiling their data, the Silvers felt certain that the animal they were studying could not be a coy-dog, and they proposed that it be considered a subspecies of *Canis latrans* and be designated as the Eastern coyote. At the same time, however, they reported that physically, and to a lesser degree behaviorally, the New Hampshire animals exhibited some unique characteristics not seen in *Canis latrans*.

One possibility—that the creature was a coyote-wolf cross—remained untested. Though wild coyotes and wild wolves were believed not to tolerate one another, Mrs. Silver theorized that pack allegiance in the New England wolf might have broken down when its population experienced sharp decline. In the absence of available mates, a few isolated wolves might then have consorted with a newly immigrant coyote population. Given the sociable nature of the wolf and

the malleable nature of the coyote, the idea deserved investigation.

And so an investigation was undertaken. A taxonomic study
was set up at Harvard's Museum of Comparative Zoology, and
examination of thirty-one skulls of the New Hampshire canids
was made by two scientists, Dr. Barbara Lawrence and Dr. W. H.
Bossert. The specimens used were provided by hunters who had
shot them in various parts of the states of New Hampshire,
Vermont, and Massachusetts. A number were also donated by
the Silvers. Using fifteen diagnostic skull and tooth measure-
ments, Lawrence and Bossert made comparisons between the
mystery canids, domestic dogs, coy-dogs, and wolves. The results corroborated the Silvers' conclusion that the New Hampshire canid could not be a coy-dog and confirmed that its
ancestry in all probability was primarily coyote.

But certain measurable factors fell distinctly between the coyote and the wolf. One possible explanation for this—that
the New Hampshire canids were coyotes which, in adapting to
alien prey and habitat requirements, had experienced rapid
evolution and were beginning to converge with the wolf—was
discounted. Nonhomogeneous traits, such as a slender jaw combined with large and consequently crowded teeth, would have
no selective advantage to an animal adjusting to a higher predator niche. At the same time, such a random combination of
nonhomogeneous characteristics strongly suggested multiple
ancestry. The wolf might very well be implicated.* Interestingly,
the most wolf-like animal and the most coyote-like animal were
both shot near Leydon, Massachusetts, apparently members of
the same pack. This is precisely what might be expected in a
sample group of hybrids.

But how could the odd couple have gotten together in the first
place? Where did the wolves come from?

In New Hampshire wolves were bountied from 1647 until
1895. Of course, the native population may not have been

---

* Recently, biologist Dr. Howard McCarley has suggested that the "red wolf"
found in the Southern states along the eastern edge of the coyote's extending
line may also be a wolf-coyote hybrid. Perhaps fraternization between the two
species is not so rare as has been supposed.

entirely extinct when the bounty law was repealed. Twelve were taken in the final year. Certainly there was no lack of food in the state to support a small number of wolves, for although by 1860 the native moose and woodland caribou were gone (victims of the transformation wrought by agriculture), white-tailed deer had appeared and were thriving.

Another possibility suggested by Mrs. Silver is that a match may have occurred somewhat later, between incoming coyotes and some pet wolves that belonged to a man named E. H. Baynes, a naturalist who lived near the Blue Mountain forest. Baynes obtained a litter of four wolf cubs from Maine in 1903 and raised the animals until the oldest died fifteen years later. In his book *My Wild Animal Guests*, Baynes recalls that his wolves sometimes escaped from their pen and ran free for a time. Obviously, a domesticated *Canis lupus* would not be so encumbered with intense pack loyalty as the wild wolf, and one of these might, therefore, be more inclined to breed with a coyote. Certainly hand-reared wolves have shown less reluctance to pair with domestic dogs. It is this cross that produced the Husky breed.

It is also feasible that at some time since the arrival of the coyote, Quebec wolves traveled down the Connecticut River, which divides the states of New Hampshire and Vermont. Along its course early sightings were made of the New Hampshire canids.

But what of the coyote side of the family—where did it come from?

Paul Doherty, columnist for the *Berlin* (N.H.) *Reporter*, recently wrote: "I have been told that more than fifty years ago a man brought a pair of coyotes from the West to Berlin. He raised them in a pen and guess what, they finally got away and were never seen again."

I met Doherty, and he told me a strange tale. Some twenty years ago loggers brought him to see a litter of pups they had found under a stump in the Diamond area. According to Doherty, the mother had been killed by the men prior to his arrival but he got a look at her body, and in retrospect he recalls that she looked much like a small wolf. As everyone present assumed the puppies to be the offspring of a stray dog, various people took them home to raise. Doherty was well acquainted with a family who adopted one of the orphans, and he told me that as time passed that animal grew up to look exactly like a wolf!

Regardless of how the animal came into being, by the 1970s it was becoming established not only in Vermont and New Hampshire but in Maine and Massachusetts as well. To the surprise of many, Massachusetts reacted quite differently from her sister states and welcomed the new predator, even allowing it protected status.

By contrast, when the first Maine specimen was shot near Millinocket, in November 1972, people came from miles around to revile and spit on its remains. In the words of John N. Cole, editor of the *Maine Times*, the human beings behaved "like primitive villagers gathered around the carcass of a man-eating tiger. Hanging gaunt and stiff like a large gray dog, the animal hardly seemed awesome enough to warrant the group hatred it seemed to engender."

Immediately, a bill was introduced in Augusta to bounty what that state looked upon as a "varmint." But to the astonishment of the highly vocal hunting lobby that was backing the legislation, conservationists, students, and biologists showed up from all parts of the state and succeeded in defeating the measure. Their victory, however, merely prevented a money reward from becoming an added incentive for those who wished to destroy the animal. In Maine, as in New Hampshire and Vermont, it is open season the year round on the Eastern coyote. In Massachusetts alone is the animal protected.

I was determined to find the creature that was stirring up Yankee passion, and in April 1972 I headed for northern New Hampshire. Conservation officer Richard Dufour generously agreed to act as my guide in the still-snowbound wilderness near Littleton-Jefferson, and together we snowshoed through a dripping green-and-white woodland on the fresh track of what citizens of Massachusetts were now calling the "new wolf." We did not sight the animal, and when we turned back, I had to content myself with Dufour's account of watching a pack of

Opposite, top:
Early sociability.
Opposite, bottom:
A baby "coy-wolf" in New Hampshire answers the howls of Wyoming coyotes recorded two thousand miles away.

seven chase a deer across a frozen reservoir some months earlier. He said: "I went back to get my snowmobile and when I returned the deer was dead. Looked like it might have been hamstrung, but I didn't autopsy it to see if it was sick or anything. If the coyotes, or whatever they are, had killed it, I must have frightened them off."

As we sloshed out of the woods, I heard a raven, and stopped, conscious of the symbiotic tie between the coyote and the raven. Dufour was surprised to learn that these two species often travel together, and he told me that ravens had begun to show up in New Hampshire only twenty years ago, about the time the new animal had appeared. Since then, flocks had been gradually building up.

Back at the patrol car, Dufour radioed several conservation officers around the state, requesting that they alert him to any coyote sightings. To my astonishment, within an hour he had a call from central New Hampshire. A voice squawked: "You're in luck. Somebody here has dug up a den. Six or seven pups."

"Hold them until tomorrow," Dufour requested.

Even before he had signed off, I was in my rented car awaiting his directions to the private game club in mid-state where the litter had just been unearthed.

But the club manager could not see me until the next day. Before leading me to the reserve, we met at a coffee shop, where he requested that both his name and the club's name be withheld. He told me that he had stumbled upon the den the previous day and was now awaiting instructions from his board of directors before turning them over to Fish and Game. Then he took me to his residence, where six chocolate-brown pups were slipping and sprawling about his kitchen, investigating everything. As soon as I sat down on a chair to load my camera, one climbed my leg with the agility of a kitten. The baby animal had no fear of me, but I was not convinced that he could see me too well through his recently opened hazy eyes. I judged him to be between two and three weeks old. In another few days his dark coat would begin to lighten and his pug snout to lengthen. At his present stage of development he was no beauty, resembling more a baby hedgehog than what I now term a coy-wolf puppy.

Already the young pups were testing their strength by standing on one another's shoulders. Two weaklings were continually being pinned by the others, and these same runts were unable to push their way into the mob of feeding puppies at the milk dish. Finally the manager filled a baby bottle with milk and began to feed them by hand.

"Might you keep them?" I asked.

"My board may want to keep some," he replied. "The females could turn out to be good decoys for luring in males, kind of help us clean them out of here. Otherwise, I'll have to turn them in. That's the law."

I knew the law. Private individuals are not allowed to keep wild animals in New Hampshire. Unless I could come up with an educational or public institution that wished to raise the animals for study or exhibit, Fish and Game would destroy them.

"Give me two days," I asked. "I think a zoo might be very interested in these animals. They're unique . . . the Eastern coyote . . . part wolf . . ."

"Oh, don't worry, I won't be doing anything for the next couple of days," the manager said. "Have to wait to hear from my board."

Before I left I tested the pups' hearing by playing a coyote tape I had recorded in the West. Upon hearing the wild music, one precocious male threw back his head and joined in. His squeaky imitation of the sonorous wails of adult coyotes was amusing to hear. I had not suspected that cubs could howl at so young an age.

As the tape progressed, suddenly all six puppies dived for shelter. One huddled under the sink ledge, another froze midway across the kitchen floor, three made it to the cardboard box, and one hid behind a curtain. During the next eight minutes none made a move.

"There's a message on that tape that is coming in loud and clear to these pups, warning them of danger," the manager said. "Where did you record it?"

"In Wyoming. These are Wyoming coyotes howling. They

must speak some universal language. At least their alarm signal seems to be understood two thousand miles away."

A half-hour later I repeated the experiment. At the same point in the recording, all six coy-wolves again took cover.

That night I flew back to New York and spent the next two days calling zoos throughout the country. Many had no facilities for a coyote or wolf exhibit, others already had wolves or had them on order. But on the second morning, just as I was beginning to despair, Dion A. Albalck of the Roger Williams Park Zoo in Providence, Rhode Island, said he would be delighted to take the unique cubs. Excellent facilities for a coyote exhibit, a hill with natural dens, had been standing empty for some time.

But when I called New Hampshire State Fish and Game to inquire into the logistics of transferring the litter to another state, I was told the puppies had already been turned in and destroyed. Immediately, I got on the phone to the manager of the private hunting club.

"Well, you see, our club members, they're hunters," he countered. "They want to see more deer around here. You know, this coyote animal killed twenty-eight deer in one year alone. They told me to get rid of them right away."

When I hung up I was shaking with anger, not so much at the game manager, whom I regarded as himself a victim, as at the pervasiveness of man's greed. Any animal that cannot be exploited, or any animal that threatens to compete with man's unmitigated exploitation of some other animal, is not long tolerated in America. Powerful forces—hunting clubs, entrepreneurs who profit from the hunting trade, gun lobbies, individuals whose self-image rests on "getting a deer," and entrenched bureaucrats whose jobs depend on how well they protect these vested interests—control wildlife management. And wildlife management in twentieth-century America has but one objective, the manipulation of Nature for the purpose of elevating target populations.

When I calmed down and began to reflect on the future outlook for the Eastern coyote, however, I grew somewhat more optimistic. Perhaps this predator's fate will be different from that of his late predecessor, the Eastern timber wolf. A new, tougher wild canine, a wolf reinforced with coyote resiliency or, if you will, a coyote infused with the strength of the wolf, seems to have emerged on the New England landscape, filling a near-vacant predator niche. Like a sunflower that has penetrated a cement sidewalk, the event seemed to suggest that man's strangulation grip on Nature may not yet be fatal.

A
Den

The pair of coyotes I was tracking through my spotscope were easy to lose as they ducked in and out of the silver-green sage. In the glaring light, their tawny coats blended well with the earth, rocks, and brushy vegetation that mantled the lower slopes of the mountain. Higher up, dark ponderosa pines swept skyward, accentuating the precipitous rise of the mountain and forming a dense forest into which the two animals vanished at will.

On this day, however, I was determined not to lose them. Two weeks had elapsed since my arrival at Wyoming's National Elk Refuge, where I had begun my search for a den of pups. Yellowstone National Park, I had decided, would not be a suitable place in which to conduct a detailed study on coyote family life. Tourists soon would be arriving there, and they would undoubtedly interfere with my observations. So instead I had returned to the National Elk Refuge, where manager Don Redfearn once again handed me keys to padlocked service roads that are off limits to the casual visitor. Here I was scouting areas where nobody else would be permitted to enter and disturb my subjects.

No detailed study had ever been written on the family life of wild coyotes at a den, although trappers had made many valuable observations. From their conflicting reports, however, I had pieced together more questions than conclusions. What role does the father coyote actually play in the rearing of the young? Are females hostile to one another's pups? Do adult coyotes confine their activities to the den areas? To these and other questions I had received innumerable answers, often from local people whose knowledge of the ways of the coyote was hardly more than a repetition of someone else's misconceptions, usually prefaced with the phrase "I've lived here all my life and I can tell you . . ." Following this opener, I might hear how all coyotes go to one particular place in the mountains to give birth **167** (in the manner of elk heading for the calving ground!) or other absurdities. I also learned much of value from local people. The difficulty always was to distinguish the facts from the fantasies.

In reading, too, I encountered statements for which I could find no supportive data. For example, I often came across sentences that began: "Unlike the coyote, the wolf . . ." But when I attempted to find the evidence on which the comparison had been drawn, I found no published studies. Obviously, the time was past due for somebody to take a close-up look at the intraspecific relationships of a family of identified coyotes in the wild. But the problem was how to find and observe such highly secretive subjects.

So far, my search of moraines, buttes, and mountains had uncovered no active dens. Thousands of ground-squirrel burrows honeycombed the earth, beckoning me to investigate them. But what actual coyote dens I found had vacancy signs hanging out front, in the form of cobwebs spun across their entrances. And what coyotes I was able to sight were cunning enough to give me the slip before returning to their sequestered pups.

Coyote pups develop rapidly, and I knew that the loss of even two weeks might spell the difference between the success or failure of my project. I therefore telephoned Yellowstone Park and the Grand Teton National Park headquarters to ask rangers in these places to alert me to any dens they might happen upon. To my dismay, I learned that not one of the men I spoke with had ever stumbled across an active coyote den! I began to worry that I had overreached myself in believing I could find the crafty coyote's hideaway.

Now my hopes were pinned on two coyotes I had been watching on and off during the past few days. They at least seemed to be a mated pair—certainly a promising sign. So, though my arms felt numb from the strain of holding a 20-power zoom spotscope to my eye, I did not lower them. Relocating the two animals in the midst of all that sage might prove an impossibility.

The male of the pair, whom I dubbed Digger since he seemed to spend a good deal of time digging up ground squirrels, now was at it again. As the dirt flew, his mate moved a few feet to one side and stood tensely at attention. When a ground squirrel suddenly leaped into her waiting jaws, I realized she had cleverly stationed herself at the besieged creature's back door. As the female crunched up the hapless rodent without dropping a morsel of it on the ground, Digger backed out of the large hole he had created and vigorously shook himself. Then the pair moved downhill, and the process was repeated in reverse. This time the female did the excavating while Digger waited for his meal to exit from its escape hatch directly into his mouth.

I consoled myself that, even if I didn't find a den, I was nonetheless witnessing some interesting behavior. The previous day the female of this pair had routed another coyote from the slope, streaking after the animal with such intensity my hopes were aroused she might be protecting a den of babies nearby. For half a mile she pursued the intruder before trotting back to where Digger stood calmly watching the whole proceeding.

I would see much more of this. In fact, when I became familiar with the coyotes in the region, I would actually learn where many belonged. Definite boundaries existed, which encompassed the hunting ranges of particular small groups of animals. When a stranger violated these lines of demarcation, he or she was summarily expelled. In every instance I observed, a coyote of the same sex as the intruder did the bouncing.

But though this told me much of interest regarding the territoriality of the coyote, my primary purpose at this time was to learn about the coyote's family life. And now, once again, Digger and his mate managed to dematerialize before my eyes. I climbed the slope and examined the ground where I had last seen them. It is always difficult to arrive at the exact spot one has sighted from afar. As one approaches landmarks that from a distance seemed proximate, they spread out and rearrange themselves. In cases of this kind, it is helpful to have a second person remain behind and direct one's approach by hand signals. I was alone, however, and though I did come upon the place where Digger had been hunting ground squirrels, I found no den. Finally I gave up in despair.

For the next three days I searched in a new area, this time on the north slope of Miller Butte, whence I had a spectacular view of the Grand Tetons. The breathtaking scenery was more than adequate compensation for my strenuous efforts. As I climbed and hiked, great blue herons winged across a backdrop of shining peaks. Below me, sandhill cranes stalked a green meadow, their improbable cries sounding like creaking gates. And under my feet, miniature flowers cushioned my steps. In springtime mountains are so fresh that the wind actually tastes of aromatic roots and smells of healthy soil. I drank the invigorating wind and rejoiced to be where I was. I found an arrowhead made from obsidian (it must have been carried from the Yellowstone area) and pondered on the Indian hunter who had long ago also passed this way and had perhaps experienced similar pleasure in viewing the Grand Tetons from such a beautiful perspective.

After a time I descended, walked a good distance across the meadow, and glassed the butte from one end to the other. But the only animals visible on the slope were a moose with her yearling calf. I was curious to see if the moose mother, who soon would be calving again, would now be exhibiting intolerance of

The male, Gray Dog, caters food for his mate, Redlegs, while their pups are growing.

her half-grown offspring, and so I watched as the two made their way downhill, their great throat "bells" swinging as they walked. Midway they stopped to browse on willow. Then, after eating their fill, they continued their slow descent. But suddenly the cow, who was in the lead, stopped to examine a fallen aspen. For ten minutes she remained immobile, totally engrossed in the tree's mystery. I could see nothing out of the ordinary about the dead wood that intrigued her, and eventually, when she resumed her meandering descent, I forgot about the matter. Sometime later, after the ungainly giants had reached the flats and cantered off, the cow's strange fixation returned to my mind, and I casually trained my binoculars on the fallen tree. To my surprise, from under it stepped a coyote! With flattened ears and wagging tail, the brownish animal dashed uphill to greet a second coyote, who had simultaneously emerged from a patch of giant Indian rye. Had these two been on the slope all afternoon without my noticing?

The brownish coyote, who turned out to be a female, made a great fuss over the second coyote, who was gray and turned out to be a male. But he seemed less interested in her than she was in him. As she frolicked at his side, he moved purposefully toward a hole on the slope and peered into it. It looked hardly different from a hundred other ground-squirrel lodges in evidence everywhere, and I wondered if he planned to dig up dinner. But he soon lost interest in the ground cavity and trotted along the hill to where a third coyote was stretching and yawning as if aroused from sleep. This animal, too, was gray, but a female, with bright red legs and a red snout. She manifested the same obvious delight over seeing the gray male as had the brown coyote. After an effusive greeting, the two took off across the butte, trailed by the third. I followed them with my binoculars until they disappeared from view, whereupon I immediately relocated the hole that had momentarily interested the gray male. It just might be a burrow. Perhaps a moose had inadvertently directed me to a den!

Immediately I set off for it. But thirty feet from my destination I decided not to approach closer. Visible claw marks around the hole, and a mound of loose dirt beside it, revealed that coyotes had recently been digging here. I backed away. If it were indeed a den containing pups, I did not want to leave excessive tracks.

Down on the meadow again, I concealed myself in a dry irrigation ditch a quarter-mile distant and watched. Three hours passed, but nothing happened at the hole. Perhaps, after all, it was only a ground-squirrel burrow enlarged by hungry coyotes. On the other hand, it might contain pups still too young to show their heads.

Vern Dorn (my first tutor on the ways of the wily coyote) had advised me by phone that at my present altitude of 6400 feet, coyotes would probably whelp during the last week in April. It was now the eleventh of May, two weeks past the predicted birth time. But as newborn pups do not surface until they are at least two weeks of age, I clung to the hope that I might still find a den in time to witness all observable stages of the babies' above-ground development.

Then all at once two of the three coyotes I had watched earlier, the gray male and the brown female, were back on the hill. I grabbed my binoculars and tracked their descent. But neither headed toward that hole which had held out such promise to me. Instead they veered and made a wide swing around it along a thirty-foot radius. Then something happened to further dash my hopes. As the female passed downhill, she touched her nose to the ground at the very spot where I had stood three hours earlier, and instantly she froze. Uncannily, the gray male reflected her mood immediately and grew hyper-alert. It seemed to me that some communication must have transpired between them.

For some time the pair stood listening and looking about. I expected they would make a sudden bolt. But to my relief, after a time the gray male began to move with all deliberate slowness uphill until he was in a position some twenty-five feet above the hole. Once there he turned, and from this lookout he seemed to take on the role of a sentry, watching in all directions. His alert stance obviously gave reassurance to the female, who now began to move toward what I still hoped might be her den. But her approach was agonizingly slow. After every few steps, she would stop and glance up at the male, as if looking for encouragement to proceed. And when, but ten feet from the hole, something startled her, she quickly retreated to the far position again, where she remained for some time. At last she summoned up courage to initiate a second approach. But again, before reaching her destination, ambivalence paralyzed her, and for eight interminable minutes she stood with neck craned and forepaw gracefully lifted, while I importuned heaven that no raven sound an alarm cry, nor airplane pass overhead.

Uphill, the male continued to remain rigidly on guard. So immobile were the pair, the two animals might have been mounted models in some museum exhibit forever cast in a moment of exquisite drama. But suddenly the tableau came to life as the female made a weasel-like scurry, dived into the hole, and quickly emerged with something dark and alive dangling from her mouth. It was a pup! Without hesitating an instant, she streaked across the slope and vanished into the giant Indian rye.

With shaking hands, I locked my binoculars on the place where she had vanished and briefly scanned the slopes with my naked eye for a glimpse of movement. I had not the slightest doubt that I had been the cause of this disruption in the coyotes' domestic tranquillity, and now I was concerned about what they might do. Parent coyotes are extremely sensitive to disturbances and in captivity have been known to kill their young when human beings approached too closely. Indeed, this tendency on the part of *Canis latrans* parents to overreact to disturbances had created serious problems for Helenette and Walter Silver when they attempted to breed Western specimens for their comparative study of wild canids.

While waiting for the female to emerge from cover, I marveled at the extraordinary cooperation I had just observed between the two adult animals. From the behavior of these two, I was convinced that some kind of intelligent planning and subtle communication had taken place between them. The male clearly assumed the responsibility of acting as eyes, ears, and nose for the female during those brief moments when she risked going underground. Even more interesting was the female's apparent awareness and trust in what he was doing. Even now, while she remained in the tall grass, he remained at his post. I was tempted to shift my binoculars away from the heavy vegetation into which she had vanished and focus on him. But precious moments might be lost trying to relocate the rye patch—moments that could cost me the trail of this pup-toting female. And it was now imperative that I see exactly where she would head.

To my delight, after a few minutes, she emerged and raced back to her former den, dived in, and surfaced with a second squirming baby in her mouth. The rye, I now realized, concealed her new den.

Now that I knew where she was relocating, I relaxed, shook my weary arms, and let myself enjoy the surge of elation welling up in me. I had found a den! The pups were as dark as chocolate and looked to be less than two and a half weeks old. I felt like leaping and shouting! But I managed to restrain myself. Already I had come close to sabotaging what was very likely my only chance of locating a den that season. So instead I made careful notations of all surrounding landmarks with the idea of finding a better angle from which to observe future happenings. A few yards uphill from the grassy patch lay a bleached elk antler. To the west grew a stately spruce, and at an equal distance to the east stood a row of quaking aspens, whose common root system was no doubt connected with that of the fallen member toward which the moose had earlier directed my attention.

When the female emerged from the grass for the second time, she seemed considerably less nervous. Having salvaged two pups, she now trotted complacently across the slope. Immediately her more relaxed demeanor was reflected by the male. He left his lookout post and sauntered into some willows, where he curled up and went to sleep.

It was only then that I noticed the third coyote. She must have been on the slope all along, perhaps concealed in the tall rye, whose waving blades, even at this early date, had outstripped all other grasses in the region. While the third pup was being toted to its new home, she vanished into the new den. What was *she* doing in there?

Though the third pup turned out to be the last one, I now watched both the females make repeated trips to the old burrow, to ascertain, I assumed, that no baby had been left behind. I waited until dark to see if others would be produced, but a severe drop in temperature finally forced me to leave the refuge and head for my motel in Jackson. That night I set my alarm for five A.M. But I was awake before it rang. My family study was under way.

A
Pack

During the next four days my binoculars were pressed to my eyes until I began to feel they had become an extension of my face, but I saw no further sign of the pups. If it turned out that the babies were as yet too immature to emerge from their underground home, I was now in an excellent position to observe a good deal of their early development. If, on the other hand, they had been surreptitiously whisked off to still another burrow, I was not only being badly fooled, I was wasting valuable time that should have been used to hunt up another den.

An encouraging sign was the ubiquitous presence of one or more of my three known coyotes on the hill. Often they rested in one another's company. At other times, I would sight one mousing on the flats and, upon tracking the animal back to the slope, would notice a previously unobserved coyote rising up from the grass to greet him (or her). With every passing day the vegetation was growing more lush. Nature was providing better cover for the time when the young of all species would emerge.

The three coyotes' manner of greeting varied. If, after a separation from either female, the gray male (whom I began to call Gray Dog) encountered one of them, he stood stiffly and accepted their affectionate homage as his due. Their displays consisted of wriggling, wagging, squirming, rolling over to expose their bellies, tapping him with a forepaw, licking his muzzle, or any combination of such canine expressions. But whenever the two females encountered one another after a separation, they were far more reserved, merely touching noses and waving their tails a bit. It appeared that they considered themselves to be equals, for they maintained an identical stance throughout their greeting. This was soon to change.

The most interesting observation I made during those slow days was the discovery that one adult invariably remained near the den. Vern Dorn, among others, had told me that the male participated in the rearing of his young, and now I was begin-

ning to verify this for myself. But what role did the second
female play? Back in 1944, Adolph Murie reported seeing
various wolf "baby-sitters" of both sexes tend cubs on Mount
McKinley in Alaska. But nowhere had I read that "aunt" or
"uncle" coyotes also performed this service.

I assumed that the brownish-colored coyote was the mother of
the pups, for she had moved them. Now, from an improved
vantage point, I saw that both Brownie (as I called her) and the
red-legged female (Redlegs) entered and emerged from the
burrow opening. Unlike dogs, coyotes do not reveal their nursing condition by developing pendulous breasts, and I was not
yet cognizant of the fact that a female with a plucked belly is
lactating.

On the morning of the fifth day, I arrived to find a red-tailed
hawk swaggering like a pirate around the mouth of the den, and
I immediately imagined the worst. No adult coyote was visible at
the time, and my first impulse was to assume the role of surrogate guardian—to leap from my hiding place with arms flail-
ing and shoo away the bold bird. But of course I could do no
such thing. If my coyote puppies were destined to become hawk
food, I was helpless. I could no more interfere with the bird's
food-finding activities than with my own subjects' predation on
the attractive little ground squirrels that sat like picket pins and
twitched their whiskers at me. All creatures, including myself,
must eat to live. Nevertheless, I was more than slightly perturbed to think that such a fate might befall the very coyote pups
I hoped to observe.

For some time the hawk flapped about on the ground, pecking at something in the grass. Finally it lifted and perched on the
topmost branch of an aspen tree, and immediately Gray Dog
emerged from the willows where he had been concealed all the
while. He trotted to the spot where the hawk had waddled
about, sniffed the area thoroughly, looked up into the branches,
and then sat down and scratched at a flea. I relaxed. No calamity
had as yet befallen the three pups.

As time passed, I would often observe birds hopping about
the den. They apparently were seeking food leavings intended
for the litter. Ordinarily an adult coyote would disperse them

with a bold charge, but on this day, before the litter had yet emerged on its own power, Gray Dog was evidently willing to take a tolerant view of the visiting hawk.

Yet less than an hour later the pups made their debut, and it was Gray Dog himself who summoned them out of their dark home into the sunshine. For a long time he stood at the burrow opening and peered inside, perhaps emitting some sound that I could not hear. Then, cocking his head from side to side, he appeared to be listening to the scratching noise of puppies clawing their way to the surface. Finally one brown bundle after another came tumbling out and began leaping about in fits and starts like three Mexican jumping beans. They moved as if they had difficulty discovering how to activate their legs. When a voluntary impulse finally did reach the right muscle, it invariably was too strong, causing the pup to lurch forward in a most uncoordinated fashion and sometimes even to topple over. Gray Dog watched them with keen attention, cocking his head in a manner to suggest that all this clumsy capering was being accompanied by some excited squeals.

Suddenly the red-legged female rushed from the willows and, with tail wagging her back end, began licking Gray Dog's muzzle and grinning up at him. Obviously the emergence of the pups was a momentous event to Redlegs, for she continued to cavort about until she was finally mobbed by the three babies. Then she held very steady while each tiny creature stood up on its hind legs and took hold of one of her teats. During the next five minutes, while she nursed them in this standing position, I slowly recovered from the shock of discovering that Redlegs, not Brownie, was the mother of the pups!

Yet my memory as well as my notes told me that Brownie, not Redlegs, had moved the litter to its present den. Had I made some mistake? Perhaps on that earlier date I was not yet sufficiently familiar with the characteristics that distinguished these two coyotes and had confused the two. Or maybe the long rays of the late-afternoon sun had cast a reddish tint on the grayer female's coat. Whatever the explanation, I have always treated field notes as final and inviolate. I had recorded that Brownie had moved the pups. I now noted that Redlegs was the nursing

mother. It would then appear that Brownie was accepting unusual responsibilities in the rearing of another female's young!

The significance of this behavior did not escape me. From
many sources, I had been led to believe that the coyote is a
semi-loner, whose associations are strictly limited to mate and
young of the year. In fact, in many circles it has become almost
axiomatic to regard the coyote as differing radically from the
wolf in degree of sociability. When adult coyotes are seen to
congregate, the group has always been presumed to be made up
of parents with their sub-yearling offspring, who soon will
migrate. But now I was observing behavior which suggested that
bonds between unpaired adults might not be so transitory as
supposed. Perhaps the "solitary" coyote was more wolf-like in
his social organization than anyone had previously suspected. I
was eager to see more.

During the next few days the pups remained outside for
hours at a time, and all three adult coyotes hovered about and
treated them with the utmost solicitude. Every four hours Mama
Redlegs nursed, always from a standing posture. This enabled
her to keep watch from all sides while constrained by clinging
nurselings. After each feeding she would clean the pups, exactly
as a dog mother does, licking them all over.

Brownie groomed the babies, too. And Brownie rolled on the
ground and allowed the fuzzy pups to crawl all over her. Whenever Mama permitted them to do this to herself, they began to
nurse, and she would be forced to move a short distance off. I
decided that one advantage of the presence of a second female
at a den might be to promote socialization of the puppies beyond
what is possible for a lactating mother to accomplish.

Meanwhile Gray Dog behaved like a stereotypical father
figure, packing in food, which he carried in his stomach and
regurgitated at the pups' feet long before they were old enough
to be interested in his offerings. I was amused to see him trudge
purposefully uphill and bypass Mama, who would meet him en
route and try to wheedle the food from him. After he had
deposited his load of nourishment and turned away, she would
rush in and eat it. Of course, she really needed it. She was eating
for four! (The following year Gray Dog reversed this behavior,

favoring Mama with the contents of his stomach before offering anything to the puppies. Perhaps by then the pair bond had grown even stronger.)

Now that the litter was spending so much time outside, the adults also became more visible. Mama Redlegs rarely entered the den anymore. Instead she summoned her young out with a signal that was inaudible to me, but nonetheless capable of reaching the ears or perhaps the noses of her underground babies.

Dens vary greatly in construction and depth, but most have a chamber that is several feet below the surface and only one exit-entrance tunnel just large enough for an adult to crawl through. Sometimes this tunnel may descend perpendicularly for two or three feet before leveling off. One den, reported in Kansas, had a tunnel that ran for thirty feet before opening into the inside chamber. Earlier in the spring, I dug into an inactive den to learn something about its construction; but my best information came from a nine-year-old boy, Leon Shaw, who told me that he had crawled into one when he "was little." Leon's den was cleverly constructed to open onto the side of a cliff. Evidently a more accessible entryway had once existed, but had been plugged up by former tenants. He drew me the diagram pictured below:

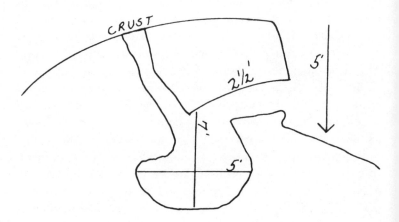

A few days after the puppies surfaced, a crisis occurred between Mama Redlegs and Brownie. Until then, the two females seemed to be on good terms, greeting one another in amicable fashion after even the briefest separation, hunting in one another's company, and trotting single file behind Gray Dog on short excursions along the butte, during which they would make innumerable stops to dig holes, investigate smells, or pounce upon unsuspecting mice. But suddenly all this changed.

One day, as Brownie headed toward the den (where, incidentally, she spent most of her waking and sleeping hours), Mama leaped out and assumed a belligerent stance over it. Brownie stopped dead in her tracks, and the short eye-to-eye

Above: When trailed, Mama Redlegs sends her pups home with a fierce gape. *Below:* During her absences the pups are guarded by other pack members.

confrontation that followed exuded tension. Finally Brownie turned aside and stole submissively into the brush.

From then on, Mama Redlegs and Brownie's relationship deteriorated. When Mama was present at the den, Brownie was not allowed to approach the litter. If she tried, Mama rushed at her and forced her to roll over on her back and expose her vulnerable underparts. Following this, poor Brownie would crawl back uphill and lie alone some seventy-five feet away, where she would wait until Mama grew weary of her pups and left to hunt mice on the flats. Then Brownie would spring toward the den and engage the litter in wild bouts of play until Mama's return drove her uphill again.

Brownie seemed more tolerant of the litter's roughhouse antics than did either of the parents. She would allow the babies to pester her by the hour—climb on her back, chew her ears, tug on her tail, and prance at her face in mock attack. Eventually, when she had had enough, she would make a dash for cover. If, as often happened, the puppies persisted in following her, she seemed to have great difficulty affecting the grimacing face Mama always put on to discourage them from tagging along. More often than not, Brownie could be lured back for more fun and games.

But if Mama returned to discover her sporting with the pups, poor Brownie would be forced to the ground and put through that humiliating ritual of submissiveness. Obviously Brownie's baby-tending services were not always appreciated, although Mama did seem reluctant to leave her litter unless the other grown female was nearby. On those few occasions when Brownie was nowhere in evidence, Mama pointed her nose skyward and emitted a single howl (which I came to call the "single siren"). Upon hearing this summons, the low-ranking female would come at a brisk trot, and the moment Mama caught sight of her approaching, she would confidently depart.*

When the puppies were perhaps three and a half weeks old, a

---

* Zoologist George B. Rabb observed the interactions of wolves in the Chicago Zoo and noted that a wolf bitch on the point of being expelled from pack membership saved her place by assuming heavy responsibility in the rearing of a litter belonging to a higher-ranking female.

number of coyotes visited them. These animals must all have shared the same territory and been members of what I later came to term the Miller Butte pack, for they were amiably received by Mama, who behaved belligerently toward any strangers who dared intrude on her domain. During a rambunctious greeting ceremony in which all the coyotes bussed noses and one of the animals rolled over on its back and kicked its paws in the air, Mama lavished such effusive attention on one male in particular that for a moment I mistook him for Gray Dog, who was not actually present. Brownie was on the hill, as usual, but was so demoralized by this time that she shrank into the vegetation and did not participate in the greeting. I did not

A pup is about to receive some dinner from an adult who has catered it in her stomach.

have sufficient time to note identifying features on the strangers before they departed with Mama in tow. The litter, as usual, was left in Brownie's vigilant care.

After this incident, a male coyote (probably one of the callers) became a frequent visitor at the den, and he, like Gray Dog and Brownie, began to regurgitate food for the pups, who by now had learned to relish predigested mouse. Often the frenzied reception made it difficult for Brownie, Gray Dog, and the new coyote (whom I called "Harness Marks") to bring up food, and eventually all the adults had to learn the trick of regurgitating *before* the advancing puppy throng had quite reached them.

At a later date, after making a thorough search of existing literature on coyotes, I found that the offering of food to a litter by a nonparent was first observed by Carol Snow in her laboratory study "Some Observations on the Behavioral and Morphological Development of Coyote Pups." Miss Snow suggested that this behavior, which she regarded as atypical, was the outcome of the confinement in pens of her study animals. She wrote: "An interesting phenomenon was observed because of the presence of an unmated female, Coyote D. In a normal situation a coyote 'family' consists of the mated male and female, plus the pups of the year. In this situation a female was present that otherwise would not have been. . . . The first time that their mother was observed regurgitating food to the pups, Coyote D also exhibited the same behavior."

Now I was discovering that in at least one "normal situation" a family of wild coyotes comprised at least four adults, who fed the litter as a matter of course. I was intrigued to know if these nonparents would also assume the more complex roles of teacher and defender of the young. If so, the coyote's social unit, I would have to conclude, was a highly sophisticated one.

Harness Marks was so named by me because of the distinct white stripes that crossed his shoulders, a marking common to the species but one that was not so evident in the other three adults I was observing. I wondered if he and Brownie, who in no way resembled one another, might be litter mates from some previous year. But during my first spring on the refuge, I had no way of guessing what familial relationships existed among my identified coyotes, and so I refrained from referring to them as an extended family.

One morning I arrived as usual at 7:30 and settled into my hiding place on the flats. The pups, I had come to know, put in their first appearance at 8:30 A.M. and seemed to be on a four-hour nursing schedule, feeding about 8:30, 12:30, 4:30, and 8:30. They probably fed at night, too, although in 1972 I did not attempt to watch my subjects round the clock but returned to a motel each night to sleep.

On this morning, I arrived to find three mule deer browsing the slopes and no coyotes in sight. This situation I thought very peculiar. Surely adult coyotes would not tolerate deer chewing away the cover that concealed their den. Nor would deer be likely to feed where adult coyotes were on guard in the brush. Had the pups been moved?

For several days Mama had been excavating a new den some five hundred yards downslope. Sometimes Gray Dog assisted her in this task, for when she descended too deep to kick the dirt she was loosening high enough to avoid blocking the tunnel behind her, Gray Dog would crawl partway down and remove the accumulating soil. When the two finally backed out, they would be covered with dirt and had to spend some time shaking and scratching to clean themselves. On the previous day, I noted that Mama had emerged from the hole headfirst and clean. Evidently the inner chamber was now sufficiently large to permit her to turn around. The den was ready.

Suspecting that the pups might have been taken to this new burrow, I trained my spotscope on it. No, I saw no sign of life there either. I lived in fear of losing my identified coyotes, and as the hours dragged on I grew convinced I had done just that. It seemed unthinkable that such importunate pups could stay belowground all morning without once seeking food, or that Brownie would overlook such an opportunity to summon up and play with an untended litter.

While the deer munched away on the willows, I glassed the entire butte, but it seemed devoid of other life. Then, just as I panned back to the den area, pandemonium broke loose. From the willows leaped Harness Marks, and at the same in-

Harness Marks routs deer caught browsing on
the vegetative cover around the pups' den.

stant the three deer sprang straight into the air and began bounding downhill at breakneck speed with Harness Marks careening after. I grabbed my camera and began shooting just as the animals rocketed past. Their strides looked to be thirty feet long. Was such a thing possible? Upon later examining my photographs, I decided that it might very well be. Even more amazing was my discovery that the mercurial coyote sailing through the air was gaining on the deer in every picture.*

I could now see Mama Redlegs standing on the hill, watching the action with keenest interest. She ran along the slope to get a better view, and when I followed her gaze, I discovered that Harness Marks had quit and was limping back across the flats. Either he had been kicked or he had caught his front foot in a badger hole during the wild chase, for he was clearly disabled.

I tracked Mama as she raced downhill and touched noses with him midfield. Then Harness Marks turned away and headed for the marsh while she trotted back to her den, where her young ones were already out and scampering about. Their ravenous behavior at her breasts raised a question in my mind: By what signal had such hungry pups been kept underground during the long siege? More and more I was persuaded that some fairly sophisticated system of communication must be employed by the coyote.

I did not see Harness Marks again for several days. Perhaps he was holed up in some isolated draw while his leg healed. I could not help but characterize his act as "heroic," however anthropomorphic that might sound. For despite the likelihood that Harness Marks may have derived some pleasure from chasing the deer, his motive to do so seemed also to be "altruistic"—to remove a menace from the den area. Since it is uncharacteristic for a coyote to take any unnecessary risk (a healthy deer need only raise its back hackles to send a coyote packing), his behavior was all the more impressive. And, in light of the fact that the pups he was defending were not even his own offspring, I was now more than ever convinced that the coyote

---

* Coyotes have been clocked at 43 miles per hour. Top speed measured for the mule deer is 35 miles per hour.

enjoys a social life similar in many ways to that of the wolf.

At the same time I could not help but muse on how different an interpretation would have been placed on this coyote's behavior by an onlooker who had no prior knowledge of what had happened at the den. Just so are rumors started that coyotes threaten game animals.

It was truly ironic, but at last I had obtained a photograph of a coyote chasing deer!

A
Female
Hierarchy

For days a feeling had been growing in me that I must somehow soon document on film the unique behavior I was observing at the den. But how to approach near enough to obtain pictures of my subjects without disturbing them? Obviously fear and flight, not sociability, would be the only behavior the coyotes would manifest should they even suspect a human being was at such close range.

Finally I mapped out a plan. In the dark of night I clawed my way up the steep and rocky back side of Miller Butte and began to move across its flat top. I was racing with the sun, for it was imperative that I reach a particular spruce tree before dawn. I hoped to conceal myself within its lowest branches and there await the emergence of the pups for their 8:30 A.M. feeding.

The wind on top of the butte was unrelenting, brutal. It roared around my ears, muffling all other sound. It caused my eyes to tear, whipped my face with loose strands of hair, and made breathing painful. As I walked, I leaned into it. Ahead in the dim light I discerned the dark outline of the tree that was my destination. To the east, against a faintly glowing sky, Jackson Peak was beginning to take shape. Soon the high butte I was crossing would be bathed in a dawn light, and against its low vegetation my silhouette, misshapen with cameras, would present a jarring spectacle. I was not surprised to feel my heart racing—more from exhilaration than from exertion—for I never fail to experience excitement when stalking unsuspecting animals.

Knowing that the four adults in my pack sometimes made use of this summit, I was watchful for coyotes. From my usual vantage point on the opposite side of the butte, I had often seen them head uphill and vanish across the top. I now wondered to what purpose. The wind up here was debilitating, and the ground as hard as pavement; I could see no sign of ground-squirrel habitations, and the place looked too dry for mice.

Nevertheless, though the butte seemed to offer little in the way of food, perhaps the coyotes found it a safe haven in which to sun, romp, assemble, howl, and view the world below.

Their favorite hunting ground was a marsh about a mile across the meadow. I estimated that they made use of five square miles of the refuge. Adjacent areas seemed to be occupied by other coyotes. Nevertheless, the previous evening, while leaving the refuge, I caught sight of Brownie, Mama Redlegs, and Gray Dog on the mountain behind Miller Butte, a place I knew to be the home range of Digger and his mate. I stopped, curious to see what the trio might be up to. From the guilty behavior of the two females, it was obvious to me that they were aware of the consequences trespassing could carry, for when they weren't poaching mice, they skulked about and looked like dogs who have swiped the roast. Every few seconds one head and then another would pop up from the thick sage and freeze in a listening attitude. Their wariness did little to further their hunting success. Stalking *Microtus* requires a coyote's undivided attention, and the females, in particular, seemed unable to concentrate on this undertaking.

As the three coyotes fanned out, I noticed that each one faced in a different direction while hunting. I suspect they were trying to cover all fronts, for every few minutes one would look back to check on the whereabouts of the others. At one point, when some tall brush blocked Brownie's view, she began to leap in place like a trampoline acrobat until she managed a sufficiently high jump to catch sight of Gray Dog and Mama Redlegs.

I had the strong impression that these three coyotes actually were out "looking for trouble," for mousing was no better here than on their own home range. And if coyotes are anything like their relative the dog, they may sometimes seek adventure. A few minutes later, when a large coyote bounded down from the tree line and headed straight for the trespassers, I became convinced their motive had indeed been to incite a chase, for all three froze in their tracks and waited until the resident animal had nearly closed the distance between them before they turned and fled, streaking into the dusk like a ribbon of gray cats. I watched as they effortlessly scaled the south side of Miller Butte and turned to watch their pursuer come to a dead halt at some invisible boundary that divided the two territories. A minute later I could no longer see them for the dark, but from the summit there pealed a chorus of vibrant voices. And from the facing mountain rang an antiphonal response. Digger's pack and the Miller Butte coyotes were talking.

I did not win the race with the sun that morning. By the time I reached the tree the day had begun, but fortunately the surrounding vegetation was higher than had appeared from afar and I crawled the last few yards without being seen.

From this opposite perspective, behind the den, everything looked different. I even had difficulty locating the rye patch until I spotted the backs of two red ears in the grass. Brownie was baby-sitting. As I settled into position, she evidently heard me or perhaps caught my scent, for in an instant she was on her feet, her pointed nose vigorously working the air.

With deep disappointment, I realized my plan had failed. Though I had proved I could succeed in making a close approach, I now knew that I could not hope to obtain the kind of photographs I wanted—natural pictures of coyotes tending pups at a den—without revealing my presence and spooking my subjects. For even though I was using a 500-mm telephoto lens, it was necessary for me to work no farther than one hundred feet away in order to obtain clear pictures of such small subjects. And at such proximity, no alert coyote charged with the task of guarding young would conceivably remain unaware of me for more than a few seconds.

Far less adroitness is exacted from a hunter. With a gun it would have been a simple matter for me to slaughter all the animals present, and in fact I would not have needed to be so close to do it. But what psychological satisfaction killing animals gives to a human being is a mystery I have never fathomed. Certainly the lives of the victims must seem unreal to the so-called sportsman, whose ego trip precludes any possibility of his experiencing the joy of being at one with Nature. No doubt he requires a carcass as proof to others that he has been clever and has accomplished a stalk. The stalk I do understand. I, too, find high adventure in it. But displaying dead bodies as trophies is a gross act. I once asked a hunter if obtaining a good close-up picture of an animal might not better demonstrate to others his skill in the field and was told he was having a camera built onto his telescopic gun so he could shoot his victim and take its picture at the same time. The man so associated violence with manly achievement that there was nothing much I could say.

By now Brownie had abandoned her post and was standing in an open place staring at me. She seemed to be offering me a clear view of herself before bolting. Perhaps she meant to decoy me from the pups. Certainly had she remained beside them, she would have served no good purpose except to alert me to their exact whereabouts. And since no coyote is capable of making a stand against a human being, her maneuver seemed perfectly appropriate. Though she remained visible for only the briefest moment before dashing off, the very act of laying a fresh track for me to follow, according to her coyote way of thinking, was good strategy. She could not know that my nose was not the equal of hers. Then, to my surprise, Gray Dog emerged from a point some fifty yards downslope and he too made himself briefly conspicuous before heading into cover away from the den.

Now that I had been seen by two adults, it seemed a foregone conclusion that the litter would soon be moved, perhaps to a place where I would never again find it. I therefore decided to make the best of the situation and at least obtain a few portraits of the pups. Since there was no longer any point to my remaining concealed, I crawled out from the tree and found a better angle. But I did not approach the den too closely, for the three babies seemed not to have noticed me and were absorbed in mounting one another's backs.

I quickly expended two rolls of film recording this activity, success at which determines the rank each pup will hold in the subsequent hierarchy of the litter. According to one study, by Dr. Michael Fox and Dr. A. L. Clark, reciprocal play-behavior is absent in coyote pups during the first three to four weeks of life and is not seen until after relative rank has been established by means of this back-standing, coupled with at least one serious fight, which occurs at about thirty days of age. In this respect,

Two of the 1972 pups at thirty days of age. At this age, siblings try to establish dominance by fighting and standing over one another's backs.

coyotes are thought to differ radically from wolves, who begin to play almost before they can walk and establish their dominance long afterward.

I tried to piece together my observations to make them jibe with this study. But my pups had engaged in bouts of play with one another, and with Brownie as well, since the day following their emergence from the den, at which time I calculated they were only three weeks old. At this tender age their principal sport seemed to be a kind of "tag," in which they would race after one another and try to bump. But in my notes I also listed the following games: hide, crouch and pounce, chase, tussle, tail pulling, nip and flee. Not until five days after play was manifested did I witness real fighting among them, and the spat I then observed appeared to have erupted over Brownie's attention. I had no explanation for the fact that the behavior of my wild coyote pups did not conform exactly with that of laboratory subjects.

After shooting my pictures, I hurried back across the butte the way I had come. In daylight, and downhill, the going was considerably easier and within an hour I reached my parked car and drove rapidly around to the north side of the butte. By 9:30 I was installed in my usual viewing place, where I set up my spotscope and waited for the return of adult coyotes to the den. But when none had arrived by 11:00, my old sidekick "Worry" began to plague me. What mischief had I done by letting myself be seen at the den? Were the adults now too fearful to rescue the litter? Or were they waiting until cover of darkness would shield them from my view?

At last, to my relief, an extremely nervous Brownie appeared. She moved swiftly across the slope in a hunched posture and stopped twenty feet short of the den, whence she signaled the pups to come to her. As they scampered through the grass, their ropy tails wagging, Brownie immediately turned and began trotting uphill. For several yards the three little pups followed her, but soon they seemed to forget what they were supposed to be doing and began to romp and play.

After several futile attempts, when Brownie found she could not lure them farther, she sat down and nervously watched over them. When one pup started to head back to the den, she jumped into its path and herded it back to the others. Then, once again, she tried to lead them off. But it was no use. The three babies started to follow but soon began to scatter. Their attention span was apparently too underdeveloped to allow them to make such a long excursion. Then Brownie spied Mama returning and dived into the brush.

If Mama was aware there had been any threat to the safety of her litter that morning, she did not reveal it. As was her custom, she looked about carefully before heading toward her babies. After nursing them briefly, she led the wanderers back to the den, where she carefully groomed one of them. After a time she began stalking mice on the slope. In quick succession, she caught two. The first one she ate, but the second she brought to her young. This was the first time I had seen her offer them an intact mouse and the pup who took it dashed about with the unfortunate creature dangling from his mouth until he succeeded in inciting his siblings to chase him. I hoped that it was dead. What finally happened to this "toy" I did not see, but I doubt it was ever consumed.

Shortly thereafter the pups charged downslope and ganged up on Mama Redlegs, who was trying to get some rest. While two made quick dashes at her head, one played pounce on her tail. Once she turned and gently nipped the tail attacker, who managed to leap out of range. But he did not take the rebuff seriously. The moment she looked away, he pounced upon her tail again. Obviously all was well at the den. At least Mama manifested no awareness that there had been an early-morning visitor there. And Brownie had proved herself to be an ineffectual baby-mover.

Then at 4:45 I spotted Gray Dog returning across the flats. Like Brownie, he had been badly spooked by my sudden appearance at the den, and now I was curious to see what he would do. As he came nearer, he veered and stopped at the foot of the butte, some two hundred yards north of the den. He did not mount the slope. Instead he stood patiently and waited until Mama happened to notice him and scampered downhill to greet him.

While she performed the usual muzzle-licking ritual, he remained in a no-nonsense posture. Then abruptly he turned and started trotting off in the opposite direction. Obviously he meant for Mama to follow him, for every few yards he stopped and looked back to see if she was coming. Was he trying to tell her something?

It was not unusual for Gray Dog to show up at this hour, nor was it odd for Mama to depart with him. Nearly every evening the two left together to hunt in one another's company. This was the first time, however, that I had seen Gray Dog return and not pay a visit to the pups. Usually he went directly to them and spent some time playing with the litter before he and Mama left them in Brownie's care. But on this particular evening he approached no nearer to the den than the length of two football fields.

Over the next two days I did not see Gray Dog at all, although Mama frequently stood on the butte and scanned the flats, apparently looking for him. Then the pups were moved. Brownie helped with this task, which took place almost entirely in my absence. Earlier in the day I had watched her excavate a den of her own. It must have been an old one that merely needed a little renovating, for within a relatively short time she had it completed and was able to turn around inside and emerge headfirst. This den, like the one Mama had been preparing, was at the foot of the butte, and the two were about one hundred yards apart.

But at just that point I had to leave the refuge in order to meet with two teenage boys in the town of Jackson who had agreed to tell me where they sold the coyotes they were shooting along the edges of Grand Teton National Park, Gros Ventre National Forest, and the National Elk Refuge. Apparently coyotes make long migrations after death. The boys told me that they brought the ears of their victims to the town of Bondurant in Sublette County, where sheepmen paid high bounties for them with no questions asked. Their ruse, of course, kept the woolgrowers in that county believing that the coyote population there, despite saturation poisoning, was virtually uncontrollable and that even more lethal methods would have to be devised to keep numbers down. It also disrupted the stability of the animals inhabiting the fringes of the parks, whose numbers, if they were not being hunted, would become self-regulatory.

When I returned to my ditch, I was filled with indignation over the boys' deeds and their self-justification.

"The coyote loves to hamstring deer and eat them alive," they had felt compelled to tell me. "You should talk to our dad if you want to learn something about coyotes. He hates them. He says people who think coyotes are just like nice dogs are just emotional." (Spoken with vehement passion!)

As a result of this interruption in my day, I missed the first stage of the coyotes' move. In fact, so absorbed was I in recalling the boys' conversation that for several minutes after my return I failed to notice that the three pups had been led to the foot of the slope, where Mama and Brownie were desperately trying to corral them into Mama's newly dug den. One made off for some rye grass, whose familiar look and scent must have reminded him of his old home, and Mama had to chase him down and herd him back again.

Then, while Brownie blocked the pups from escaping by facing them and dancing from side to side like a quick-stepping cutting horse, Mama trotted uphill to check the old den for stragglers. While she was there, the ground began to vibrate. A herd of government horses had been released to pasture on the refuge, and now four were galloping across the flats. Alarmed, Mama bounded pell-mell downhill and put her pups down their new hole as quick as weasels. When the situation called for blind obedience, Mama was obviously able to muster it.

During the next hour and a half the pups remained underground, and Mama made use of this respite to make repeated trips uphill to inspect their former home. At last she seemed satisfied that no pup had inadvertently been abandoned and she returned downhill to lie down and rest.

While peace momentarily reigned, Brownie took a turn at investigating the former den. She, too, seemed to be looking for a forgotten pup. Cocking her head from side to side in a listening attitude, she peered into the hole, then decided to enter. She soon emerged, however, and headed downhill toward the new den. But as she neared it Mama jumped to her feet, and her warning stance brought Brownie to a halt.

Accustomed to such treatment, Brownie withdrew with an amusing air of nonchalance, even stopping once to investigate a ground-squirrel habitation in what looked like an attempt to save face. Then, as if in reproach, she looked back at Mama and regurgitated a food offering. Ordinarily Mama would have made a rush to eat this mess, but in her present mood she exhibited no interest in it whatsoever, and after a short time Brownie reingested it.

Although for a time that day the two females had got on well, now Mama Redlegs, having just brought her family under control, was no longer in a mood to tolerate Brownie's disruptive presence at her den, and the rejected female crawled into the private hole she had excavated earlier that day. But Mama did not have things so well in hand as she thought. Later, when the pups emerged to nurse, they once again went on a rampage, dashing in three directions at once. They were totally uncontrollable. One traveled so far that he even discovered the hole

Checking a newly vacated den to be sure no pup is left behind.

Brownie had entered and proceeded to climb in after her, a development that instantly flushed out Brownie, who tried to summon up the renegade by standing at the entrance and peering in.

Just then the other two sped past, and Brownie, ever on the alert for wayward pups, jumped into their path to block them from passing. But Mama, who was right on the tails of her babies, did not welcome any assistance. She rushed at Brownie, who sank to the ground cowering. For several seconds Mama stood over her menacingly while neither coyote moved.

Meanwhile, the two pups succeeded in covering considerable distance, and by the time Mama released Brownie they were hiding in some tall vegetation some fifty yards to the west. Immediately Mama went off to retrieve them, and all might have been well had not Brownie unwisely gone to her aid. For a few minutes, Redlegs tolerated Brownie's helpful herding, but when the pups tagged after her instead of their own mother, poor Redlegs had had enough. Once again she forced the low-ranking female to the ground and held her there for several seconds. When at last she was released, Brownie ran off.

By this time the pups were totally unmanageable and far from their new habitation. Their distraught mother sat down and let out a plaintive howl: oh—oo—oo. Then she looked about in all directions, perhaps hoping to see Gray Dog approach. When he did not immediately appear, she acted. With head up and tail low, she took off at a brisk pace, heading for her former burrow. It was growing dark, but I could count one—two—three pups trailing up the slope after her as obediently as ducks in a line.

Apparently the move to the new burrow had not worked out.

I still had not solved the problem of how to obtain photographic evidence of the "loving" and "cooperative" behavior of my subjects, though in making notations I now freely referred to my band of coyotes as a pack. I knew that objections might be raised to my use of this term. A number of knowledgeable people have thought that coyotes, since they do not depend on one another to obtain food, never had the need to evolve such a complex social unit as is implied by the word "pack." Wolves, by contrast, have had to band together to kill animals sufficiently large to provide them with adequate nourishment. A wolf can weigh five times more than a coyote, and therefore he is unable to subsist entirely on a diet of small rodents.

In support of the prevailing view of the coyote as a loner is the undeniable fact that he is almost always observed singly or in pairs. A winter study by Robert Chesness in northern Minnesota reported 61 percent of the animals sighted traveling alone and 34 percent in the company of only one other animal. In winter observations, only once did Chesness observe as many as four coyotes together.

But these figures cannot possibly tell the complete story. I, too, more frequently than not observed coyotes hunting alone or in pairs, especially in winter. But often after watching a particular animal for many hours, I would see it be joined by others or would catch sight of coyotes mousing nearby. To *Canis latrans*, one thousand yards or more is not a separation. Togetherness cannot be determined by human standards.

And now, in spring, the coyotes I was watching were positively wolf-like in their tendency to form exclusive relationships with one another. They recognized and greeted "accepted" individuals and expelled all others from what clearly seemed to be delineated territories. They also cooperated in the rearing of young. And often in the early evening I observed as many as six **201** of my subjects convening on Miller Butte, enjoying a good howl, and then, just like wolves, setting off together as if to hunt game. Upon arriving at their destination, usually the marsh, they would simply scatter and individually begin to look for mice. Thereafter they would pay no further heed to one another.

I was by no means the first to notice that coyotes sometimes "pack up" seemingly for no other purpose than to enjoy one another's company. Explorers who visited the Far West during the nineteenth century (Audubon included) reported coyotes to be more sociable than wolves. J. Frank Dobie, noting that in recent years such behavior was not being reported, tried to reconcile past and present trends by postulating that the versatile coyote may have been forced to adapt himself to a more solitary life to survive the advance of civilization. He wrote: "Had they, bison-like, persisted in following an inherited instinct for gregariousness, they would by now have been eliminated from much of their territory."

Perhaps, then, my Miller Butte coyotes, living as they did on a protected refuge, had reverted to the more gregarious life-style once natural to the species. Or perhaps all coyotes become clannish in the spring of the year, when pups are born. Such behavior would certainly have high survival value. It might even help to explain how *Canis latrans* has managed to survive the efforts aimed at its extermination. For should Redlegs and Gray Dog both be killed, their three pups would undoubtedly be raised by Harness Marks or Brownie, or the two together. Nature had provided the litter with surrogate parents. At the same time, Brownie and Harness Marks were enjoying the advantage of serving an apprenticeship in pup-rearing for the day when they would produce litters of their own.

Then again, perhaps the pack association I was observing was only temporary. Certainly Mama's growing intolerance of Brownie suggested that the bond between these two females was weakening. Might not the dynamics of coyote survival demand that these two animals ultimately sever their relationship? Miller Butte could not support an indefinite number of coyote litters, and therefore Brownie's maturation would ultimately present a threat to the well-being of any future pups born to Mama Redlegs. But since coyotes are rarely able to reproduce before their second year, the rupture between these two females might not occur before the younger one had served for a season as "nursemaid" to the other's whelps.

I was reminded again of the Minnesota study cited earlier. By means of telemetry, Robert Chesness plotted the movements of a number of coyotes and successfully pinpointed their respective ranges. He found that the adult females that he had successfully trapped, fitted with radio transmitters, and released occupied exclusive territories. His male subjects wandered across larger areas, some overlapping the boundaries that enclosed two separate female ranges. Preliminary findings of an in-progress study of eight or nine coyotes in south Texas seem to support Chesness's conclusion that territoriality is controlled by the adult female segment of the population.

Excellent as these studies are, one weakness is inherent in the use of telemetry. Only those animals that have been fitted with radio collars are accounted for. Chesness learned nothing about the unmonitored females who may have been cohabiting in perfect harmony with others of their sex. To discover the complete answer, it is therefore essential that "bedroll" fieldwork supplement modern gadgetry.

Without fixing collars to them, it was apparent to me that the animals I was watching were territorial, and that my female subjects acted belligerently toward strange females for the sole purpose of driving them off their range. On the other hand, I also observed that more than one female occupied a territory. To ascertain that my Miller Butte coyotes were not unique in this respect, I briefly watched a contiguous pack on forest-service land and discovered it to be made up of at least three females and two males. Moreover, the following year another coyote-watcher, Franz Camenzind, discussed with me his findings, which were similar to my own. He even described two females who were so compatible they cared for their respective litters in the same den!

Even though Brownie had her troubles with the dominant female, Mama Redlegs, she was by no means an outcast. Sometimes after Redlegs had spent a long day watching over her babies, if she happened to sight Brownie approaching, she would run out on the flats to greet her. Her friendliness on these occasions would elicit a few convulsive heaves from Brownie, which would separate the rufous-colored coyote from an entire day's harvest of rodents. Mama, of course, would promptly devour the booty. Afterward the two females might remain together in loose association without discord.

At times the coyotes would maintain low visibility, and I would be surprised to discover how many had been sleeping around the den while the pups had been playing all day by themselves. Sometimes one of the litter would discover an adult in the brush and begin to pester him or her until the beleaguered animal would rise, walk a few yards away, pounce on a mouse, and then deliver the wretched creature to the dancing babies. Upon receiving this prize, the three would dash off and start a game of keep-away. I decided that catching mice must be an exceedingly easy task for a coyote, who seems able to do it upon request, and I began noting down the above sequence of behavior in a kind of shorthand, which read: "You want a mouse? Okay, here's one. Now leave me alone."

Mama had again moved her family to the new den at the foot of the slope, and this time she seemed to have no difficulty controlling them there. I was curious to know what had motivated her to change residences. As far as I was aware, nothing had happened recently to disturb her at the former burrow.

Many people have noticed this tendency of coyotes to shift a litter from den to den. H. T. Gier in *Coyotes in Kansas* suggests they may be trying to escape the tracks and telltale food traces that inevitably accumulate around a burrow. Another theory, advanced by Jane Goodall and Hugo Van Lawick, who noted the same behavior in jackals and wild dogs in Africa, is that infestations of vermin may be what drives adults to abandon an otherwise suitable den. This idea made sense to me. I was only too aware that insects in general were becoming intolerable. Even the arrival of large flocks of green and purple swallows seemed not to put a dent in the swarms of mosquitoes and gnats that hovered like a low cloud in late afternoon. It was that time of year, and the pups were obviously plagued by some kind of

pest, for they scratched themselves incessantly. One other explanation occurred to me. Since a coyote during his first year of
life will automatically begin to develop fear reactions to
changes in his environment, it may be important that he be
exposed to a variety of terrains and situations while still very
young. John Paul Scott and John L. Fuller, in their work with
dogs, found that litters raised in the enriched environments of
homes performed better in experiments than those reared in
pens. It follows that the exposure of young coyotes to a succession of different surroundings might improve their future
performance in life situations and therefore might have some
intrinsic survival value.

To Mama's apparent delight, now that the puppies were no
longer inhabiting the "dangerous" slope, Gray Dog began show-
ing up again. He never appeared without receiving an enthusiastic welcome. In part, Mama's demonstrativeness was probably
motivated by her desire to be fed; this would not fully explain
her behavior, however, for whether or not an offering was
forthcoming, she would continue to dance joyfully about the
slope, and on several occasions she even ignored the food
Gray Dog presented to her while she persisted in making a
fuss over him. Moreover, when Mama was not present, Brownie
gave Gray Dog a similar greeting. Brownie's tail-wagging and
muzzle-licking, however, never stimulated Gray Dog to offer *her*
food.

Though he accepted all female homage with good grace, I
never saw Gray Dog wag his tail. He was a dignified animal who
appeared to take himself very seriously. He was always extremely gentle with the pups, though. They, of course, pestered
any adult who came within visual range and at times they even
tried to nurse the males. This behavior always caused Gray Dog
to lose his aplomb completely, and he would leap for brush.

One day I watched him try to avoid the pups. A moment
earlier they had made the mistake of trying to suckle his
rudimentary teats just as Mama poked her head from the
brush. Noting that her offspring were seeking milk, she sneaked
off in a most amusing manner and crawled into Brownie's
hole. She was gradually trying to wean the litter, and lately

I had noticed that she stood still to be nursed only twice a day.

Gray Dog dived for cover. But the pups quickly found him and swarmed all over him again. Again he shook himself free and sought peace elsewhere. By this time, however, the pups were enjoying the game of "find Gray Dog," and when it became apparent to the big male that he was not going to be left alone, he departed, setting off at a determined pace that his tormentors could not keep. Like an anxious little dog who has just awakened to the fact that she is being left behind, Mama now came to life and streaked after him. And behind her streamed the three little pups. I wondered if they were about to take their first long excursion from the den.

Mama had no difficulty overtaking her mate, who was only loping along, and when she did, the pair put on a short burst of speed. But the litter did not turn back and when the two adults stopped to look back the three babies were struggling onward through high grass. At last the pup in the lead caught up with his parents, and the delighted youngster stood up on his hind legs, his tail twirling like some kind of propeller which at any moment would provide him with lift. But neither parent would look

Gray Dog allows a pup to clamber all over him.

down at him. Instead their gazes were fixed on the other two puppies, gamely lurching toward them. Then Gray Dog seemed to make a decision. Turning back, he assumed command over the stragglers and led the whole entourage to the den. The safety of the litter was still paramount and apparently superseded his wish to escape these nuisances and go hunting.

Once back at the den, Mama, too, relented and yielded to the pups' desire to nurse. It was obvious that they were teething, for frequently she had to nip one who began to chew on her. The litter was developing rapidly now, and I got the impression that this short adventure would soon be followed by a real, adult-led, purposeful excursion.

I often tried to distinguish the litter mates one from another, but they changed so rapidly I seldom could recognize the same individual from one day to the next. One did lag in growth, but unless I saw all three together, the difference was not evident. With every passing day their snouts were lengthening, their coats were lightening, and their ears were growing bigger. Sometimes they would strike such charming poses, I had to fight an impulse to run across the flats and gather them up in my arms. At this stage of their development only one word, "irresistible," could adequately describe their appeal. It was not easy to maintain a detached attitude toward such beguiling subjects.

The day the badger came I did not feel one bit objective. And when he entered the den, I nearly leaped from my hiding place, and had to hold my hand over my mouth to keep from shrieking.

A badger is an interesting and useful animal. He is also a fierce and pugnacious predator who is himself all but impervious to attack, since he wears a skin several sizes too large. This enables him to do everything except turn around inside. As a result, no animal is able to get a firm grip on a badger. His diet consists of gophers, moles, mice, and other earth-dwellers, which he obtains by rapidly excavating burrows, removing dirt like a high-powered steam shovel. It is impossible to exaggerate the speed with which he digs after his prey. Bill Gilbert, in his book on the weasel family, describes the badger's burrowing ability as "one of those natural phenomena, like the Grand Canyon or a tropi-

Top: Redlegs expresses affection for Gray Dog.
Wild coyotes wag their tails in greeting.
Bottom: Tag-along pups interfere with their
parents' plans to go hunting. Gray Dog (right)
waits for a straggler to catch up, then leads
the litter back to the den.

cal storm, that has to be seen to be believed, and even then the performance seems incredible." A dog who has caught a badger by the tail is apt to find himself standing knee-deep in a mound of dirt and looking at a hole being plugged up.

Badgers are not unfriendly toward coyotes. On the contrary, Indian legend has it that the two are companions, even soul mates. The Aztec word for badger is *tlalcoyotl*, meaning "earth coyote," and, according to the Navajos, "Coyote" and "Badger" called each other cousin. The white man, too, did not fail to notice that coyotes and badgers occasionally keep company. J. Frank Dobie wrote of watching a coyote and a badger hunt wood rats together in the manner of Digger and his mate, described in a previous chapter. While the badger dug, the coyote waited expectantly for the besieged creature to leave by its back door. At other times, of course, it is the badger that exploits the coyote's aptitudes. When the swifter coyote has run a rabbit into a hole, a badger may burrow after it and not surface again until dinner is over.

Despite this symbiotic tie, the unprotected young of either badger or coyote would probably be regarded as fair game by the other. So when I saw the badger poised on the edge of the coyote burrow, I sadly concluded that I had seen the last of Mama Redlegs's puppies.

But I had not counted on Brownie. Until she charged, I was under the mistaken impression that the pups had been left untended. Suddenly the rufous female was on the spot and circling the badger, who had backed away and was turning around and around, trying to keep her in view. His guard hairs stood high on his back like boar bristles as he hunched and hissed at the coyote making quick darts at him. Her moves were all feints, however, for Brownie was sensibly staying out of range of the badger's formidable claws.

I wanted to cheer her on, but hated myself for my bias. The badger, I knew, must find food and might also have young to feed. But I had not seen the badger babies and Mama Redlegs's pups had begun to seem like my own dogs.

In no time, Brownie succeeded in driving the badger off the mound, whereupon she stretched her body across the den entrance and eyed the would-be invader menacingly. When he showed no sign of departing, she jumped to her feet and resumed her terrier-like harassment until she had the slower creature whirling again. Gradually she worried him farther and farther from the den, and when last I saw them disappearing behind a rise, the badger was still bristling and turning and Brownie was still circling and darting.

An hour later, when Mama returned, the pups did not pop out of the den to greet her as was their habit. I wondered if they had gone into shock at the sight of a badger about to descend on them in their underground sanctuary. When they finally emerged, Mama seemed to sense that something had happened. She looked them over carefully and then began to explore the surrounding area, sniffing the ground as if she were some kind of vacuum cleaner sucking up the details of the recent drama.

The next day the pups were moved again.

I expected the pups would be too large by now to be carried, yet that is how they were moved to their next home some three-quarters of a mile away. I witnessed the entire operation, which began so abruptly it seemed to have come about more by impulse than design. In retrospect, I realized otherwise. After Brownie's confrontation with the badger, Mama Redlegs must have spent the entire night and most of the following day preparing a new lodging, for I did not see her again until 5:07 in the evening, when she showed up looking dirty and disheveled. Within a few minutes, the move was under way.

Still, it caught me by surprise. Throughout that hot and still day Brownie had been lying beside the den, and all seemed tranquil. She had just retired into some shade when Redlegs appeared. Directly, Mama moved to her pups, and for the next two minutes she nursed them. Then began the grooming process, which provoked the most ferocious scrap between litter mates I had yet witnessed. The battle did not cease until Mama picked up the pup she was trying to clean by his rump and dropped him some seventy-five feet away from his attacker. There, once again she proceeded to wash him with her tongue. But the obstreperous sibling had followed, and immediately another fight erupted. At this point, Mama seized the victimized puppy by a hind leg and began to run with him, his head bumping the ground as they traveled. At first I thought she was merely trying to break up the fight, but when she rounded the butte and disappeared, I realized the coyotes were moving.

In the hope of spotting her again when she returned to pick up a second baby, I quickly shifted my hiding place, moving a quarter of a mile eastward. While waiting there, I caught sight of Brownie sneaking along the side of the butte, and I got the impression that the low-ranking female was surreptitiously tracking Mama. She brought to mind a dog I once owned, who, when told to go home, merely made a big show of 211 turning back, but would in fact continue to follow behind cover.

By watching Brownie I was able to gain more directional clues and so seek out a new hiding place one-quarter mile farther along. Thus it was that forty-five minutes later, when Mama passed with a second pup dangling awkwardly from her mouth, I was all but sitting on her route. She obviously caught my scent or heard me, for she suddenly bolted.

The moment she was out of sight I dropped downhill, advanced eastward again, and settled into another concealed vantage point. The next time Mama passed, she, too, had altered her course, crossing the butte at a much higher altitude. She must have felt reasonably secure up there, for she sat down and gave vent to the wail I had come to call "single siren." Seconds later, an identical theme echoed from far across the flats. Perhaps Gray Dog had just been informed of Mama Redlegs's sudden change of residence. Then I descended to the flats and hiked to the easternmost tip of the butte, where, like a surveyor, I used all Mama's various routes to calculate a point of intersection. I raised my binoculars to my eyes and there, in precisely the location I focused upon, stood Brownie.

She was having difficulty keeping the two relocated members of the litter from straying, so I decided to leave. I did not want to risk upsetting the coyotes while they were settling into their new home, and where I was standing I was all too visible. Besides, I had a plan in mind for the following day, and I went in search of one of the refuge maintenance men.

At the foot of the butte was a large hay shed. It had no walls and its tin roof was supported by great log pillars more than two stories tall. The shed was tightly stacked to its rafters with baled hay, elk feed for the following winter. I planned, if the men would agree to lend me a ladder, to climb up and camp under the roof beams. From the far corner of the shed I would have an excellent view of the new den.

I must confess that throughout my life I have suffered from an irrational fear of ladders. Scaling the face of a cliff seems less perilous to me than climbing one of these insubstantial man-made devices. At least a rock wall is fixed to the earth and won't topple. But the next morning when I arrived and found the men had already complied with my request and propped a fire-department-size ladder against the concealed side of the shed, I knew I would have to get myself up it.

By pretending I was never more than two feet above the ground I fooled myself into ascending. Not until I was safely ensconced behind a rafter did I allow myself to look down. Then the terrible realization struck me that descending was going to be a lot more difficult than climbing up had been, for to go down I would have to back out of the shed and feel for my footing on the ladder without seeing the rung. I suddenly knew how a treed cat feels.

At the moment, however, since I was exactly where I wished to be, I dismissed this horrifying prospect and managed, by crawling and squirming, to wriggle my way between hay and beams, past an enormous raven's nest woven of coarse twigs, to the far corner of the shed, where I set up my spotscope.

The view was perfect. Even without lenses I could identify the two animals tending the litter as Gray Dog and Brownie. And I could clearly see with naked eye that the object being dragged about by one of the pups was a dead ground squirrel.

Routinely, I began to jot this information down, and as I wrote across the top of the page the words "Den Number Four," I experienced a kind of thrill to think that I was still on the trail of my identified subjects. One of those Aztec coyote gods, I decided, must be looking out for me.

The shed, I now noticed, was surprisingly cool and smelled good. It had one other desirable feature. Its tin roof rattled in the wind, muffling any sounds I might inadvertently make. I tipped some bales on end and built myself a fortress-like blind to prevent my subjects from noticing my silhouette or picking up my scent. Then I stretched out in a prone position to observe my subjects in comfort. Very soon I became aware that my setup, along with its many advantages, also contained a serious drawback. My hair and clothes quickly became matted with hayseeds, which got into my eyes and mouth and fell down my shirt, as well. Even my lenses had to be kept covered to protect them from the loose chaff. And after a while, I, who have never been afflicted with hay fever, began to suffer from a running nose.

Despite this unexpected development, I soon became too engrossed in what was happening on the hill to be aware of my physical discomfort. Gray Dog, I now noticed, was in an exceptionally restless mood. He shifted his lying-up place from one bush to the next and scanned the flats repeatedly. I presumed he was looking for Mama Redlegs. Brownie meanwhile was keeping a sharp eye on Gray Dog. When he moved slightly nearer to her, her tail thumped the ground. But Gray Dog ignored her, grabbed one of the pups, and gave it a thorough grooming. Finally Brownie began to stalk ground squirrels, freezing like a champion pointer whenever she singled out a potential victim.

Except for the preliminary freeze, a coyote's technique for catching ground squirrels differs from its method of harvesting mice. As described earlier, when a coyote attacks a mouse, he leaps high in the air, brings his forepaws together, and pounces on *Microtus* with his two front feet. In the case of ground squirrels, however, the attack must take place more swiftly, for these wary creatures stay handy to their many burrow entrances. Consequently there is no time for a coyote to execute a vaulting pounce, and ground squirrels must therefore be caught directly by mouth. A sudden low scurry either secures the prize or sends a hunter into a nose dive. On several occasions I have seen coyotes somersault, head over tail, while making unsuccessful lunges at ground squirrels.

On this day Brownie was concentrating exceptionally well on her prey. I timed her freeze at eleven minutes, during which time she stood on three legs and did not allow a single muscle to twitch or relax or betray to her intended prey that she was anything more threatening than a rock. But for all that, her strike failed. The ground squirrel escaped to safety.

While Brownie was thus occupied, the restless Gray Dog departed, and when Brownie finally came to and noticed he was gone, she bounded downhill herself. By then Gray Dog had already reached the flats, but when he saw that Brownie was coming, he waited for her to catch up. Then the two coyotes headed into the marsh. With my spotscope I was able to follow their movements for an hour: Gray Dog trotting ahead and marking numerous bushes with urine, Brownie lagging behind to mouse. Suddenly Brownie began to cavort about in quite a cat-like manner. The leaps she performed were strangely perpendicular. Higher and higher she jumped in the air with her back arched, her tail straight out, and her legs stiff. Neither then nor now do I have even a theory about what her actions might have signified, though at a later date I again observed coyotes exhibiting the same peculiar behavior.

Despite my trepidation, which did not diminish with time, I somehow managed to climb in and out of the hay shed every day without plummeting to my death. Thus I was able to watch my subjects at closer range than previously, and, more important, I was able to obtain some sorely needed pictures of my cast of characters interacting. Although these photographs were of poor quality due to distance, nevertheless I was grateful to have them and relieved that in this eleventh hour I was at last documenting some aspects of the unique social behavior I had been watching over the past few weeks. It was this development, of course, that motivated me to get up and down that ladder every day!

One day I witnessed a strange interaction between Mama and Gray Dog. The pups had just been rebuffed for trying to nurse when Gray Dog dashed at Mama, forced her to the ground, and maintained a belligerent stance over her. Though Mama submitted by rolling on her side, she simultaneously drew back her lips and exposed her teeth in a most ferocious gape. Gray Dog quickly backed off. That was the first and only time I witnessed such an expression of conflict between the pair and I wondered if the dominant male had mistaken Mama's rejection of her pups as a threat to himself. Actually, none of the pack members ever engaged in real battle. Differences were always resolved by ritualistic displays of one kind or another.

On another day Mama returned and could not find her family. Brownie had taken the litter uphill into heavy vegetation. As Mama circled and sniffed, she appeared to be very distressed. Frequently her head jerked up and she froze in a listening attitude. Finally she picked up some clue or other and headed uphill just as Brownie came into view with the litter in tow. Belligerently Mama rushed forward, gathered her pups round her, and, after allowing the babies a brief suckle, led them back to their den.

A few minutes later Brownie reappeared carrying a mouse, which she obviously intended to give to one of the pups. But as she headed toward them, Mama stopped her with a look so ominous that she dropped her offering and ran. Mama immediately rushed over and picked up the dead mouse. Then *she* presented it to her three prancing babies!

But on the same day, when Gray Dog showed up, Brownie would not be intimidated by Mama. While Mama was lavishing attention on the male, Brownie pushed her way in and did likewise. She behaved like a new dog who is vying for human attention, while at the same time taking care to avoid the jealous maneuvers of another already established pet.

Wild coyotes, I had by now come to see, manifest most of the qualities I had often observed in dogs. Only the object of the two species' devotion differs. The coyote's emotional and social life quite properly revolves about other coyotes, whereas a domesticated canine, as a result of centuries of association with human beings, now makes man the object of his affection. Actually the devotion of the dog is just a perversion of an innate capacity of wild canids to love their own kind.

A little while after witnessing the rivalry between Mama and Brownie over Gray Dog, I observed Mama and Gray Dog depart together on their usual evening jaunt. But on this night Brownie was in no mood to remain behind. When she awoke after a short snooze to discover herself alone, she began pacing the hill and scanning the flats. Finally she sat down and howled. From the top of the butte a chorus of yaps and howls answered her wail. Brownie turned and headed straight uphill toward the sound. She was trailed by the three pups.

I tracked them until they disappeared into thick vegetation. On that particular evening I had no reason to register the scene in my memory, for I had no way of knowing that I was enjoying my last look at the 1972 litter. But I was. They never again returned to the den.

Over the next several days, I made exhaustive efforts to locate my subjects. Frequently I was teased by the sound of coyote howls, which reassured me that the pups were still thriving, for their squeaky voices were readily discernible above the canine clamor. But just as those coyotes in Dryhead had tricked me long ago, now these animals seemed able to throw their voices and thus confuse me as to their whereabouts.

At last I did succeed in pinpointing where the sound was coming from—a place that was virtually unapproachable, the heavy vegetation that crowned the northeastern tip of the butte. I made several unsuccessful forays up the precipitous slope, but it was devoid of high cover and the coyotes could see me coming long before I was near enough to see them. I had to concede that they had chosen an ideal place to complete the rearing of a litter that had outgrown the need for an underground burrow. Here the pups could develop in safety and relative freedom until they were old enough to fend for themselves. I thus had to accept the sad fact that my study had come to an end.

Leaving my subjects was not easy. I did not expect I would ever again see any of the characters I had come to know so well, though I entertained a tiny hope that my reports of "unortho-

Adult coyotes acting as surrogate parents. Here a pup has received a mouse from a returning adult while a baby-sitter remains vigilant.

dox" coyote behavior, which I could now substantiate with a few pictures, might excite sufficient interest to gain me funding or an assignment to return to the refuge in 1973 to make a follow-up study on the same animals. But I dared not become too optimistic about this possibility. The coyote has for so long been cursed with a false and evil reputation that money is seldom spent to study any aspect of his existence other than how to get rid of him more efficiently.

On the June day I packed my gear, Franz Camenzind, a graduate student in biology, arrived at the refuge to conduct a study of the territoriality of *Canis latrans* for his doctoral thesis. We compared notes briefly, and Franz, sensing how I felt about leaving my subjects, promised to keep an eye out for Miller Butte coyotes and write me in the event he happened to see any of them. In October I received a letter from him: "I have a feeling that one of the pups from your den may have been lost as I saw only two into the end of summer. Adults were, of course, conspicuous and even now are in the area."

In all stable animal populations, it is biologically essential that young be produced in excess and that they experience high mortality. Thus only the fittest survive their first winter to be recruited into the population as replacements for animals that have succumbed to old age and disease. The dynamics of this natural population flux have always intrigued me and filled me with profound awe. Conversely, man's arrogant efforts to miti-gate the effects of this natural order of things often incite me to wrath. Still, when I read Franz's letter, I felt a pang. I could not help but wonder what fate had already befallen one of Mama Redlegs's three little pups.

The
Crash

To my great joy I did win an assignment from the National Geographic Society to write about my findings on coyote behavior for their magazine. Thus I was able to return to the refuge the following spring and remain as long as necessary to obtain photographs to illustrate the article.

Unlike many publishers and even film producers who make use of spectacular-looking pictures and footage that have been obtained by confining hand-reared wild animals in naturalistic settings, the *National Geographic* editors insist that the pictures they publish be taken the hard way. Only shots of authentically wild animals who are behaving spontaneously are considered for use. For this I was grateful. Although it is certainly possible to create valid wildlife pictures using trained animals as models, such staged photographs seldom produce new information. On the contrary, they often reinforce long-standing and sometimes erroneous ideas about animals.

Ideal as all this was from my point of view, one aspect of the assignment worried me. Could I deliver high-quality pictures of wild coyotes at a den? If I failed to do so, I hoped the *National Geographic* editors would realize that the North American coyote is not so approachable as some of the African wild canids that had previously been featured in their publication. African animals are not the flighty, man-shy species that constant harassment has conditioned the North American coyote to become.

At the same time I felt reasonably confident that, once equipped with one of the magazine's 1000-mm lenses, I stood a fair chance of succeeding. Moreover, over the winter I had thought up a stratagem that might gain me closer access to a den. Thus I returned to the National Elk Refuge in high spirits, a state of mind soon to be deflated.

Immediately upon my arrival and for a number of days thereafter, I stationed myself in positions where I could keep a sharp watch on the four burrows Mama Redlegs had used the previous year. But none of these showed signs of occupancy. I then combed the territory of my Miller Butte pack for a glimpse of my identified adults. But they all seemed to have vanished. No nightly serenades or dawn howls emanated from the windy butte to blend with the plaintive cries of curlews or the creaks and groans of the sandhill cranes who stalked the meadow below. Miller Butte without coyotes seemed a desolate place, devoid of all the energetic activity that had made it so interesting the previous spring. I got the eerie feeling that since my departure a century, not a year, had passed.

I now began to notice that some of the adjacent packs with which I had a degree of familiarity seemed to contain fewer members than previously, and an uneasy feeling gripped me that, during my absence, the refuge coyotes had experienced a population crash.

Animal populations build up gradually over a number of years, and when one species becomes too dense, natural factors precipitate a reduction.* A population crash of the refuge coyotes, however, might as likely have been induced by the past winter's mild weather as from density. Some hundred-and-fifty miles to the north, where I had carried on my winter fieldwork in Yellowstone National Park, this very thing may have occurred. Throughout the cold months elk had experienced such an easy time feeding through the shallow snow that they had thrived; as a result, carrion-eaters were severely deprived of food. Now Franz Camenzind, who was still in the National Elk Refuge collecting data for his thesis, told me that during my absence exactly the same conditions had prevailed here. As a result, in February, numbers of coyotes had weakened and died

---

* The following illustrations show how some of these factors operate: Malnutrition afflicts oversized populations, and this lowers food-finding efficiency, which increases susceptibility to disease and causes infertility; density expedites the spread of communicable disease and creates social stress, which in turn leads to intraspecific aggression as well as poor breeding success and maternal neglect; lack of a sufficient number of birth sites to accommodate a large breeding population results in high mortality of the young.

of a variety of secondary causes. An autopsy report on one of them had implicated canine hepatitis.*

I now grew fearful that Mama Redlegs, Brownie, Gray Dog, and Harness Marks might have been victims of this epidemic. So after spending ten critically important spring days looking for them, I reluctantly forsook the Miller Butte territory and directed my search for a den to sections of the refuge that were relatively unfamiliar to me.

By now, however, I was extremely pessimistic that I would find pups anywhere. According to Franz, the epidemic had swept through the region during the early part of the mating season, and I feared it may have also affected the fertility of survivors. If so, I would have to report this fact to the *National Geographic*, in which event they might suggest that I give up my search. It was my anxiety over this prospect that impelled me to apply myself the more diligently and drove me on into a chain of circumstances too bizarre to have been foreseen.

It all began when the rear wheel of my van dropped into a badger hole on a remote section of the refuge. The agency that had rented me the vehicle had failed to equip it with a jack, and after wasting two hours trying to dig out with an elk antler, I finally concluded I would have to walk to the town of Jackson, some twelve miles away. However, since it was very late in the day, I did not plan to make this hike until the following morning. In the event of any such emergency I always keep a supply of food and water, as well as a sleeping bag, in my vehicle.

I hated to lose the entire next day, which could better be spent hunting for a den than fooling around with a disabled vehicle. So when I recalled that a house had recently been built along the eastern edge of the refuge, not four miles from where I was stranded, on an impulse I decided to make a dash for it. I had heard that its occupants were writers, thus I was hopeful that they would be sympathetic to my plight.

Off I set at a brisk pace, and when the sun began to sink behind the jagged Tetons, tinting their snowy faces with rose

---

* Later, Franz was able to calculate that from 75 to 90 percent of the previous year's pup crop had been lost over the winter.

and gold, there seemed little danger that I would fall short of reaching my destination during the next few minutes of twilight. I could not then have anticipated what I was about to encounter.

Suddenly, as I climbed a small rise, I thought I was witnessing elk resurrection day. At least five thousand *Cervus canadensis* had gathered in the valley, and in the fading light I could see scores more streaming down from surrounding slopes and feeding into the milling herd. Along the periphery of this swirling mass, bulls were pacing. Their heads, seasonably lightened of their customary burden of antlers, were carried high like camels'; thus, even without their magnificent headgear, they were easily distinguishable from the cows.

I knew at once what was happening. The entire population of elk were in the process of assembling in preparation for their annual migration to summer pastures in Yellowstone National Park and the Grand Teton Wilderness Area. In a few short hours some mysterious signal would be given, and the animals would begin to move en masse on their age-old trek.

I watched with a sense of horrified fascination. It would have been suicidal to try to walk through, along, or around this volatile barrier of animals, whose primordial urge to be on the move was so evident. Their tension was electric, and in such a mood the slightest disturbance might spook them into a stampede. Some were already agitating to be under way, their shrill whistles and loud barks evoking answering cries from various parts of the herd.

Ironically, at that moment lights were turned on in the house that was to have been my destination, and thus I was able to see what a short distance remained for me to travel. But as I was not equipped with wings, the beckoning house might as well have been situated on another planet. Only a fool or a saint would have ventured to walk through that teeming river of animals, which at any moment threatened to flow swiftly in any direction. At the same time, it was now too late for me to retrace my steps to the van. Very shortly, I would be enveloped in darkness.

As the full realization of the seriousness of my predicament slowly made itself felt in the pit of my stomach, two things immediately became clear to me. It was imperative that I move out of the path of these eruptible elk without delay. And it was essential that I quickly find or erect some kind of shelter. Though at this altitude May days are usually balmy, night temperatures can plummet as low as twenty degrees. I was by no means dressed to spend a night out-of-doors, and a sharp wind was already beginning to signal the precipitous drop in temperature that was about to take place. To compound the problem, I was suffering from a severe chest cold.

As often happens when one is confronted with a real emergency, my brain came up with an instant plan. Vaguely I recalled having passed an empty hay port, similar to the one that had served as my blind during the previous year. Some half-dozen of these sheds were scattered about the refuge, and though they had no walls, this one, I seemed to recollect, still contained a number of unused bales of hay. How far back had I seen it?

Half-groping, I managed to cover a quarter-mile in the dark and, to my relief, discovered that a shed did indeed exist which was partially stacked with hay. Quickly I arranged some bales into a shelter. But like the one made by the little pig, the straw house I constructed was poor insulation from a wind that was already gusting up to fifty miles per hour. I had picked a fine night to be stranded! Inside my straw igloo I grew so cold that finally I was forced to break open one of my rectangular building blocks and bury myself directly under the scratchy stuff.

I did not sleep at all that night, for to keep warm I was forced to lie on my back and pedal an imaginary bicycle. To add to my misery, the loose chaff severely aggravated my cold and I hacked and sneezed and dripped all night without benefit of an intact piece of Kleenex. So wretched was I that when at last the sky began to lighten, I decided to hazard fording the elk rather than remain a minute longer in all that hay. I pushed my way out and discovered the valley to be quiet and, except for one bewildered cow who apparently had missed the exodus, devoid of elk.

Immediately I headed for the house, but upon arriving at its doorstep, I suddenly realized what a sad appearance I presented, and I hesitated a long time before I summoned up the courage to knock on the door.

If Frank and Rodello Calkins were shocked by the apparition that flung itself upon their mercy at such an ungodly hour that morning, they politely concealed the fact. They gave me breakfast, and after I had cleaned up a bit they allowed me plenty of time to explain myself, a task complicated by the fact that I had lost my voice. Nevertheless, little by little I did manage to convey the story of my night in the hay, and when Frank comprehended the fact that my difficulties had all arisen from a stranded vehicle, he offered to get out his jeep, drive me to my van, and jack it out.

In the light of day, the same ground I had covered the previous night seemed almost embarrassingly short. And when we pulled up to my yellow van, there sat Franz chewing on a blade of grass. Unhurriedly he got to his feet and I saw at once that he had already jacked the wheel out of the hole. I was touched by all the solicited and unsolicited help I was being given. But without a voice I could express my thanks only by going into the kind of pantomime routine performed by American tourists outside the English-language zone.

I was unaccustomed to having anybody around to look out for me while I carried on my fieldwork, but I quickly grew to like it. In one sense it wasn't easy for either Franz or me to adjust to the fact that the other was researching refuge coyotes. However, our work was complementary. Franz was taking more of an overview of the coyotes in the region, whereas I was concentrating my efforts on making a close-up examination of the social relationships that existed within an exclusive group of animals. Nevertheless we were both somewhat apprehensive at first that one of us might disturb the other's subjects.

"Your coyotes!" Franz had interjected at one point in an early conversation. "Those aren't *your* coyotes!"

I understood only too well how he felt.

But after one difficult day, Franz and I decided we liked and respected each other, and we began to share our observations openly. Besides, we each approved of the other's method of working, which put minimal stress on the coyotes and demanded maximum effort on the part of the observer. He even found me a den of pups—but it was impossibly situated for photography, so I couldn't use it for my purposes and had to resume my search. Then one day I caught a glimpse of five coyotes performing a greeting ceremony on Miller Butte. I was too far away to identify individuals, but my hopes skyrocketed. I tried to remind myself that these animals might not even be members of my 1972 pack. Nature abhors a vacuum, and good coyote territory does not remain vacant for long. But my own nature being optimistic, I refused to listen. With quickened enthusiasm, once again I began to search old familiar territory, combing the butte, quartering the meadow, and even glassing the marsh. But I did not see these animals again.

"How can I climb up to the top of the hill behind the fish hatchery to get an overview of the far end of the marsh?" I asked Franz one morning when we met on the road.

"Your coyotes wouldn't den in a marsh," he answered. (At this point even he referred to the Miller Butte pack as mine!) "But maybe it isn't such a bad idea to have a look from the other side," he added.

From the opposite direction, the marsh looked totally strange. Suddenly Franz spotted a narrow strip of green.

"Conceivably that's a little piece of high, dry ground in there," he commented.

"Let's go," I said. There was no place left to look.

When I found the den, my beaming face told Franz to retreat even before I announced victory. A suspicious mound had caught my eye and when I edged closer, two milky eyes blinked up into mine. Sitting in the mouth of a burrow was an improbable creature, dark brown with a high domed brow. It reminded me of the German stuffed animal, the Steiff bear. For just one moment I was too dumbfounded to move. Then I retreated swiftly.

By mid-afternoon I was installed in my bright yellow van and parked not eight hundred feet from the burrow. This was my big gamble. Since stalking a coyote den on foot had always proved an exercise in futility, I was now trying out my new stratagem. Perhaps my subjects could learn to tolerate a very obvious, but apparently empty, vehicle parked on their land-scape. In the event they could, I had stocked it with enough food, film, and plastic bags (for collecting wastes) to last me a month. If the trick worked, I would hide in the back of the van for as long as the coyotes remained at this den, live like an astronaut, sleep on the floor, eat cold food, and view my subjects exclusively through a lens poked through a heavily curtained sliding side door.

A major impediment to the ultimate success of this plan was, of course, the problem of moving my vehicle into position with-out frightening off the subjects. As I zigged and zagged around ditches, potholes, and quagmires, I knew that the parent coyotes would be watching in a panic, and I died every minute of the way. When at last I switched off the motor and dived into the van's windowless back end, I was actually relieved to be entering into a state of solitary confinement. Quickly I curtained off the door and set up my five-foot lens on a tripod. Then I settled down to wait.

The first few hours of my watch seemed interminable. In part, I was suffering from the fear that I would not be able to adjust to the lonely life-style I had devised for myself. But my restless apprehension quickly turned into excitement when I spied an animal on the horizon. As it gradually moved nearer, I began to distinguish its features. And when at last it stopped some one thousand feet away and turned its long gray face to stare at my vehicle, I could have shouted for joy. It was Gray Dog! All my identified animals were not dead after all!

Then, as Gray Dog moved even closer, he crossed our tracks of the morning, picked up the scent, and shot off. With my anxiety again on the rise, I waited. But I no longer felt the need to "break out" of my self-imposed prison; now I was suffering from a fear that the mother of these babies would be too spooked by the proximity of my blind ever to return to her family. If so, I would have to abandon my plan. I was also going through something of a curiosity crisis. I had to know which animal had given birth to these pups. Were they Brownie's? Or had Mama Redlegs remained the dominant, breeding female on this territory?

Then, imperceptibly, out of haze and heat halation, a creature materialized. As it came into focus, I could see that its belly was plucked and I knew I was looking at a lactating female. Then I saw she was gray with red legs and a red snout. It was Mama Redlegs! Both she and Gray Dog had survived to produce another family.

Redlegs approached with mind-boggling caution, slowly nosing the ground and making frequent stops to fix her baleful gaze on my van. When at last she reached the mouth of the burrow, she was instantly greeted by a tangle of dark and squirming pups who tumbled out and piled one on top of another as they sought teats along her belly. Redlegs quickly slipped behind the burrow mound, thus placing her babies out of my line of vision. From across the top, however, she continued to keep watch on the great eyesore of a van that had suddenly blighted her landscape. She nursed only briefly. Then she shook off the litter and ran away.

It had all happened so quickly I was unable to obtain a proper pup count. Were there six or seven? At one point I could have sworn I saw nine!

A litter of nine would be unusual, but not outside the realm of

Very young pups, still in dark color phase, cling to Mama's breast while she regards my van with evident suspicion.

possibility. A study of uterine scars indicates that female coyotes have given birth to as many as twelve.* However, litters average between five and six. Could it be that the surviving coyotes were already producing oversized families to compensate for the recent death toll here on the refuge?

Errington explains the principle of population intercompensation as follows: As animals are removed from a population, the remainder find living easier and begin to reproduce more abundantly. However, since the epidemic and oestrus had in this instance coincided, this principle would not have had time to operate. But had the epidemic really struck while the coyotes were mating? Later, when I was better able to calculate Mama Redlegs's date of conception, I discovered it to have occurred on the first weekend in March. Coyote mortality had peaked in early February. Thus Mama had indeed enjoyed a full month of reduced competition for available food prior to her ovulation.

That night as I lay in the dark, a mournful chorus told me that not only had Mama returned to the den, but the whole pack had assembled there. I wondered if Brownie were out there adding her ululations to the primordial song. Apparently the coyotes were tolerating my van.

Now only one question remained: Could I?

---

* Trappers have reported digging up as many as nineteen pups from a single den. But, inasmuch as double-denning by two females has been reported, this information is probably misleading.

It had slipped my mind that the next day was to be Antler
Pick-Up Day. Every spring, shortly after elk migration, local
boy scouts are invited onto the refuge to clear the ground of
thousands of antlers that have been shed over the winter. In
1973 the sale of these decorative racks netted the scout troops
some $20,000. (In recent years Japanese buyers have bid up the
price. In Japan powdered elk antler is thought to be an aphro-
disiac.)

So when I awoke to hear trucks grinding back and forth across
the meadow, my heart sank. I remembered that this was the
one and only day in the spring season when outsiders would
be admitted to off-limits sections of the refuge. And though
manager Don Redfearn had thoughtfully instructed the truck
drivers not to drop any boisterous antler-hunters in the imme-
diate vicinity of my parked van, nevertheless my animals were
greatly stressed by the event.

When at last the trucks departed, piled high with racks and
topped with happy youngsters, no adult coyote returned to the
burrow. After glassing all day, I was ready to pull out myself,
when I spotted Mama Redlegs at some distance, sniffing the
myriad tracks that crisscrossed the refuge. Clearly she was in a
nervous state. With her tail hanging low and her spine arched,
she made a tortuous approach to her burrow. Then, after sig-
naling to her babies to emerge, she seemed unable to stand still
to nurse, but dragged those able to hang on about the mound
while she continued to investigate it. Soon she ran off, and I
tracked her with my spotscope. When she stopped a half-mile
away and began to dig, I suspected she was preparing a new
home for her family.

I watched with keen interest as dirt spewed into the air and a
mound slowly began to take shape behind her. After a while,
Mama backed out of the hole she was creating, sat upon this tiny
elevation, and looked about. Then, curiously, she abandoned **229**

the project. Had the outlook not been to her liking? In two more places she repeated the same performance. In both instances, like a human house-hunter, she spent several minutes checking out the view before giving up.

From her behavior, I was now certain that Mama planned to move her litter, and I only hoped she would postpone doing so until daylight would make it possible for me to track her. But no! Darkness was fast obliterating the scene when I caught a final glimpse of her racing away from the den with a pup hanging from her mouth. Then I could see no more.

It took me just twenty-four hours to find Mama's new den in the aspen stand where she had whelped the previous year. But I was unable to account for all the pups. Though I was still somewhat uncertain that I had actually seen as many as nine, I knew the number exceeded the six now in evidence. Had some failed to survive transport? Recalling how awkwardly Mama clasped her young, it seemed likely. Moreover, the last pup to be moved would, while awaiting its mother's return, have had to endure a period of bitter cold with no sibling to huddle against. By midnight the temperature had fallen into the teens and even I, ensconced as I was in a down-filled sleeping bag, had suffered.

I allowed Mama another few hours of grace before crowding her again, then took a double-or-nothing gamble and drove my van partway up the butte, this time to within four hundred feet of the burrow. For several hours I was the object of much scrutiny, but when Redlegs did not relocate her pups again, I knew that at last my siege had begun.

During the days that followed, my strongest impression was of Redlegs's fatigue. Perhaps she had overtaxed herself transporting all those babies across such a distance. In any case, she did not leave the slope even to hunt, but was fed by Gray Dog and a number of other coyotes. And when she wasn't nursing or grooming the litter, she retired into a willow stand some one hundred yards across the slope, I presumed to rest. It came as a great surprise to me to discover, a few days later, that this vegetation concealed an auxiliary den which contained the missing pups. There had indeed been nine! But why had they now been divided, six and three? Had she split them up as a kind of precautionary measure, not wishing to put all her eggs in one basket? If so, she was revealing a capacity for conceptual thought that many people would not believe within an animal's capacity.

I designated the two burrows "north den" and "south den" and timed Mama's stopovers at each place. I was curious to see if she might slight the pups at one place or the other. She never did. Even after being relieved of the discomfort of full breasts by part of her litter, she would unfailingly trudge across the slope to feed the others. In fact, she budgeted her time almost equally between the two dens and even varied her routine so that sometimes she nursed her offspring at the north den first and at other times she would give the south den pups the benefit of first suckle. A week later, when she reunited the family, all nine had developed to identical size.

By then I had become adjusted to life in my van. My rhythm of sleeping and waking soon became attuned to hours of daylight and night. I seldom turned on my flashlight, for when darkness shut off my view of the outside world (which was limited to what could be seen through the long lenses I had trained on the two dens), I simply climbed into my bedroll and went to sleep. And when the sun rose, so did I. Nevertheless, living within four hundred feet of a family of high-strung coyotes did put something of a crimp in my life-style. I tried to move about so as not to make any noise. I was careful never to be visible through the front windows of the vehicle. And I did not cook my food, a process which, besides requiring fuel, produces strong aromas.

I did not go hungry, however. My wooden lens case made an excellent food chest, which I had stocked to capacity with oranges, apples, granola, peanut butter, cheeses, cans of tuna and chicken salad, jars of marinated beans, bread, cookies, cold cuts, fruit juices, Cokes, and even hard-boiled eggs. I had no need of the lightweight, dehydrated products one generally takes on a camping trip, for I had not backpacked in. Thus, my single unfulfilled desire was for hot coffee. It would have helped soften the shock of climbing out of a warm sleeping bag into twenty-five-degree air each morning. By midday, though, when the temperature had reached a pleasant seventy degrees, I enjoyed the luxury of drinking a cold Coke that had chilled overnight.

I was also well supplied with jugs of water for drinking and washing. In addition, I had brought in a stock of clean clothes, several books to read (which I never found time to open), a tape cassette for recording howls, paper for note-taking, and one hundred rolls of unexposed film.

I seemed always to be busy. When my coyotes were not visible, I made use of the time to log and label film, transcribe my scrawled notes, clean my cameras, package wastes, wash, eat, and sleep. Surprisingly, I did not become depressed by isolation. I had equipped my friend Franz with the other half of my walkie-talkie set, and every second day or so he would drive to within a mile of my van and honk three times. If my adult coyotes were beyond hearing range of my voice, we spoke: I assured Franz I was still alive, and he gave me news of the outside world. When it became necessary for me to leave my post to ship film to the *National Geographic* or to obtain fresh supplies, I left my van in place, hiked out to Franz's pickup, and was chauffeured to the town of Jackson. And on those occasions when the coyotes moved to a new den, which required that I shift my vehicle anyway, I made a preliminary run into town and treated myself to a night in a motel, where I invariably experienced insomnia. Even with the heat turned off, windows open wide, and blankets on the floor, I had difficulty breathing anything but the pure twenty-degree mountain air I had grown accustomed to. I did appreciate having an opportunity to shower, and I luxuriated in being able to walk upright. I sometimes worried that life in the back of a van would leave me a hunchback. On the other hand, reports from the *National Geographic* to the effect that the film I was shipping contained some good pictures made the deformation of my spine seem a minor sacrifice.

I am certain that the coyotes were aware from the start that the bright yellow vehicle stationed in their front yard was inhabited. No doubt they could smell and sometimes even hear me. But during my seven-week watch I did not allow them a glimpse of me and perhaps they decided that such a hermit could not be very threatening. Even on those occasions when Mama relocated her family to a new den, I did not relate her moves to my presence; sometimes she would transfer her litter to a new burrow no farther from my van than before.

Yet there were limits to the coyotes' tolerance of me. Clearly, they altered their approach routes so as not to pass one step closer to the van than absolutely necessary. And later, when the pups began to scatter about the slope, a watchful adult would invariably summon or herd them away from my blind just as I was about to take a close-up picture of them.

I soon became acquainted with the seven pack members who fed and cared for the 1973 litter. Besides Mama Redlegs and Gray Dog, a gray male I named Jethro was in constant attendance. He looked almost exactly like Gray Dog except that he lacked the caudal spot seen on most coyotes' tails; thus if either of these two males failed to give me a rear view of himself, I had no way of knowing which one I was looking at.

A red-nosed male I called Rudolph was the easiest member of the pack to identify. Even when the long rays of a late-afternoon sun bathed all the coyotes in reflected colors, I recognized "Rudy," who could be counted on to walk around with a stick in his mouth. He had distinct hackle marks and I wondered if he might be Harness Marks grown more sturdy.

A very small female became Tiny. She was extremely timid and avoided the other coyotes, although she seemed to get along well with Rudy. I wondered if she were an outsider he was courting.

And then there were the twins. At first I did not realize that Tippy and Tuffy were two animals, and I had difficulty sexing the tiptailed coyote who couldn't decide which posture to assume when urinating. Not until I saw these two look-alikes together did the truth dawn on me: Tippy was a female and Tuffy a male. I suspect these two were the surviving members of the previous year's litter of three. Not only did they appear to be young, but they were exceedingly attached to one another and often played together.

Brownie, my favorite coyote, was nowhere to be seen. I sadly speculated that she may have been one of the victims of the

February die-off. Or perhaps Mama had forced her to migrate. Remembering how assiduously she had cared for the 1972 pups, I hoped that the latter was the case and that she was now tending a litter of her own somewhere.

Now Jethro assumed Brownie's role of chief baby-sitter, and during the first two weeks of my watch he was rarely absent from the slope. Maybe because he was a male, Mama did not resent his ubiquitous presence as she had Brownie's. Or perhaps with so many babies to care for, she felt the need for help—especially during the week she housed her family in separate dens. But Gray Dog was not so tolerant of Jethro, and when Jethro saw the dominant male approaching he would very sensibly vanish into brush. Once, Gray Dog came upon him unaware and forced Jethro to lie on his side while he stood over him.

It would seem from this and several similar incidents that some kind of male hierarchy existed in the pack and that Gray Dog was top dog. His appearance on the slope often had the effect of dispersing the other males. They did not cower or run, but simply meandered off as nonchalantly as possible. Yet at other times the males would assemble around Gray Dog and even tag along after him as he headed for the marsh. En route Gray Dog would remain his usual sober self while the others would gaily caper in his wake.

The ordering of dominance is of the utmost value to aggressive species who live in closed societies, for such animals must establish ways to promote harmony among themselves. A hierarchy is not, therefore, a system by means of which the superior can enslave the inferior. On the contrary, in a well-ordered hierarchy individual members learn to know their respective places and thereby avoid fighting. When conflict does occur, the more dominant of the two animals need only stand over the subordinate individual to remind him or her of some past defeat; no blood need be shed. By the same token, a low-ranking animal can use the posture of self-abasement to appease a riled-up superior. It is of critical importance to a creature endowed with the ability to kill that such pacifying techniques exist.

Even so, it is worth noting that these responses within a hierarchy are not necessarily automatic and stereotyped. Be-

Opposite: Rudy, a male, assumes the role of baby-sitter for the 1973 litter.

sides the techniques of self-assertion and self-abasement already described, "love" seems to be a component in determining the outcome of any conflict within a pack. If this were not so, self-abasement would only invite punishment from a superior animal, as indeed it does when two strangers fight. A begging-for-mercy attitude can defuse hostility only between individuals who have previously enjoyed a positive relationship. (By contrast, flight is the only recourse open to a losing combatant who is a stranger.) Rudolph Schenkel, who has conducted the master study on hierarchical behavior in wolves, uses the word "generosity" to describe that impulse on the part of the superior animal to grant quarter to a submissive animal with whom he is bonded. He defines generosity as "superiority combined with tolerant love."

Some ethologists believe that the ability to love is found only in those social species that are also aggressive. They suggest that discriminant love may have evolved as an adaptation for curbing aggressivity, which otherwise might threaten the survival of members of an exclusive group. In a TV interview, Nobel prize–winner Konrad Lorenz pointed out that a school of herrings, which is a most nonaggressive species, "doesn't give a damn who their companions are. They are mutually exchangeable; a stranger is not noticed; any individual is as acceptable as any other." He describes the wolf, on the other hand, as being not only the paradigm of cruel aggressivity, but capable of the most devoted kind of "love" toward members of his pack. "The fidelity of the dog," said he, "comes from the wolf. It was not bred into him by human beings."

In my Miller Butte pack I suspected there were two or possibly three coexisting hierarchies: a male hierarchy, a female hierarchy, and a pack hierarchy. The female Tippy, for example, appeared to rank higher with Gray Dog than she did with Mama, and as time passed she (like Brownie before her) began to spend considerable time with him.

Yet all my animals got along so well that I was actually unable to determine their relative ranks. Two things seemed certain, however. Gray Dog ruled both sexes: Every coyote deferred to him either by giving him space or by displaying excessive affection for him. And Mama, too, was a dominant animal. All the coyotes brought her food, and only before Gray Dog did she display what might be regarded as ingratiating behavior. When she greeted other males (Rudy, Jethro, or Tuffy), her bearing appeared to me to be the same as theirs: Both greeters would stand nose-to-nose and wave their tails in a dignified manner.

In the light of her past behavior toward Brownie, I was surprised to see how well Mama treated the two females, Tippy and Tiny. I never saw her make a threatening move toward either one. Still, these two animals often demeaned themselves without any apparent necessity to do so, and their behavior may have prevented Mama from having to assert herself. Tiny, in particular, was careful to survey the scene before rushing in to regurgitate food for the litter, and she seldom lingered to socialize with the pups. Often she cached her food contribution at some distance from the den without even contacting the litter. I got the impression that she was trying to avoid the adults. It is possible, however, that this high-strung animal was actually more fearful of my van than of the other coyotes. My vehicle was a variable in my own study that I was unable to eliminate.

It interested me that even the subordinate animals in my pack did not always remain abject when in conflict with a superior. Thus, they were not invariably losers. Though Tuffy was definitely dominant over Tippy—sometimes during play he would force her to lie down and make an inguinal presentation *—her tolerance of his domination had limits. Once she responded with a defensive gape similar to the fierce face I had seen Mama make the previous year when pinned down by Gray Dog. And just as Gray Dog had done, Tuffy withdrew.

During the first week of my watch, I also saw Mama defy Gray Dog. While her pups were very young, she did not allow any other adult coyote to enter her dens, although she did not seem to mind who associated with the litter aboveground. So when Gray Dog tagged after a puppy and appeared ready to dive into

---

* In the inguinal presentation, the submissive animal rolls on its back and displays its groin in the manner of a very young pup submitting to the grooming process.

the burrow after him, Mama dashed uphill and barred his entry. Gray Dog, unaccustomed to being thwarted, stiffened. But this did not intimidate Mama. Instead, she maintained a perfectly erect posture, which clearly expressed her unrelenting attitude. Then all at once, she laid back her ears, wagged her tail, and presented the would-be intruder with a most beguiling dog smile.

Rudolph Schenkel probably would have characterized Mama's smile as an expression of "active" submission, which he defines as "behavior on the part of the inferior designed to reestablish friendly and harmonic relations with the superior." But however her manner may be defined, Gray Dog succumbed to it. Suddenly he lost all interest in entering the den and walked away. Mama's friendly face and gesture had struck some responsive note in him—call it "generosity," call it "love."

The
Pups

Oone day, when the pups were three weeks old, I became aware that they were cutting teeth. Mama had just fed her babies at the south den and was dutifully nursing the north den puppies, when she abruptly vaulted straight into the air and violently pushed away the nurselings. One of them had bitten her.

In the days that followed, the pups spent much time gnawing on grass and sticks and gave every indication that they were ready to handle food more solid than the predigested pabulum the pack members had been regurgitating for them. Then Tiny brought them a whole mouse.

What surprised me most about this timely presentation was that Tiny had carried it not in her mouth, but in her stomach. From that day forward other adults, too, presented the litter with whole rodents catered in their stomachs. I wondered what prevented digestion from automatically taking place. Mama was the only adult who was not regurgitating for the litter. Her body was producing quarts of milk a week, and she relied on the other pack members to supplement her own food supply. Not until the pups were weaned did I observe her offering them regurgitated food.

Meanwhile, Mama did give her babies a lesson in the art of begging. On the very day she felt their teeth (and three days before they were presented with their first whole mouse), she paraded in front of them with a piece of solid food firmly clenched in her teeth. She seemed to be deliberately trying to entice the litter to investigate her mouth. When she finally succeeded in exciting interest at the south den, she trotted over to the north den puppies and strutted before them. Soon the curious pups were standing on their hind legs and sniffing and licking her lips. I was reminded of the instructions on the back of a box of dog "yummies," which advised how an apathetic response to that product might be transformed into a frenzy of 239 excitement simply by withholding the treat in a clenched fist. An experiment with my own dogs proved how effective this technique of denial can be in whetting the canine appetite. Whether or not Mama was now using such a ploy to stimulate puppy interest in solid food or even trying to induce infantile begging behavior (which ritual would gain for her offspring both food and approval from other pack members) is, of course, speculative. But in the end she ate the food herself.

The development of the 1973 litter closely paralleled that of their 1972 siblings. During their third week of life, though the litter mates frequently mounted one another's shoulders, they seemed more interested in clambering over the bodies of tolerant adults than in playing with one another. Early play bouts among themselves sometimes evoked sounds of distress as one pup would be too vigorously shaken by a leg or rump. Nevertheless, these grappling matches were accompanied by much tail-wagging, clear evidence of playful intent. (It is only through experience in play that a canid learns to inhibit the intensity of its bite.) Another early game was bump and flee. Soon every puppy was bent on trying to induce the others to chase him.

According to my best estimate, the litter was twenty-nine days old when real fighting occurred. One battle, which took place under a log, was not stopped until Rudy dragged the ignominious combatants out and separated them. On the same day I observed another pup being bullied by her brother. And on the following day a male who was blissfully wallowing in a pool of regurgitation objected when his sister joined him. He forced her to the ground and maintained a threatening stance over her while she made the classic inguinal presentation. Then the two forgot their differences and, side by side, proceeded to lap up the object of their dispute.

In two days this contentious phase passed and good relations were restored. If the litter succeeded in establishing a dominance hierarchy during this period, the results escaped me. Fighting rarely occurred, but when it did, any two pups might be involved. It appeared to me that playmates were interchangeable. Just as in 1972, however, the babies developed so rapidly I was unable to distinguish one from another for more than two or three days at a stretch. I did note that the litter sometimes split up into two groups numbering six and three, and I wondered if this could be the product of the early division of the pups into two dens.

The young coyotes were taught many things by the adults. One day I watched Rudy induce all nine to follow him over the top of the butte by regurgitating food for them a little at a time. And even before the babies were a month old they understood the signal to take cover. On one occasion, when I was forced to shift my van to keep up with a den change, Mama nervously sent her family underground by emitting a soft vocal signal that sounded like a short half-wail, descending in pitch. I was glad for the opportunity to note how obedient the pups could be when the situation called for discretion. For two and one half hours they remained in hiding, with no message reinforcement to remind them. Then they began creeping out of their dark den, where regrettably they had been forced to waste a beautiful afternoon.

Mama also used her gape to convey opposite instructions at different times. Sometimes her wide-open mouth induced the pups to approach, possibly in the expectation that she was about to regurgitate food (which she finally began to do when the litter was five and one half weeks old). Yet at other times her gape meant exactly what it looked like—a threat—and produced a hasty retreat. Though I could not differentiate between the two expressions, her babies seemed to have no difficulty doing so.

The pups also knew that a raven's alarm cry signaled danger and upon hearing it would take cover. Their response to this sound seemed to me to be entirely stereotyped and unlearned. At least I witnessed no instance when they might have come to associate the bird's call with a threat to their own safety. Nor did I observe them taking their cue to hide from a more experienced adult. Furthermore, the simple presence of a raven at their den did not disturb them in the least.

At night a single adult schooled the pups in the art of howling. I recorded many of these sessions, which always made me want to laugh. A long, drawn-out adult wail, sonorous and controlled, would be followed by a chorus of wavering squeals, echoing the same phrase several octaves higher. This exercise would be repeated a number of times in succession and always the pups would remain silent during the adult's demonstration. Then they would break into full voice, replete with sour notes and bravura. By summer, when I left the refuge, the puppies' chorus sounded terrific.

While the litter was still very young, the adults howled only at night, but as time passed the pack began to raise its common voice to a cobalt sky, seemingly for no other purpose than to celebrate being alive in Jackson Hole. In June the days were so perfect I wanted to sing along with them. The air smelled of summer grass, which by then was long and iridescent and concealed ground sparrows whose unexpected burbles of song brightened my solitary life inside the van. Along the slope the quaking aspen fluttered as if in perpetual dance. This was a happy time for the coyotes. The weather was perfect, food was easily obtainable, and pups were underfoot. But it was also passing quickly.

The pups were weaned in a single day. In one harsh lesson, Mama succeeded in discouraging all future assaults on her breasts. Astonishingly, her milk had dried up overnight. Even so, the litter did not want for food. Seven adults seemed capable of keeping pace with their growing appetites. Throughout the day, Gray Dog, Rudy, Jethro, Tiny, Tuffy, Tippy, or Mama Redlegs would approach the den and try to induce as many of the pups as could be rallied to follow him or her to a secluded lying-up place. Sometimes only two or three would do so, the others being too preoccupied in play to notice their departure. Those left behind might later be found and spirited away by other returning coyotes. In 1973 the supply of puppies on Miller Butte nearly equaled the adults' demand for them.

One day Mama Redlegs returned to her den and found no one there. Immediately she visited the various burrows along the slope where she had stashed her family over the course of that season. Then she investigated every known haunt frequented by adults, until at last she came upon three of her babies in the custody of Tiny. But she was not satisfied until all nine had been located and assembled, a process which took longer than an hour. At the end of that time I was all but convinced that Mama could count. Even with eight puppies trooping after her, she continued searching until the ninth was found.

Coyotes must have some sense of number or at least a notion of quantity. At this stage, the litter would sometimes break up into small groups and scatter across the now familiar slope. Returning adults would take this into account and apportion food donations accordingly. Often I watched an adult search for out-of-sight puppies after making an initial food deposit for at least a half-dozen eager recipients. Upon locating the missing ones, he would regurgitate what he had withheld.

One day, when the litter was not yet six weeks old, they initiated their own howl. For several hours no adult had visited the den, and the puppies had begun to display classic signs of anxiety. Several were standing with their forepaws on slight elevations, craning their necks and scanning the horizon. Finally they all sat down and produced a genuine howl. On that windy day their mewling chorus could not have carried very far, so when Mama appeared shortly I was forced to conclude she had never really been out of range.

At this point adults, too, sometimes made use of vocal signals to summon the pups across short distances—for example, over the top of the butte. But I never observed an adult use a vocal summons when he was within visual range of the litter.

Now that the pups would come to a "call," it occurred to me that there was really no longer any necessity for them to be kept in a specific place where they could always be found. I began to wonder when the coyotes would abandon the denning slope and move to the rendezvous site. I also gained some insight into the ability of the domestic dog to respond to his name. Canids, it would appear, must be born with a species-characteristic behavior pattern for recognizing and approaching a familiar vocal signal. Whether that signal will be "Here, Fido" or the "single siren" depends on a learning experience.

Like all members of the dog family, coyote pups play with objects. Here, an old elk vertebra becomes a toy.

The thought shed some light on those baffling howling lessons. Knowing that captive coyotes learn to howl spontaneously, I had never fully understood the natural purpose behind what seemed so obviously to be training sessions. Now I suspected the puppies were not only learning to differentiate voices, but were being led to understand that they should make some meaningful response to these familiar voices.* Of course, the nocturnal songfests promoted pack harmony, too—if only in a social sense!

* A study of the significance of howling in wolves, made by John B. Theberge and J. Bruce Falls, suggests that animals learn to recognize one another's voices and then use vocalization as a means of communicating specific information across long distances.

Perhaps because the 1973 litter was so large, the pups were
not brought to the rendezvous site until they were eight and a
half weeks old. Thus, I was able to continue observing them for
two weeks longer than I had watched the 1972 litter. They
quickly passed through many phases of development. From the
fifth to the seventh week they were hyperactive and extremely
playful with one another, and they began to incorporate objects
into their games—clods of earth, sticks, and a shaggy piece of
elk hide that had been presented to them by one of the adults.
They never tired of worrying this treasured object and snatching it from one another's jaws. Then they discovered insects,
and a new world opened to them. For hours on end, group play
was forsaken for the solitary pursuit of stalking grasshoppers

Old bones, pieces
of hide, sticks, and
clods of earth
assume great
importance in
wild games of
"keep away."

and beetles.* I was amazed at their single-mindedness. Dog puppies of the same age do not have such a long attention span. Even so, after a certain time lapse, the young hunters would begin to seek out their siblings and once again engage in wild games.

The adult coyotes had created what I called a "play burrow" at the foot of the butte. Here any pup who inadvertently traipsed after an adult heading for the hunting marsh could be deposited. As the surrounding area was devoid of cover, I presume the hole had been cleared out just to serve as an escape hatch in the event the babies should be disturbed. They never spent a night there. At dusk an adult would check this burrow and lead any bivouacs back to the south den (which the litter had recently reoccupied after a ten-day stint in one of the 1972 burrows). As time passed, the pups learned to find their own way to and from the play burrow, but in the beginning they had to be guided back and forth by an adult.

One day three of the four pups who had earlier been dropped off at the play burrow were rounded up and led uphill by Tippy. The fourth baby, who a minute earlier had descended into the hole, was overlooked. I was curious to see her reaction when she emerged to find herself alone. For a long time she sat on the mound in a hunched posture, looking about for her vanished playmates. "Forlorn" is the word that best conveys the impression she gave. As if to make herself conspicuous, she sat high on the tiny mound, like a shipwrecked waif awaiting rescue.

At last she was sighted, not by an adult, but by a sibling, who made the long trip down the slope and across the flats to retrieve her. Upon seeing her brother approach, the little female bounded joyfully to meet him. Then, unguided, the tiny pair struggled uphill to the south den.

When the litter was seven weeks old, one of their number caught a mouse. I did not see the pounce that gained the prize, but I knew it could not have differed much from the high leaps

Opposite: Left behind at the play burrow.

* Adolph Murie found that even grown coyotes actively hunt grasshoppers as late as November, when that insect is dormant. Some droppings he collected in the fall contained more than 90 percent grasshopper remains. It is likely that the coyote acts as a check against insect explosions.

Right and opposite:
No rubber toy,
this mouse! A pup
flaunts his prize
catch—only to
lose it to a
covetous sibling.

that were securing beetles and grasshoppers beneath stabbing
paws. I became aware of what had happened when the puppy
began to shake his head vigorously. Instinctively, he knew this
method of killing small prey.* Then I had to laugh when the
little Nimrod began strutting back and forth before the others,
with the dead mouse swinging from his mouth. In a flash another pup was on top of him and a noisy battle ensued, which
quickly relieved the proud little hunter of his trophy.

Only five days later all the coyote pups were trying to stalk
ground squirrels, formidable prey indeed. Even a grown coyote
must be both quick and careful when catching these feisty creatures, who in the event escape is cut off will stand their ground
and fight. I assumed the pup would quickly be cured of this
new mania. But no. Baby coyotes are resolute hunters. I timed
one pup who held his "freeze" for one minute and fifteen
seconds, then watched him lose his prey by no more than a hair
after executing a perfect adult-style scurry. Even in the

* Adult coyotes rarely shake their victims to death but usually kill them with a
bite.

face of defeat, he then tried to dig out his vanished quarry.

That same day two pups actually did each succeed in catching a baby ground squirrel, apparently from a single nest. But even young squirrels will put up a fierce battle, and one of the pups soon found he had got the devil by the tail and was powerless either to subdue or escape from his prey. He tried alternately dropping and seizing the savage little fighter, who was inflicting painful bites on his muzzle. His shrieks at last brought rescue in the form of Tippy, who was baby-sitting on the slope. She dashed downhill and quickly put an end to the rodent.

The second pup subdued his ground squirrel unaided, but then lost it to Tuffy, who confiscated and ate it. In view of the fact that Tuffy had fed the litter daily, it seemed odd behavior indeed for him suddenly to steal food from one of the babies. Was something changing? Perhaps. Only once, on the day the litter was weaned, had I seen an adult carry out the threat signaled by a gaping face. Tuffy was soon to underscore the lesson that an adult gape is no empty bluff but a very serious warning when one of the pups made the mistake of trying to pull a bone from his jaws. Suddenly, I heard a squeal and watched in horror as the little one received a terrible trouncing. Again I thought it strange that Tuffy, who had spent endless time and energy toting food to the litter, should now deny one of the babies an old, dried-out elk bone. Was the litter beginning to lose its privileged status in the pack?

Sooner or later this would have to happen. By winter what pups had survived would find themselves relegated to the sidelines, while dominant adults stripped carcasses of choice parts. But this reversal of status would not occur abruptly. At least until October the pups' own meager pickings would be supplemented by contributions from indulgent adults. Not until the pups had shed their deciduous teeth and grown more effective hunting weapons would they be abandoned to their own devices.

Learning to hunt begins in a small way with insects. Orphaned coyote pups have been reported to survive on a diet of bugs.

Such prolonged dependency of the young on adults is called "neoteny." Neoteny is a characteristic of all species that have not inherited a fixed repertory of behavior, but must *learn* how to survive. The higher a species ranks on the phylogenetic tree, the more prolonged is infancy and correspondingly the more that

species is required to learn. Thus, Nature exacts a price from creatures she has endowed with real intelligence. At the same time, only to these chosen ones has she given much potential for development, for individuality, and for adaptation. While her more programmed offspring may seem to be born to the easy life, environmental changes can quickly doom them when they inappropriately continue to make the same automatic responses. The neotenal coyote, on the other hand, meets change by learning new responses and is therefore capable of developing a whole new life-style. And so, just as he was depicted in Indian legend, Trickster sometimes shows up in disguise.

For two years I had been on intimate terms with the archetypical coyote. My subjects, being relatively undisturbed, had no need to alter their habits, and so they lived in an ever-teetering but harmonious balance with other native species, as they had done since time immemorial. Often I wondered how the Yellowstone coyotes I had watched or my Miller Butte pack on the refuge would compare to their less fortunate relatives throughout the West, who were daily being assaulted by bullets, poison,

At six weeks of age, a pup maintains a "point" for one minute and fifteen seconds.

and traps in one of the most massive extermination campaigns ever waged against a species. Were these persecuted coyotes being pressured into transforming themselves in order to survive an environment suddenly turned lethal?

Unexpectedly, I was about to match my knowledge of the ways of *Canis latrans*, gleaned through two years of work and disappointment, discomfort and delight, boredom and high adventure, with the views of a group of people who looked upon the same animal as nothing but a pair of walking jaws, a cruel varmint with no redeeming qualities.

Man
the
Predator

Franz gave me the news over the walkie-talkie. United States Senate hearings on predator control were to be held the following week in Sun Valley, Idaho, and Casper, Wyoming.

"You'd better plan to attend in Casper," he advised. "The town is going to look like it's holding a woolgrowers' convention. There won't be a good word said for the coyote."

"But Senate hearings were already held on predator control in Washington, D.C.," I protested. "All sides of the issue were aired in March before the Senate Subcommittee on the Environment."

"I know, but now the Senate Subcommittee on Public Lands wants an inning, and it seems to be loaded with Western senators out stumping for the sheepmen's vote."

I brooded over the significance of this political maneuver. Woolgrowers would, indeed, attend the field hearings in full force. By contrast, the trained biologists and scientists who had given testimony before the Senate Subcommittee on the Environment in Washington would not be likely to appear as witnesses a second time, especially in remote Casper, Wyoming. As a result, all of the valuable information they had given, their warnings regarding the irreparable harm poison can wreak on entire biotic communities, could be conveniently overlooked by members of this subcommittee who had usurped the issue and who might possibly make recommendations for some very destructive legislation.

Franz read my thoughts across a half-mile of flats.

"I know you hate to leave your coyotes just now," he said, "but you and I are two of the few people within traveling distance of this hearing who really know something about coyotes. I'd be willing to bet we'll be among a handful of people in Casper who've ever bothered to read the Cain report. And between the two of us, I guess we've racked up more hours of sustained coyote-watching than all the woolgrowers in the state."   255

Franz was right. Most sheepmen never bothered to watch a coyote longer than a minute before putting a bullet in him. To the sheep rancher, the coyote is evil incarnate. No need to learn anything factual about him. From the sheepmen, the senators would be led to believe the coyote is guilty of massive depredation on livestock. The presumption would be supported by exhibitions of gory pictures of half-eaten carcasses, and the senators, being better politicians than biologists, would not be likely to question whether all or any of the dead lambs depicted had actually been killed by coyotes or whether they might in truth be carrion, upon which the scavenger coyote normally dines. Moreover, no mention would be made of the fact that sheep, after centuries of man's manipulative breeding, have very little fortitude and, as a result, die of a variety of causes, including birth defects, inadequate mother's milk, lack of maternal protection, a long list of diseases, parasites, accidents, inclement weather, the ingestion of toxic plants, and malnutrition caused by the overgrazed condition of their pastures. That is not to say that sheep do not at times fall victim to predatory animals. A domestic sheep, unlike its wild cousin the bighorn, is quite incapable of self-defense, and since its introduction into the Western ecosystems less than a century ago, some coyotes have learned to prey upon it. Nevertheless, a common saying among sheep ranchers themselves is that lambs come into the world "trying to die."

Yet before the Senate subcommittee, all livestock losses would be attributed to predators—if not to coyotes, then to eagles or even to the four-pound kit fox! And though statistics reveal that overall lamb losses in Ohio, where coyotes and eagles are virtually nonexistent, are substantially no different from those in Wyoming, the Western woolgrowers would cite predation as the major cause of their economic woes.

I suddenly realized that Franz was waiting for my answer, and I radioed him that I would get busy and prepare some testimony. I would go with him to Casper.

During the next few days I remained in my van by the den, but my attention was divided between observing my study animals and reviewing the historical developments that had led up to the scheduled hearings. I also reflected on my personal experiences on public lands, the abuse of which was now central to the issue. During the four-year period I had tracked and written about wild horses, my field studies had all been conducted on public lands. In addition, I had spent considerable time searching the public domain for the very coyotes the sheepmen now complained were so numerous there. Even with the help of a former government trapper, I had not been successful at locating subjects. In fact, owing to the sheepmen's unremitting war on wildlife, I had found much of the land bereft of all fauna.

Paradoxically, the importance of the public domain, which belongs equally to every American citizen, lies in the fact that so little of it is arable. Much of the West receives less than twenty inches of rainfall annually; thus, in the days of the big land giveaways, acreage that did not include direct access to waterways was rarely homesteaded, or reverted to the government when injudicious homesteading failed. Even the states and railroad companies passed up much of this barren and rocky real estate when it was offered to them in the form of land grants. And so, by default, what was left became the joint property of all Americans. Today, in just ten Western states (Arizona, California, Colorado, Idaho, Montana, Nevada, New Mexico, Oregon, Utah, and Wyoming), this unsettled territory amounts to an area which exceeds that of France* and is of incalculable value to the long-range health of the entire continent. Such an extensive stretch of undeveloped land provides breathing space to offset the corrosive effects of unrestrained industrial development. Besides serving to transform carbon dioxide into oxygen, the vegetation that lightly mantles these miles of desert, plains, and canyons provides a natural habitat for complete ecosystems.

Late in the nineteenth century sheep ranchers began to herd their large flocks onto this public domain and thus to initiate its deterioration. Arid land is fragile land, and the sheep is an animal that crops forage to the roots. When vegetation is re-

---

* Excluding federal land set aside for military installations, monuments, national forests, and national parks.

moved, topsoil erodes. Whereas it took the earth a thousand years to produce a single inch of life-sustaining topsoil, it took sheep but a few decades to destroy much of the West.* As early as 1949, J. Frank Dobie, in *The Voice of the Coyote*, deploring the devastation of millions of acres of public lands, wrote:

> Unless long-term public good wins over short-term private gain and ignorance, vast ranges, already greatly depleted, will at no distant date be as barren as the sheep-created deserts of Spain. Metaphorically, the sheep of the West eat up not only all animals that prey upon them—coyotes, wildcats and eagles especially—but badgers, skunks, foxes, ringtails and others. The surface of the earth does not offer a more sterile sight than some dry-land pastures of America with nothing but sheep trails across their grassless grounds. The free-enter-prisers of these ranges, many of them public-owned, want no government interference. They ask only that the government maintain trappers, subsidies on mutton and wool, and tariffs against competitive importations.

Dobie's dire predictions of twenty-five years ago have largely come to pass. While sheep were overgrazing property belonging to the American public, their owners were being granted everything they asked for and more from the federal government. Yet despite economic advantages derived from pasturing subsidized animals on the public domain for absurdly low fees, and despite the additional protection of federal price supports and tariffs on wool, the industry still pleads poverty. Many sheep ranchers contend that without the federally financed killing of predators, they would surely be driven into bankruptcy. Thus the taxpayers have also been footing the bill for the slaughter of the nation's wildlife in order to sustain an industry which, if what its own members say is true, must ultimately be doomed

---

*In the short time the white man has imposed his will on the West, he has irretrievably destroyed an area twice the size of the fertile croplands of California, and seriously damaged, perhaps beyond reclaiming, five more Californias.

anyway. Professor Charles Laun of the biology department of Stephens College, testifying before a congressional hearing in 1966, said: "The history of sheep on public lands has been a history of destruction. Their removal from public lands would be an asset for the American people."

The American people, however, have largely been kept in the dark regarding the carnage their tax dollar has been helping to purchase. After ferreting out some of the more appalling details regarding this wholesale destruction of wild animals, Jack Olsen wrote in *Slaughter the Animals, Poison the Earth:* "If there is a single point on which Western game wardens and conservation officers are agreed, it is on the bloodthirsty tendencies of certain sheepmen, propensities that are directly reflected in the poisoning programs now going on under their control. To question a warden on the subject of sheepmen and predators is to invite oneself into a conversational chamber of horrors."

Not that a better-informed public would find it easy to withdraw its long-standing support of this entrenched industry. Sheepmen are unquestionably the best-organized political force in the West. Considering that they represent a rather small fraction of the total Western population, it is surprising to what extent they control state capitals, run state conventions, and send representatives to Washington. Much of their clout comes from the fact that they have managed to form an alliance with some of their traditional enemies, cattlemen, who like themselves are concerned lest grazing fees be raised on the public domain. Privately, most cattlemen will admit that, on the issue of predator control, they side with the woolgrowers only in order to strengthen this coalition. Few of the former believe they suffer any real damage from coyote predation.

Additionally, a powerful elite among the woolgrowers can afford to buy special protection for their so-called dying industry through campaign contributions to sympathetic politicians. It is, of course, these same individuals who receive the big subsidy checks and who demand ever increased federal predator control. Former state senator Arnold Reider from Montana pointed out: "The little sheep operators, the ones who take care of their stock, you seldom hear from them."

Thus most of the money spent in federal wool subsidies goes to a few large growers. Public land statistics for 1974 show that a privileged 5 percent of leaseholders running sheep on public lands in ten Western states have been allotted more than half of the available sheep range. These powerful ranchers number fewer than three thousand. One wonders how such a relatively small number of individuals, representing what can only be regarded as a minor industry, succeeded in gaining so much cooperation from the federal government in the first place. The story bears telling.

Until World War I the Department of Agriculture acted only in an advisory capacity to Western stockmen, woolgrowers, and cattle-raisers alike, who at the time were trying to exterminate the wolf. During this early period, the coyote was largely ignored, being regarded (quite correctly) as only a minor predator. The last of the wolves died hard. Those wily individuals who managed to survive blind sets and scented baits were the cleverest of their kind, and persistently outwitted hunters greedy for the high bounties put on the elusive animals, hunters who boasted of the diabolical cleverness and savagery of their quarry. One of the last of the Western timber wolves to be killed was the "Custer Wolf," an animal reputed to have taken up with a pair of coyotes for want of any remaining wolf companions.

By the time tales of the wolf's rapacious qualities finally filtered back east and reached the ears of Congress, its population in the Western states had in all likelihood already fallen below a viable number. Nevertheless, aroused by the horror stories and anxious to increase beef production to feed the army of World War I, funds were allocated and the Department of Agriculture was directed to extirpate the vanishing wolf.

Having no animal to extirpate might have proved embarrassing to the Department of Agriculture's Biological Survey, charged with the task of carrying out this directive, had it not been for the existence of the coyote. Heretofore ignored, the coyote's occasional depredations now became a matter of overriding concern, and additional funds were obtained to eradicate him. So a new bureaucracy was born.

By 1930 enterprising employees of this new bureaucracy (which later was to be known as Predator and Rodent Control, or P.A.R.C.) encountered some opposition to their plans for expansion when their request for a one-million-dollar allocation from Congress aroused protests from the American Society of Mammalogy. The august members of this society questioned the wisdom of instituting a program to eradicate predators in advance of any scientific knowledge of the possible consequences. The removal of carnivores, they said, would very likely be followed by an explosion in the rodent population, which could destroy large areas of grasslands. Such a situation would in all probability prompt the sheepmen to seek government assistance in the elimination of mice, rabbits, ground squirrels, and other plant-eaters that competed with their flocks. Where would it all end? For a brief moment, it looked as if sanity might prevail and the allocation would be denied. But forces favoring predator control won the day, and Congress voted to grant the moneys requested.

The following year, sheep-raisers and those government employees whose jobs had momentarily been put in jeopardy by the opposition of the scientists fortified their positions by convincing Congress to pass legislation calling for "the destruction of all mountain lions, wolves, coyotes, bobcats, prairie dogs, gophers, ground squirrels, jackrabbits and other animals injurious to agriculture, horticulture, forestry, husbandry, game or domestic animals, or that carried disease." In short, every wild animal not already designated as "game" and claimed by hunters was put on the death list. The U.S. Biological Survey team now had plenty of work cut out for it!

Today, few senators would knowingly endorse a program aimed at eliminating not just an entire species but whole categories of animals. But it is considerably easier to start a program at the taxpayer's expense than to put an end to one. Incredible as it may seem, the 1931 law still stands, and the bureaucracy it spawned is alive and thriving.

In the 1940s, the expansion of this bureaucracy, which by then had been renamed P.A.R.C., was nothing short of phenomenal. Not only did it succeed in quadrupling its funding,

Above: A chain of death results when a poisoned
coyote is fed upon by birds.
Opposite, top: Traps set for coyotes
commonly catch other species. Here a
terrified fox awaits its final fate, which
may be days in coming.
Trappers protest proposed regulations that
would require them to check their lines every
twenty-four hours—hardly a stringent
requirement.
Opposite, middle: A badger clearly reveals what
agonies are suffered by animals caught by
leg-hold traps.
Opposite, bottom: Proposed legislation that
would require traps to be designed with offset
and padded jaws to ease the victims' pain,
and tranquilizers to be placed in the bait, has
invariably been tabled by congressional
committees.

manage to become transferred to the Department of the Interior, and deploy hundreds of trappers across the West, but,
most significantly, it acquired the highly lethal poison known as
"1080."

Discovered during World War II, 1080, or sodium fluoroacetate, was hailed for its efficacy in killing canines. That is not to
say that any bird or animal who fed upon any bird or animal who
fed upon any bird or animal who fed upon 1080 would escape
the death agonies experienced by the original victim. The stability of the compound was terrifying. But this was no deterrent

KENNETH CORMACK

ED PARK

DICK RANDALL (*Defenders of Wildlife*)

to government trappers intent upon racking up impressive tallies of animals killed. Nor did anyone seem upset by the fact that victims sometimes took two hours to die, while experiencing painful retching and agonizing convulsions. Compared to some of P.A.R.C.'s other "management tools," compound 1080 was humane indeed. The following descriptions of the effects of a few of their alternative methods of killing will give some indication of how inured to animal suffering were these "mammal-control agents," as the trappers were euphemistically titled.

A denning technique that spares a trapper the trouble of digging. The burrow is filled with gas and ignited.

Thallium, for twenty years the principal toxicant used in predator control, kills only six out of ten of its victims. Survivors go blind and all their hair and toenails fall out.

Animals caught in traps may struggle so violently for release

DICK RANDALL

that they dislocate all their joints. While awaiting death, often for days, they must lie in painful positions under scorching sun and drenching rain without food or water. Flies and insects and even other predators feed upon them. To gain release, many chew off their clamped paws. But such dearly bought freedom is usually short-lived, followed by death from gangrene or starvation when the amputee finds it can no longer hunt.

Gassing pups in dens does not induce a merciful death. Cartridges are pushed into the mouth of a burrow and ignited. Smoke soon drives the pups to seek air, but when they attempt to crawl to the surface, they meet fire. One Defenders of Wildlife writer reported: "It's not hard to tell when the pups reach the fire or the gas cartridge. You can hear them from quite a distance."

Another denning technique, described to me by Vern Dorn, is no less hideous. A long wire with a hooked end is inserted into a burrow until it contacts and pierces a puppy. It is then twisted until the soft little body, which until that moment had known nothing of life on planet earth beyond the tender breast of its mother, is fished out. This saves the trapper the trouble of having to dig.

Coyotes are chased by means of airplanes or helicopters until they begin to stagger and finally roll over and expose their vulnerable underparts in the canine plea for mercy. They are then blasted with gunshot.

One recipe for death calls for a number of live coyotes to be tied up and their mouths wired shut. While they are being tormented in this way, adrenalin pours into the terrified animals' systems, creating strongly scented bladders and anal glands, which, when cut out of the still-living animals, provide "passion" bait for poison stations.

In winter the coyote is pursued with snowmobiles, in summer by relays of men in trucks, who signal one another with walkie-talkies. When a victim has been surrounded, trained dogs are released to tear their wild cousin to pieces.

The "coyote getter," touted as a humane tool, is described by Cleveland Amory, president of the Fund for Animals:

I have here on my desk something called a "Humane Coyote Getter" which is advertised as the "Marvel of the 20th Century." Humane? It is literally a whole trap gun. A bait is soaked in urine and covered with a jacket, then placed over a bullet cartridge, the whole being set in the ground. When the coyote investigates, the bullet is set off by a spring and shoots the coyote in the mouth with sodium cyanide. This, in turn, on contact with the moisture in the coyote's mouth, or eyes, or wherever it hits him, releases gas, and the coyote gasses himself to death. Or perhaps just blinds himself.

While the above-described devices were proliferating and the unrestrained slaughter was escalating, the majority of Americans remained unaware of how their tax dollars were being spent. The West is large, and the Department of the Interior is circumspect when it comes to projecting a public image. P.A.R.C.'s propaganda included color posters and slick literature portraying its employees as dedicated to the protection of resources and crops, health and public safety. Nevertheless, little by little, more and more people were beginning to see through this pious facade.

One such individual was Dr. Raymond F. Bock of the Pima (Arizona) Medical Society, who registered his indignation in a letter to the Department of the Interior, which read in part: "One wonders whether someone in your department has gone mad from a personal hatred of predators. . . . We have found consistent objection to your methods by trained biologists. . . . We wonder what kind of misfits may be perpetuating this campaign."

But any agency that measures its success or failure by body count is not likely to be disturbed that its methods are gruesome. Even the fact that the new wonder poison 1080 was so slow to degrade that there was a danger it would seep into the water table did not seem to alarm its dispensers. Nor did thirteen alleged human fatalities, five suspected deaths, and six nonfatal cases cause P.A.R.C. to reorder its priorities. Though 1080 has no antidote, 1080 was cheap, and the most effective poison yet developed. A few cents' worth injected into bait and scattered by plane across hundreds of miles could clean out wildlife from places that man was unable to penetrate on foot. Why animals in such remote places should have to be "cleaned out" was never made clear. Predator-control agents defended their assiduity as evidence of unstinting dedication. After all, they were protecting sheep.

In actual fact, the fragile sheep who drifted aimlessly about the public domain looking like so many wads of cotton were about the least protected animals ever to suffer the misfortune of falling into man's custody. In the 1950s, due to a rise in labor costs a majority of sheep ranchers dispensed with the hiring of herders and thenceforth began turning out their flocks untended in fenced pastures. Even shepherd dogs were no longer sent out to guard the vulnerable stock, for with so much poison bait scattered about, a meat-eating dog would not long survive. And so flocks were left to weather the season and face the perils of birth, toxic plants, illness, and injuries alone. It should come as no surprise to learn that in the fall, when animals were gathered for market, attrition was often found to be exorbitant.* Naturally, the coyote was blamed for it all.

Given so much opportunity, perhaps coyote predation on sheep did increase. All creatures must eat to live, and the coyote's natural food sources were systematically being eliminated. No longer did game animals provide him carrion in winter, for surplus elk, antelope, or deer were now being carefully managed by state fish and wildlife departments for hunters to harvest. And just as was predicted by the American Society for Mammalogy, the removal of so many predators had caused small rodent populations to peak, which then had to be suppressed by more poison. Whether as a result coyotes more frequently utilized sheep as a food source is not known. Statistics on coyote depredation on lambs and ewes are singularly unreliable, being no more than compilations of questionnaires filled out by sheep ranchers, who, fearful that government

* Dr. Sander Orent, who directed a fifteen-man study team observing sheep bands, concluded that a large portion of missing sheep simply wander off and become lost. I occasionally came across such lost stock while studying wild horses in remote places on the public domain.

predator control might be discontinued, consciously and unconsciously inflate their estimates.

Certainly man's arrogant tampering with Nature's intricate checks and balances had created unforeseen problems, not only for future generations, but for the very sheep ranchers who were responsible. Paradoxically, increased pressure on the coyote seems to have produced a corresponding increase in the woolgrowers' allegations of losses! If their allegations could be believed, the phenomenon deserved serious study, and a number of biologists attempted to postulate theories. Some wondered if the adaptable coyote, as a result of the extirpation of stronger predators such as the wolf and the grizzly bear, might not be trying to occupy a higher predator niche. Other biologists sought an explanation in the theory that the poisoning of carrion obviously would tend to eliminate the innocuous, scavenging coyotes and leave room to expand for those individual animals who ate only fresh meat that they themselves had killed. And Dr. Alfred Etter postulated that constant harassment of the territorial coyote perhaps was so stressful as to cause many individuals to become itinerant and behave atypically.

Yet despite indications that their methods were only exacerbating their problems, sheep ranchers reacted irrationally to rising lamb losses by demanding more predator control from the federal government. They got it. To give some idea of the devastation of wildlife inflicted by P.A.R.C. agents on behalf of the woolgrowers, one need only examine Department of the Interior figures for a single year in the 1960s, when the following body count was made public: 89,653 coyotes; 20,780 lynx and bobcats (the lynx is endangered in the Western states); 2,779 wolves (the red wolf is endangered); 19,052 skunks; 24,273 foxes (the kit fox is endangered); 10,078 raccoons; 1,115 opossums; 6,941 badgers; 842 bears (the grizzly is slated for the endangered-species list); 294 mountain lions; and untold numbers of eagles and other rare and endangered birds. This tragic toll does not take into account the large number of poisoned animals that were never found. It does reflect what can be accomplished by one thousand government trappers who have been given seven million dollars to spend.

However ghastly such a death toll may seem to the average American, P.A.R.C. officials, eager to distinguish themselves in their department, blithely viewed each year's tally as the next record to be broken. J. Frank Dobie, in *The Voice of the Coyote*, summed up the government's attitude: "The hierarchy of 'Control' cares nothing at all except to keep killing and to keep increasing their jobs."

By the 1960s, P.A.R.C. agents were blatantly soliciting business across the West. Through the negotiation of special contracts with state and county agencies and livestock associations, moneys could be added to their coffers that would enable the bureau to "build new programs." To drum up business, government field agents made speeches before livestock groups exhorting them to sign up for predator control. Cattle-raisers, who heretofore had not been heard to complain of coyote damage, were particularly courted.

Ironically, all this proselytizing was to backfire, for it attracted the notice of many people who previously had been unaware of what was going on. Increasing numbers of scientists and biologists now began to deplore the official rapine of the nation's land and wildlife, and joined with nature-lovers in their protests against the wholesale massacre of North American birds and animals.

In view of the dichotomous roles being played by the Department of the Interior's Fish and Wildlife Services (of which P.A.R.C. was a division), it is difficult to see how employees avoided schizophrenic breakdowns. On the one hand, the department was charged with the protection of wildlife; on the other, it was extirpating these same animals. In 1963, Secretary of the Interior Stewart Udall, in an effort to resolve this dilemma, appointed an impartial panel of scientists to study the whole question of Interior's participation in predator control. This blue-ribbon committee was headed by Dr. Starker Leopold of the University of California and included four other distinguished men: Dr. Ira N. Gabrielson, president of the Wildlife Management Institute; the late Dr. Clarence Cottam, former assistant director of the Fish and Wildlife Services; Thomas L. Kimball, later executive director for the National

Wildlife Federation; and Dr. Stanley A. Cain of the University of Michigan.

If conservationists expected that the Leopold report would be a total whitewash, they were in for a surprise. In 1965 the committee announced its findings. The situation, the report stated, was exactly as the conservationists had described: The rampant killing of wildlife was unjustified and the biological assumptions were specious. The committee recommended that overkill be halted at once.

Lamentably, the only outcome of this two-year investigation was that P.A.R.C. changed its name to "Wildlife Services," and its employees were thenceforth forbidden to proselytize. Killing went on as before.

In 1970, when it became apparent that no reforms were going to be implemented, conservationists again tried to make an assault on this formidable bureaucracy, this time through the courts. Two prominent organizations, The Defenders of Wildlife and The Humane Society of the United States, filed suit against the Department of the Interior and Secretary Rogers C. Morton, asking for a restraining order on the poisoning of animals on the public lands. Meanwhile, seven conservation groups (The Defenders of Wildlife, The Sierra Club, The New York Zoological Society, National Audubon Society, Inc., The Humane Society of the United States, Friends of the Earth, and the Natural Resources Defense Council) petitioned the Environmental Protection Agency, demanding that it institute regulations prohibiting the use of poison on the public domain. While court action was pending, several unexpected things happened.

First, an eagle scandal rocked the country. It began when the badly decomposed bodies of more than ten bald and golden eagles were found near Casper, Wyoming, victims of an outlawed poison, thallium sulphate. The sheep rancher responsible, Van Irvine, claimed the poison was intended for coyotes. An investigation of this incident led to the discovery that certain sheep ranchers in Colorado and Wyoming were engaged in a massive eagle-killing operation. According to a hired helicopter pilot who turned state's evidence, more than eight hundred eagles had been gunned down on missions he had been hired to fly. Perhaps because the eagle is the symbol of the United States, the incident aroused great public outcry, and for the first time in history, a number of sheep ranchers were indicted for violating the Bald Eagle/Golden Eagle Act.

Then a report from the Cain committee, a second panel of impartial scientists who had been appointed by the Department of the Interior to make still another study of the government's role in predator control, was made public. The Cain committee findings were even more imputative of Wildlife Services and of the sheepmen the bureau served than had been the Leopold report. The scientists announced that while a scattered few ranchers did at times appear to sustain heavy losses to predators, massive extermination of coyotes across the public domain had produced no economic benefits. The cost of such a "prophy-lactic" program exceeded any realistic measure of the worth of the livestock being preyed upon. Moreover, the committee was unable to grant the woolgrowers their claim that, in the absence of the government's program, their losses would have been considerably higher; according to the woolgrowers' own figures, the more coyotes that were killed, the heavier were their re-puted lamb losses. Since no study showed livestock to be a major food item of the coyote, the panel of scientists could only con-clude that a small number of atypical animals must be respon-sible for what real damage was occurring. Therefore, saturation poisoning of millions of acres of public lands was not only extravagant and inhumane, but pointless.

In addition to recommending that poison be banned and aerial shooting outlawed, the Cain committee suggested that sheep-men look into the possibility of purchasing insurance for their flocks that would reimburse them for losses from all causes.* In lieu of such a program, the Cain committee recommended that a trapper extension system be adopted, similar to those in the states of Kansas, Missouri, and parts of South Dakota, aimed at the selective removal of only offending animals.

* After inspecting the Western sheep ranchers' careless operations, insurance companies have set premiums too high to interest the woolgrowers.

In Kansas a single trapper, biologist F. Robert Henderson, responds quickly to livestock growers' complaints and is usually able to locate and eliminate a marauder coyote without disturbing the remaining animals. Non-killer coyotes, along with other predator species, are regarded as a valuable resource in Kansas, for they suppress rodent populations that would otherwise peak. In addition, Henderson offers advice to ranchers on how to increase their operating efficiency and prevent coyotes from picking up the habit of preying upon livestock. In testimony before the Senate Subcommittee on the Environment, Henderson told of Kansas livestock operators who had been in business for thirty years without ever losing a sheep to coyotes.

The results of the Kansas system of "damage" control have been spectacular. Whereas Wyoming is spending over one million dollars annually in an intensive coyote-extermination program, Kansas, at a cost of less than twenty thousand dollars a year, is selectively weeding out only those coyotes that actually cause damage. Yet Wyoming complains of ever-escalating sheep losses, while Kansas, because she is so satisfied that she is sustaining minimal depredation, has thus far refused any federal assistance urged upon her by zealous officials of the Fish and Wildlife Services. To appreciate the full significance of this, it is important to know that in 1972, figures showed Kansas to be supporting the highest density of coyotes in the nation, while Wyoming's coyote density, after decades of saturation poisoning, was the lowest in the West.

Unlike the Leopold study, the Cain report did have an impact on politicians in Washington. In February of 1972, one month after its publication, President Nixon ordered that all poison be removed from the public lands, and the Environmental Protection Agency immediately followed suit by instituting regulations restraining all interstate shipments of toxicants. It is difficult to say who was most astonished by this sudden reversal of government policy—Wildlife Services, the woolgrowers, or the conservationists! But even while conservationists were still reeling from the unexpected victory, Western sheep ranchers were not remaining idle. Having for so long believed themselves astride a tiger, the idea of having to dismount filled them with indignation and terror, and they quickly launched a counteroffensive. Most were sincere in their conviction that without 6.5 million strychnine baits, 140,000 "1080" baits, and 410,000 cyanide stations strewn across the public domain, their industry could not long survive.* In January of 1973, just seven months after the poison was presumably removed from the public lands,** the National Woolgrowers Association staged a convention in Washington, D.C., at which its members were highly vocal. Not only did they demand that the presidential order be rescinded, but reporters at news conferences were given graphic accounts of depredations caused by the "burgeoning coyote population" that allegedly had resulted from the ban on poison. Journalists who wrote these stories were not told that *Canis latrans* has a single annual breeding season, which had not yet occurred since the removal of the poison baits. No mention was made of the fact that poison was the single weapon in the woolgrowers' vast arsenal of death-dealing tools now being denied to them, and that, even as the woolgrowers were crying "coyote," guns, traps, gas, and fire were annihilating wild animals by the thousands. Thus, a good deal of misguided public sympathy was generated for the ranchers.

In March the sheep ranchers once again converged on Washington, this time to testify before the Senate Subcommittee on the Environment, which was holding hearings on proposed legislation to implement the recommendations of the Cain committee and incorporate the presidential ban on poison into a federal law. Before this subcommittee, the sheepmen's testimony conflicted widely with that of trained biologists and scientists. So with the help of some of their elected friends on the Hill, the indomitable National Woolgrowers Association succeeded

---

* Psychologist Dr. Christian J. Buys conducted a study on rancher views on predators and found an "attitudinal set" not unlike that attributed to them by environmentalists. His study strongly suggests these entrenched beliefs to be highly resistant to change. He concludes: "The validity of ranchers' attitudes . . . is less important than the prediction that ranchers can be expected to behave in a fashion largely consistent with their attitudes that predators inflict severe damage on livestock."
** Due to the inaccessibility of the bait stations in wintertime, poison was not picked up until June 1972. Many ranchers even then ignored the order.

in reopening their case before an entirely *different* Senate sub-committee, one they hoped would be more sympathetic to their cause. When this subcommittee scheduled its hearings in far-away Sun Valley, Idaho, and Casper, Wyoming, where few experts would be likely to appear, the sheep-owners were jubilant.

And that is where matters stood on the day I took temporary leave of my coyotes, pulled off the refuge, and headed for trouble in Casper.

Franz and I drove the 350 miles to Casper together in his van. I spent most of the trip trying to shorten my testimony. Prior to our departure we both had received telegrams from Washington, D.C., granting our requests to appear as witnesses before the Senate subcommittee, but stipulating that we must each restrict our statements to five minutes.

Five minutes! Was it worthwhile making the trip? What could either of us possibly say about coyotes in five minutes? Yet we had to try, for what we were learning from our *undisturbed* subjects about their territoriality and cooperation in raising young was information that was relevant to the whole question of the wisdom or folly of massive extermination programs.

The day was hot and the land we were crossing was devoid of wildlife. For miles on end we drove through sheep-tufted scrubland.

"See any herder wagons?" Franz asked at one point.

"No herders. And I don't see any eagles or coyotes either. This country is totally sterile. It positively gives me the creeps to look at such an endless expanse of blue sky without any birds in it."

Franz was silent, and I knew he was thinking about the eagle study he had conducted three years earlier. In 150 visits to thirty-one active golden-eagle nests, not once had he found sheep remains, despite the fact that several of his nests were located on lambing grounds. He had been greatly upset by the public disclosure that so many slain eagles had been found in southern Wyoming. Now we had learned that sheep ranchers who had been indicted for the crime of killing 363 of these birds had been let off with a slap on the wrist. Moreover, one of the defendants, Herman Werner, even while awaiting trial, had been the recipient of $110,000 in federal wool subsidies.

Finally Franz broke the silence: "I think you should quote at **275** least one of the ranchers you interviewed. You and I know that only those livestock growers who are advocating a return to massive poisoning will appear tomorrow. The Senate subcommittee might be surprised to learn how many people out here are opposed to a return to the good old days of saturation poisoning."

Some of the livestock growers I had interviewed owned ranches adjacent to the National Elk Refuge. In particular, I was interested to find out if these ranchers were troubled by refuge coyotes, for these animals had never been subjected to systematic harassment.

Rancher Hugh Soest had said, "Never been bothered. The coyotes, in fact, are beneficial to me and I have made it known publicly that I will turn in anyone who shoots one. I've done it. Some people think they have a right to kill a coyote anywhere they happen to see one. I turned in a man from California who just pulled up and shot one right there on refuge ground. I figured that that very animal, while it was alive, was worth a hundred dollars a year to me. Kept down pocket gophers in my fields. If it weren't for refuge coyotes coming on my land, I don't know how much time and effort, as well as dollars, I would have to spend getting rid of rodents."

"How many coyotes do you think there are around here?" I had asked him.

"Oh, it all depends. I see the same animals year after year. There's one with a tag on her ear always crosses in the same place. I would say, though, that their numbers fluctuate. Some years the population is quite high, then it drops."

"And what about your newborn calves?"

"The coyotes aren't interested in them. One of our newborn calves got its nose froze right to the ground. The coyotes just walked around it and spent the day mousing. They tell me, though, that the coyotes south of town are quite a problem. I don't know what the difference is, but I've never had trouble with the ones we have out here."

Soest's observations agreed with scientific findings, which show coyotes to be territorial and their numbers to fluctuate cyclically within limits. Even more interesting to me was his observation that the unmolested refuge animals evinced little interest in livestock, while coyotes south of town, who had been subjected to years of harassment, persecution, and slaughter, were creating problems for livestock growers. I had collected many such statements and letters from Western ranchers and even from some sheep herders whom I had searched out in their isolated wagons and interviewed. But in the five minutes allotted me I would not be able to introduce many of these.

I also wanted to speculate on my own findings, particularly the significance of the behavior I had observed within the female hierarchy. Among the female members of my Miller Butte pack, in two years' time only one, the dominant Mama Redlegs, had bred. Other females of lower rank had acted only as "nannies" in the rearing of Redlegs's annual litters. And in short-term observations of coyotes whose territories were contiguous with that of my Miller Butte animals, all displayed the same pattern of reproduction—only one female per pack gave birth. Did a dominant female on each territory prevent the others from reproducing and thus limit the size of the coyote population?

Judging from the behavior of other wild canines, I thought the idea deserved attention. Dominant wolves gang up on low-ranking pack members to prevent subordinates from copulating. And among the wild dogs of Africa, the female hierarchy may function in a slightly different way to achieve the same end. Jane and Hugo Van Lawick-Goodall describe how the dominant female, "Havoc," killed pups that were born to the low-ranking female, "Angel."

I had never observed a female coyote interfering with the actual breeding of another female. Nor had I seen one destroy the offspring of another pack member. However, agonistic behavior among female coyotes might operate in some other, more subtle fashion to achieve the same end, the suppression of population. For example, the psychological stress endured by a low-ranking female might be sufficient to inhibit her ovulation or perhaps prevent her from forming a bond with a male. Even the occasional report of two females denning together did not alter my suspicion that coyote density is in part regulated by behavior within the female hierarchy. For if on occasion it should happen that a second female does succeed in becoming bred, she might very well find it expedient to incorporate her young into the dominant female's litter in order that they might benefit from the pack's pattern of care-giving.

It would follow then that indiscriminate killing of coyotes as a prophylactic measure could be counterproductive. Continual disruption of established hierarchies through the casual removal of high-ranking females might create a situation in which low-ranking animals begin to breed, excessive numbers of coyotes are produced, and territorial boundaries are broken down. Since it seems likely that uprooted coyotes are to a large extent responsible for what livestock damage occurs, I felt these ideas should be explored.

The hearings were to be held on the following day at the Ramada Inn on the outskirts of Casper. When we pulled into the parking lot, we found it filled to capacity with pickup trucks, many of which displayed bumper stickers that read "Eat More Lamb: 20,000 Coyotes Can't Be Wrong."

"We're clearly outnumbered," I commented.

"I see a dissenter over there," Franz said, pointing to a single bumper sticker that read "Give a Coyote Pup a Home!"

Inside, while waiting to register, we watched Senator Clifford Hansen from Wyoming glad-handing his constituents. I picked up copies of the witness list and discovered I was scheduled to be the eighteenth person to testify and that Franz was number twenty-seven on a list of twenty-eight. Calculating that each speaker would be given five minutes to make a statement, followed by perhaps ten minutes of questioning, I assumed I would be called upon shortly after the lunch break the following day. Such was not the case.

All through the morning witnesses droned on and on, exhibiting pictures of dead sheep which they asserted had been ravaged by predators (coyotes, eagles, and even foxes), complaining of impending bankruptcies, and intoning scriptural passages about good shepherds who protect their flocks. (If they only would!) Where only one man had been listed to speak, whole panels appeared, and each member was not only granted time to make a statement, but was interrogated at length by the Senate subcommittee members.

The witnesses were seeing coyotes everywhere, and they related this phenomenon to the ban on poison. Their specious rhetoric was often colorfully persuasive. One skillful orator, who was simultaneously a sheep rancher and a Wyoming state senator, succeeded in equating coyotes to big government, to the delight of the audience of several hundred woolgrowers: "Next year we'll have more coyotes than the Department of the Interior has employees, and then the next year we'll have more coyotes than the entire government has employees. And, gentlemen, that's a lot of coyotes!"

At the press table, the sound of scribbling pencils could be heard across the room. That remark was destined to appear in news stories throughout the country. By contrast, reporters failed to see anything newsworthy in the less flamboyant description of coyote population dynamics given by an expert government witness, Dr. Donald Balser, who said: "On balance, mortality equals natality. If this were not true, any given species would either overrun the earth or become extinct. The limits of the population fluctuations are controlled largely by the environment. This means that our coyote population is primarily under natural regulation."

Next, Charles Crowell, president of the Wyoming Game and Fish Commission, made a statement that was later described by one conservation-minded journalist as "the worst performance yet seen by someone representing Game and Fish." With no evidence to support his contention that coyotes were killing all the game, Crowell told why the Wyoming Game and Fish Commission had decided to increase to $50,000 its annual contribution to the state's coyote-eradication program*: "Our game department is entirely financed through the sportsman's dollars. . . . It is consequently understandable why a game department would favor the hunter over the coyote

---

*The Cain committee wisely recommended that federal funding of predator control be retained as a means of allowing general citizen review and input in decision-making. Citizen input is absent in state control programs, in which long-term vested private interests hold political control.

when harvest time comes around. The role of the coyote in predation upon game herds may be arguable. . . . However, Wyoming and most of the other Western states are of the opinion that such predation constitutes a significant loss of antelope and deer population and must be controlled in the interest of game management."

Crowell, for lack of data to substantiate this admittedly "arguable" claim, cited the fact that the Yellowstone Park managers had discontinued the practice of culling excess elk as supportive of his opinion. He reasoned that the park had found it possible to end its policy of killing surplus elk only because an enlarging wolf population was now doing the job for them! Aside from his distortion of fact, Crowell's logic was extremely faulty. By analogy and inference what he was trying to say was that the exact reverse should apply to an entirely different predator species, the coyote. By decreasing the coyote population, more elk should become available across the state for hunters to shoot. As for his facts, Yellowstone biologists are finding that park elk herds are self-regulatory. Moreover, if Crowell has seen extant wolves in Yellowstone Park, he had better inform park officials of the fact. Though a remnant wolf population is believed to exist within park boundaries, the animals are all but invisible. Every report of an oversized coyote or coyote-like animal that is brought to the attention of park biologists is carefully studied.

The Senate panel, in its eagerness to appear knowledgeable, nodded in agreement to Crowell's misinformation that wolves were controlling the Yellowstone elk population. I, on the other hand, was having difficulty stifling an impulse to interrupt the hearings and object, and Franz wisely suggested we leave the room for a while.

My name was not called until four o'clock, and by then it seemed Franz might not be heard at all. I requested that the Senate panel allow us to testify together, stating that our findings were corroborative. We were given permission.

I testified with my back to several hundred sheepmen, whose exasperated sighs were at times audible. I will never know how I managed to get through my statement. Several times I heard the bell ringing, meaning that I had exceeded my allotted five minutes. I rushed on to the end. Then Franz barreled through his statement, and we both sat back anticipating a period of questioning. Senator Clifford Hansen banged the gavel. "Thank you very much for your testimony," he said. "We will now take a fifteen-minute recess."

So it was all over for us. No questions would be asked. I felt weak as I left the table. Tom Garret from Friends of the Earth came to greet us.

"There's a rancher in the audience who is spreading the word that you were lying about tracking coyotes," he told me. "He's telling everyone that if you had spent so much time in the field as you say, you would be sunburned."

"That's pretty woolly logic," Franz said. "She's been holed up in a blind for seven weeks."

We went into the only restaurant in the inn. It was jammed with ranchers, some standing at the bar, others table-hopping. Franz had been right. It was like attending a woolgrowers' convention. Two men, beer mugs in hand, edged their way to our table.

"So you two are the coyote-lovers," one of them bellowed by way of introduction. He then pulled up a chair and demanded to know what we thought was so wonderful about coyotes. When it became apparent that he would not go away, I made the mistake of responding.

"I think coyotes are interesting animals," I said in a level tone. The remark couldn't have been more provocative. In a moment I was engaged in a heated argument without knowing quite how it had come about.

"Interesting, eh!" the rancher retorted. "Well, you might not find them so damn interesting if you ever saw what they do to sheep."

My temper flared. "If you ranchers really cared about what happens to your sheep, you'd try looking after them," I shot back.

The man stiffened. "I suppose you know better'n I how to operate my business."

"At least I would know enough to hire herders, train a few dogs, and build lambing pens," I shouted at him.

The rancher sneered. "You armchair experts make me sick. What do you know about ranching? Have you ever ridden the range in a freezing blizzard? Have you ever baled hay? Let me tell you one thing, girlie. I've operated sheep for twenty-five years and never lost money. So don't you give me any advice how to run my business."

Ashamed of having been lured into this argument, I now tried to end it by keeping silent, but the man was enjoying the quarrel. Over and over again he demanded to know if Franz had ever baled hay, but refused to listen to his reply. Franz, being the son of a Wisconsin farmer, had spent more time than he cared to remember baling hay, for whatever that was worth.

Finally Franz interjected, "If what you are saying is true and in twenty-five years running sheep you never lost money, the coyotes must not be hurting you fellows as much as you've been claiming."

"I've never lost money, that's true, but if it weren't for the damn coyotes I could make more. The coyotes reduce my profits. Now you agree that a man has got the right to make as much money as he can, don't you?"

I wanted to ask him what he would regard as a reasonable profit in view of the fact that he was grazing his livestock on public property and not laying out a penny for herders to watch over them. I also wanted to ask him why he, a rancher, should be receiving government protection against such a predictable cost of operation as lamb loss, whereas dairymen were not being supplied with government refrigerators to protect them from milk spoilage, ski resorts were not given snow-makers by a government concerned about warm winters, and taxpayers were not underwriting the risk I was taking in studying the coyote and writing a book about him. Why, then, did *he* deserve the taxpayers' help to contaminate land that was not his own so that *he* could maximize *his* profits? And finally, I wanted to ask him what made him think that killing coyotes *would* maximize his profits, since based on his industry's own evidence the more coyotes that were killed, the more lambs were allegedly falling victim to them. But I decided to let the matter drop.

I recalled the words of Kansas extension trapper F. Robert

Henderson, who had testified earlier that year in Washington, D.C.: "The sheep ranchers generally refuse to accept new methods and research findings. Western sheep producers spend entirely too much time and energy talking about coyotes. Since biblical times sheep have required more direct care than any other type of domestic livestock. When the Western sheep producers abandoned the use of herders and demanded intensive predator control at public expense, it was the point at which they lost their way."

Obviously, with these men, as with so many sheep growers, the problem was largely a psychological one. With synthetic fibers threatening the very future of their industry, no amount of profit would give them the security they sought. And God forbid they should be denied their favorite scapegoat—the coyote.

The second rancher, who was by now decidedly in his cups, slid into the booth beside me and, noting that I had written down his friend's words, he, too, decided to go on record.

"I don't condemn the coyotes for killing lambs," he said. "The coyote has gotta eat, too. But it kind of hurts economically." Then he picked up my hand and kissed my wrist. "This year it was actually the big storm that killed all our lambs. You know we could go broke overnight."

His friend shot him a dark look, but the signal escaped him. I gave him my full attention, and he eagerly continued: "You know, where there's lots of rabbits and sage chicken, a coyote won't kill a lamb, 'cause that's their natural food. That's the truth and you can quote me on it." He slid over closer to me. "I sure wish I could have heard you today."

I felt no shame as I beamed what I hoped was a fetching smile at him and asked, "How do you feel about poison?"

"Actually, I don't believe in it," he said. "A coyote, you know, is as intelligent as people. An animal has as much spirit as a human being. If we live beyond death, I think they will, too. Now don't quote me on that! At the same time, you gotta understand our problem. They took poison away from us without giving us time to develop any alternative methods of protecting sheep."

Now both men began to relax. They seemed irresistibly drawn

to us, their "enemies." And though we were all four uncomfortable in one another's company, I began to think there might be some value in our awkward efforts to hold a dialogue. It is easy enough to air opinions among friends, all of whom are in accord anyway. To speak candidly with one's opponents, however, particularly on a day when battle lines have been so clearly defined as to preclude evasiveness, is another matter.

"You talk about developing new methods of protecting sheep," I said. "Everybody's always waiting for modern science to come up with some newfangled gimmick like a coyote repellent. Well, that may happen someday . . . but in the meantime, what's wrong with going back to some of the old tried-and-true methods, like hiring herders?"

"Can't get 'em," the first rancher replied.

The second man spoke up: "I got the best herder I ever had a couple of years ago. He was a wetback. When my son found out I had hired a Mexican, he was mad. Now he tells everyone what great workers they are. They can rope, too. But the authorities caught this guy and sent him back to Mexico. I'll tell you one thing, though. If he ever makes it across the border again, I'll hire him again."

This piece of information intrigued me as much as any testimony I had heard all day. Consistently, woolgrowers have defended their neglect of flocks on the grounds that (1) the high cost of labor prohibits them from hiring help and (2) in twentieth-century America nobody is willing to perform the lonely task of herding sheep. Might Mexican labor be a possible answer to the latter argument? I once made a documentary film on the agonizing poverty and unemployment in northern Mexico and among the Chicanos of southern Texas.

"Are the Mexican sheep herders really good?" I asked.

"They're as good with sheep as the Basques. But you can't get them. The U.S. Government won't let them in."

It seemed to me that two apparently unrelated economic problems might provide interlocking solutions here. All too vividly I recollected the faces of Mexican men and women who each morning would rise before dawn in the hope of getting aboard one of the trucks bound in convoys for harvest fields.

With equal clarity, I could remember the expressions of despair on the faces of the many who were passed over and given no opportunity to work all day in the blazing sun harvesting crops. The thought flashed across my mind that we Americans might better subsidize Mexican or Chicano sheep herders with a decent wage than pay for the morally repugnant devastation of wildlife.

By the time we parted company with the ranchers, it seemed preposterous to me that the two human beings with whom we had sat and chatted could actually be responsible, directly or indirectly, for the reprehensible cruelty inflicted on so many wild animals. After our initial confrontation, the men relaxed and began to seem like anybody else. Some trick of the human mind obviously prevented them from realizing the appalling consequences of their self-serving policies. In this respect, they were exactly like the trappers who carried out their destructive mandates. I recalled Jack Olsen's description of the government "control agents" in *Slaughter the Animals, Poison the Earth*. He wrote: "A trapper with his poison kit is not viewing anything in its entirety. He is looking at life in an oversimplified unrealistic manner, in which all relationships are one-to-one, all wildlife evil or good. Like everyone else, he is hopelessly inadequate to the task of determining complete ecological relationships, but unlike everyone else he keeps busy interrupting and distorting them."

Franz and I were silent during most of the long journey back to Jackson Hole. Both of us were wondering if our trip to Casper had been a waste of time and effort. At one point I remarked that the first rancher had admitted that he wasn't really going broke, just wanted to maximize his profits, and the second one had divulged the news that it was a storm and not coyotes that had killed all his lambs last year.

"It's too bad the senators didn't hold their hearings in a bar," was Franz's only comment.

Aftermath

The Western field hearings in Casper and Sun Valley demolished all hope that federal legislation would be enacted to implement recommendations made by the Cain committee to end massive extermination of predators. A syndicated news story headlined "Idaho Ranchers Declare a Shooting War on Rapidly Increasing Coyote Population" left the general public with the false impression that evidence at the hearings showed coyote numbers to have burgeoned as a result of the poison ban. Thus, a great deal of sympathy was generated for the woolgrowers, who, emboldened by the good press, pushed harder for concessions from the federal government.

A number of Western politicians seized the opportunity to jump on the sheep wagon. Led by Wyoming's Senator Clifford Hansen, twenty-one senators signed a joint letter accusing Interior Secretary Rogers C. Morton and his department of suppressing important data from two in-progress studies on coyote predation being conducted by Interior. They demanded a face-to-face meeting with him.

In point of fact, since Interior's Wildlife Services had been forced by presidential decree to cease and desist poisoning the West, employees of that bureau were behaving as if they were relieved to shed their black hats, and they refused to lend support to the woolgrowers' campaign to have the poison ban rescinded. This reversal of Interior's policy on toxicants not only angered sheepmen, but apparently annoyed a number of the representatives the woolgrowers had elected, too. Or so it would seem from news accounts of that highly critical senatorial letter sent to Secretary Morton.

News accounts of the letter's contents were highly inaccurate, however, as were reports about its authorship. For example, one signatory, Senator Henry Jackson, was falsely named by the press as the letter's author and the leader of the attack on the
Department of the Interior. In actual fact, the letter was drafted

by two sheep ranchers, polished by a member of Senator Clifford Hansen's staff, then cleverly circulated by Senator Hansen among his colleagues on the Senate Interior and Insular Affairs Committee just minutes before Congress adjourned for Christmas. Evidently most of the senators who signed it did so perfunctorily and without making a careful study of what they were putting their names to. As a result, a number of signatories (including Senators Jackson and Metcalf) later felt compelled to write follow-up letters to Secretary Morton, repudiating portions of the letter. But these follow-up disclaimers were given no publicity whatsoever, and thus the public was somehow left with the erroneous impression that twenty-one leading U.S. senators were so convinced that a coyote population explosion was wiping out the sheep industry that they favored a return to the practice of lacing the West with poison.

To its credit, *The New York Times*, in an effort to rectify the damage done by all these news stories, carried a strong anti-poison editorial. But the specter of the "bad predator" had been resurrected in public consciousness, and the well-organized National Woolgrowers Association, noting a favorable climate of opinion, grew more adamant in its demand that the "right to poison" be restored.

In actuality, since the poison ban had gone into effect, the percentage of sheep lost to predators had actually declined below that in 1969 and in 1970, when the public lands were saturated with toxicants. Moreover, even if coyote numbers had risen in 1972–73, such a phenomenon could not have been attributed to the removal of poison baits, since only one pup crop had been born after the ban went into effect, and these animals had not yet reached maturity. (Not that coyote density has ever been shown to be related to lamb losses anyway!) And finally, the Department of the Interior, despite its shift in policy on the poison issue, had by no stretch of the imagination relaxed its war against the coyote; another recommendation made by the Cain committee—that only those coyotes who were offenders should be eliminated—was being completely ignored by Wildlife Services. Though government trappers were now being more selective regarding which *species* they shot, trapped, gassed, burned, and kicked to death, predator-control operations as applied to *Canis latrans* were as massive and indiscriminate as ever and aimed at reducing the overall size and density of the entire coyote population. By its own count, Wildlife Services reported killing ten thousand more coyotes between June 1972 and June 1973 than it had in the previous year, when poison was still among its arsenal of tools.

But things were to become even worse for the coyote. Despite a praiseworthy action by Senator Jacob Javits of New York, who obtained the signatures of nineteen other senators on a letter he wrote to President Nixon, in which he spelled out the facts on predator poisoning and urged the chief executive to remain steadfast against lobbies pressuring for a revocation of the ban on toxicants, the federal ban on poison began to weaken.

While the Department of the Interior managed to stand firm, the Environmental Protection Agency did not. Under intense pressure from such politicians as Congressman W. R. Poage of Texas, chairman of the House Agriculture Committee, the E.P.A. began to look for ways to appease the woolgrowers. Meanwhile, Chairman Poage's committee, keeping up the pressure, passed a resolution asking that the executive order be reexamined and that permits be granted for the use of such devices as the M-44 and other nonpersistent poisons, as well as small baits of strychnine.

In a first step toward capitulation, the E.P.A. authorized the use of the M-44 (a new model of the old cyanide-filled "coyote getter") in an experiment in Texas. Though E.P.A. administrator Russell Train tried to reassure an alarmed public that the program to be set up in Texas was only for the purpose of determining the relative effectiveness of this type of killing device, hardly anybody was fooled. The M-44 had been sufficiently studied during several years of use prior to the poison ban. Moreover, as pointed out by Dr. A. Starker Leopold, chairman of the Leopold committee and member of the Cain committee, any data coming out of the Texas experiment would have absolutely no validity, because information was being collected not by scientists but by ranchers.

But the E.P.A. remained deaf to criticism and blind to the

significance of its own actions. The Texas experiment immediately provided sheep ranchers with the loophole they had long sought, and a number of states applied for permission to conduct the same so-called experiment with M-44s on public lands within their borders. At the time of this writing,* California, Montana, and Idaho have all been granted the right to do so. M-44s now stud the public lands like noxious weeds.

Most servicemen would quickly recognize one of these devices. It is similar to a "bouncing Betty," a military mine that mutilates as often as it kills. Though touted as "safe" and "selective against coyotes," the M-44, like earlier versions of cyanide guns, is not so discriminating that it prevents skunks, raccoons, foxes, bears, red wolves, and particularly dogs from tugging at its lethal head. In January 1974 the *Denver Post* reported that a Colorado rancher stepped on a similar type of "getter" and was killed.

Poison is seeping back. Not that it was ever totally absent. In a letter from ex-trapper Vern Dorn I was informed: "There is enough poison in the hands of the individual sheepmen to saturate the state of Wyoming for the next 20 years. The airplane furnishes them with a method that is almost impossible to police."

To date, although more than one hundred thousand cyanide capsules have been issued for use in the phony experiments, the sheepmen are still not satisfied. Emboldened by the momentum generated by one success, they have begun to attack the poison ban in its entirety. In August 1974 Western governors released a resolution on behalf of their sheep-raising constituents, which asked that the superpoison 1080 be made available again. The resolution further stated that predator control should be taken out of the hands of the Department of the Interior and placed under the jurisdiction of the Department of Agriculture, which has no mandate to protect the nation's wildlife and therefore would make every decision in the exclusive interest of sheepmen.

None of these developments came as a surprise to me. After

---

* 1975.

the brouhaha in Casper. I had a premonition that it was going to be a bad year for the coyote, and it was with a deep sense of foreboding that I returned to the refuge to conclude my study. Nevertheless, the sight of Mama Redlegs' pups rollicking on the slope temporarily assuaged my anxiety, and for the remainder of my stay, at least, the oppressive experience of the Senate hearings faded.

In my peaceful quarters, once again my tempo began to harmonize with the movements of the earth, the weather, and the lives of my subjects. Each quiet day was filled with impressions of animals going about the business of living, satisfying their own needs, giving care to one another. How fantastic it now seemed that the fate of such creatures should be determined in a distant air-conditioned room by a group of arrogant individuals who talked in euphemisms about "control" and "management." I asked myself: Where were these men when the foundations of the earth were laid? Fifty-five million years of *Canis latrans* evolution they would snuff out by any obscene means at their command. Yet many had introduced themselves as "conservationists," meaning, of course, that they favored the efficient exploitation of natural resources for their own profit.

My last days on the refuge were marked by a heightened awareness, the result, no doubt, of a realization that I would soon be leaving. Moments were recorded in my brain like snapshots—pups trailing adults, a family howl, the orderly chaos of a greeting.

All nine pups were led, a few at a time, to the same rendezvous site that had served Mama's litter the previous year. Over the winter an elk blind had been erected atop the northeastern point of the butte, and to this strategic hut I climbed, there to remain for three days and three nights in the hope of continuing my observations. But the fast-developing litter seldom emerged from the jungle of willows, which now and over the next two months would screen them from view. And the adults, aware that I was inside the blind, chose not to pass that way, but signaled the pups to come to them from a place outside my line of sight. What brief glimpses I obtained of my pack did not add up to meaningful observations. Finally I was forced to accept the fact that my study had come to an end.

As I assembled my gear and prepared to leave, I tried not to think about what might lie ahead for the coyote. By virtue of the fortuitous location of my Miller Butte pack, these animals, at least, were relatively well protected. Nevertheless, poison bait, leg-hold traps, and human bounty hunters surround and sometimes even invade the refuge. If the dominant male, Gray Dog, should extend his range but a short distance, trained dogs could tear him limb from limb. Should Mama chase a marmot across an invisible boundary, a steel trap could snap around her delicate red legs. And I was unable to contemplate the future of the playful Rudy and his mate-to-be (Tiny?) should they den apart from the pack in some new location.

As for less sheltered members of this species, their future looked very grim indeed. Chances are coyotes will outlast mountain lions and even bears, for *Canis latrans* is a genius at evading

One of the pups at nine and a half weeks of age.

The coyote—flexible in his habits, cooperative with his kind, opportunistic by nature, catholic in his tastes, capable of observational learning, suspicious, tough, ingenious. Many claim he is the smartest wild animal in North America.

man's lethal devices. In the long run, however, even the crafty coyote cannot hold out against modern man's determination to rid the earth of everything that competes with himself.

Biologist Durward Allen wrote in *Our Wildlife Legacy:* "In the face of traps, dogs and strychnine, the adaptable and prolific coyote held its own and even extended its holdings, but the appearance during the war of sodium fluoroacetate, compound '1080,' completely altered the outlook. Widely spaced injected carcasses are deadly baits to the far-ranging brush wolf, and its extirpation in large regions is now but a matter of time."

At the time of this writing, 1080 is banned by presidential order, but as yet no act of Congress has fixed this tentative decree into permanent federal law. Nor is it likely that the congressional committees that have heard arguments for such legislation, dominated as they are by Western politicians, will ever recommend that such a law be enacted. Conservationists feel the outlook for North American predators is dim. Time is short, and help, they say, can come only from the East, where elected officials do not shake in their boots over a woolgrower's frown.

Perhaps what is really needed is more awareness among the American people of their own property rights in the West. Since every citizen of the United States is a co-owner of the public lands, each and every citizen has an equal stake in the long-range health of that real estate. Ultimately, then, it is incumbent upon the American people to acquaint themselves with this network of land, along with those plants and creatures it has shaped. For if vested interests continue to regard their demands upon this communal property as the only valid ones, the public domain will at no distant time lose its regenerative power. Nature, too, must be served if she is to renew the bounty upon which all her diverse life forms depend and to which each must also contribute. For ultimately the green leaf has a more legitimate purpose than any technology; and each creature, linked in a chain that is also man's lifeline, has more purpose than economic growth.

Aside from these pragmatic realities, there are philosophical considerations to be observed here, too. Even were it possible for man to survive outside that nitrogen cycle which powers all of life (and it is not!), another question would remain: Would existence be meaningful in the absence of other life forms? One of Nature's most eloquent spokesmen, the late Joseph Wood Krutch, tried to visualize a futuristic world in which man, through his own technology, had somehow succeeded in severing his dependence upon Nature and could, therefore, lay waste the planet in the pursuit of ever more comfort and wealth. Krutch's description of such a man-made utopia is chilling:

He [man] will no longer find the world, in Thoreau's words, "beautiful as well as convenient, something to be admired as well as used." The emotions which have inspired a considerable part of all poetry and music and art will have ceased to exist. Man will have all his experience with things which man has made, rather than with the things which God or nature, choose whichever word you like, has made. No flower will suggest thoughts too deep for tears. Man will know only machines, no longer know anything which, like him, is living, alive.

A world without wild creatures! A part of me would die should coyotes ever cease to pour their throats in nightly celebration of life. Even the sublime grandeur of the West's towering mountain ranges would no longer evoke in me a sense of the divine mystery should those ancient faces ever cease to reverberate to the old wild song of Trickster.

On the last night before my departure I tried to fix my pack's primeval music in my very being even while I recorded it on tape. The pups were in full voice, and the pack sang as if in rapture. It was an impressive farewell.

The next day I left. But after shipping camera equipment to the *National Geographic*, I could not resist an urge to return for one final look at my study animals. Through my binoculars I spotted three pups wildly sporting high on the windy butte. On guard below them sat the sober-looking Gray Dog. For one mystical instant, as he turned his long gray face and fixed his gaze on my idling van below, I experienced a moment of contact with him.

"Take care, Gray Dog," I whispered to the distant coyote.

Then I put away my binoculars and left quickly.

While driving off the refuge for the last time, I met Franz on the road and stopped. But I found it difficult to speak.

"Take care, Franz," I finally managed. "And keep an eye out for my coyotes."

"What do you mean, *your* coyotes?" he shot back.

As I pulled away, I had to smile, even though I was having difficulty seeing the road.

And everywhere that I appeared
The lamb squad was sure to go.

L ike Mary in the nursery rhyme, I was being followed. The
first edition of this book had just come out and I was doing
the "author's circuit." That is, I was appearing on television talk
shows, describing my new book. On these programs I showed
slides of Mama Redlegs, Gray Dog, and their pups and spoke
about the bonds of "affection" these animals displayed. The
pictures elicted "oohs" and "aahs" from interviewers and a great
many letters from the public. Most of the letters contained
wonderful stories about coyote behavior, revealing more about
the animal's keen intelligence. I also talked on the air about the
government's predator-control program. That brought a strong
reaction from the sheep ranchers.

One morning my phone rang. It was the producer of *The Mike
Douglas Show*, on which I had appeared the previous week. CBS,
I was told, had received a request for equal time from the
National Woolgrowers Association. The sheepmen wanted to
challenge the positive view of the coyote that I had presented.

"What are you going to do?" I asked.

"Nothing. We've looked into your comments about predator
control and find them to be accurate. The sheepmen will not be
invited to appear."

NBC's *Today Show* also heard from the wool lobby. The idea of
controversy, however, appealed to the producer of that program. And so representatives of the sheep industry were invited
to be guests on *The Today Show*. One morning I turned on my
television set and there, in front of two big blowups of *my*
photographs of Gray Dog and the pups, sat a panel of sheepmen
expounding on the bloodthirsty nature of the coyote. The sheep
industry had had the last word.

More often than not, the vested interests do have the final say.
They have the time, money, staff, and economic incentive to
defeat all the unpaid citizens who fight to protect natural resources. Whatever be at stake, whether coastal wetland or native   **295**

animal, conservationists are always at a disadvantage. They must win every time or the resource they seek to protect may be lost. The exploiters, on the other hand, know that they need claim victory only once. It will be a final one.

Thus, it was predictable that the executive order banning the use of poison on public lands would come under repeated attack from the woolgrowers. Their persistence gradually eroded the opposition. The following concessions were granted to them:

In 1972 Congress allowed M-44s, baited with sodium cyanide, to be used *experimentally* on public lands for the purpose of research.

In 1975 President Ford issued Executive Order 11870, which allowed for *emergency use* of M-44s to kill coyotes on the public domain.

In 1975 the Environmental Protection Agency permitted the *registration* of sodium cyanide for use by certified individuals.

In 1976 President Ford issued another executive order, 11917, which permitted *operational* use of M-44s baited with sodium cyanide on the public domain.

Now that sodium cyanide was back in their arsenal, the sheepmen intensified pressure on politicians to revoke the ban on 1080 (sodium fluoroacetate)—so deadly to coyotes, and capable of killing any bird or animal that feeds on the corpses of its victims.

To hear the woolgrowers tell it, one would suppose that, since 1080 had been declared illegal, they had experienced economic hardship. Not so. In 1978 sheep ranchers were realizing higher profits than they had done in many years. It is true that the number of people raising sheep on public lands had fallen off. But this fact (in itself a boon to the overgrazed public lands) could hardly be blamed on the coyote. No increase in predation had occurred. Moreover, since the poison ban had gone into effect in 1972, government trappers had succeeded in killing more coyotes annually than ever before. Despite the Cain committee's recommendation to Interior to eliminate coyotes only where sheep-kills actually occur, coyote-population reduction was still the order of the day. As a result, between 1974 and 1977 coyote numbers dropped by 26 percent in the Great Basin and Mountain states.

Still the sheep industry was not satisfied. One wonders how much government support this group of people can expect to receive. The Wool Act of 1954 compensates sheep-raisers whenever the support price for wool exceeds the national average price. In addition, high import duties discourage foreign competition and raise consumer prices on wool. More government subsidy is given in the form of cheap grazing on public lands, which reduces the industry's overhead. And, finally, government predator-control programs relieve the woolgrowers of the need to hire shepherds to guard their flocks.

As a result, in the Mountain states herders are employed by only 16 percent of ranchers running sheep on public land. In the Great Basin states only 24 percent hire shepherds to protect their livestock. Of the large sheep enterprises operating on the public domain, only 8 percent have bothered to construct lambing sheds to shelter newborn animals. Still fewer use guard dogs to ward off predators. And none seems willing to try any of the nonlethal chemical repellents that have been developed to discourage predation. Why should they bother when a responsive government agency so willingly slaughters the nation's wild carnivores on their behalf?

Since 1972, federal predator-control expenditures have nearly doubled. Coyotes are being shot from the air, poisoned by M-44s, and trapped in record numbers. Last year more than one hundred thousand were killed by federal, state, and county predator-control programs. This body count is 30 percent higher than in 1972, when poisons of every kind saturated the public domain. Yet the sheep-raisers continue to complain that the government is not doing enough for them. Unless 1080 is again made available, they say, they will all go out of business.

As a pressure group the industry is without equal. In June of 1978, in a move to dramatize their demands, woolgrowers in Idaho closed all their private land holdings to hunters. Strongly worded pamphlets and posted signs explained that access would be denied sportsmen until the Secretary of the Interior revoked the ban on 1080. *The New York Times* quoted the ranchers as saying the action was meant to "call attention to their plight and lead to increased predator controls."

And how many people actually stand to benefit by "increased predator controls"? Aside from the army of government employees paid to kill off the nation's wildlife, not many. It is shocking to learn that over half of the sheep utilizing public lands (56 percent) are owned by only 6 percent of the nation's woolgrowers. In real numbers this means that 2820 individuals are the major recipients of government programs costing millions of dollars annually. The cost of these programs in long-term ecological damage cannot be guessed.

Today a vogue for "fun fur" further imperils the coyote, even in regions where the sheep industry does not operate. Last winter the animal's pelt brought two hundred dollars at fur auctions. Hordes of professional and amateur trappers beat the bushes for the easy money. As a result, an unprecedented number of coyotes—303,932—were "harvested."

I have not returned to Miller Butte to see how my study animals have fared in the carnage. Something prevents me from going. But I have enjoyed glimpses of coyotes while studying bobcats in Arizona. *Canis latrans* is smaller and paler here. He is the same clever creature, though. I am told by one local cattle rancher that an old male often sits under his pear tree, waiting for ripe fruit to drop into his mouth.

That's Trickster, all right. The coyote always was an opportunist. I can only hope this trait will continue to favor his survival. Because times are bad for the animal the Indians called God's dog.

Hope Ryden
July 4, 1978

Sources

PREFACE

Chesness, Robert. "Home Range and Territoriality of Coyotes in North Central Minnesota." Paper presented at 34th Midwest Fish and Wildlife Conference, Des Moines, Iowa. December 12, 1972.

Correll, J. Lee, research supervisor for the Navajo tribe, letter to author. May 30, 1973.

Dobie, J. Frank. *The Voice of the Coyote*. Boston: Little, Brown and Company. 1949.

Hall, E. Raymond, and Kelson, Keith R. *The Mammals of North America*. New York: The Ronald Press Company. 1959.

Lowie, Robert H. "Myths and Traditions of the Crow Indians." *Anthropological Papers of the American Museum of Natural History*, XXV, pt. 1. 1918.

Niehuis, Charles C. "Coyote." *Arizona Wildlife Sportsman*. July 1967.

AUTUMN

The Billings Gazette, Yellowstone National Park 100th Anniversary Issue. 1972. "The Bad Guys Look Like Good Guys Now."

Cole, Glen F. "An Ecological Rationale for the Natural or Artificial Regulation of Native Ungulates in Parks." *Transactions of North American Wildlife and Natural Resources Conference*, 36. March 1971.

Conversations with Vern Dorn, Lloyd Tillett, Buzz Robbins, Bob Pearson, Don Redfearn, Glen Cole, Mary Meagher, Adolph Murie, Chuck McCurley, Victor Jackson.

Dobie, J. Frank, *op. cit.*

Errington, P. L. "Factors Limiting Higher Vertebrate Populations." *Science*, 124, pp. 304–307. 1959.

Errington, P. L. "Predation and Vertebrate Populations." *Quarterly Review of Biology*, 21, pp. 144–177. 1946.

High Country News. "More Species Endangered." November 12, 1971.

Houston, Douglas B. "Ecosystems of National Parks." *Science*, 172, pp. 648–651. May 14, 1972.

Meagher, Mary. "The Bison of Yellowstone National Park: Past and Present." Ph.D. thesis. University of California, Berkeley. 1970.

Mech, L. David. *The Wolf*. Garden City: The American Museum of Natural History Press. 1970. P. 139.

Murie, Adolph. *Ecology of the Coyote in the Yellowstone*. National Park Service Fauna Series #4. Washington, D.C.: Government Printing Office. 1940.

Murie, Adolph. *The Wolves of Mount McKinley*. National Park Service Fauna Series #5. Washington, D.C.: Government Printing Office. 1944.

Roosevelt, President Theodore, letter to Lieutenant General S. B. M. Young. January 22, 1908.

Theberge, John B. "Wolf Music." *Natural History Magazine*. April 1971.

WINTERTIME

Beach, F. A., and Le Boeuf, B. J. "Coital Behavior in Dogs: Preferential Mating in the Bitch." *Animal Behavior,* 15, pp. 546–558.

Beston, Henry. *The Outermost House*. New York: The Viking Press. 1962.

Conversations with Helenette Silver, Frank Calkins, David Hiser, Franz Camenzind, Almer Nelson, and people in and about Yellowstone National Park.

Crisler, Lois. *Arctic Wild*. Boston: Little, Brown and Company. 1958.

Dobie, J. Frank, *op. cit.*

Eiseley, Loren. *The Immense Journey*. New York: Random House. 1957.

Fox, Michael W. *Behavior of Wolves, Dogs and Related Canids*. New York: Harper and Row. 1971.

Gier, H. T. *Coyotes in Kansas*. Kansas State College of Agriculture and Applied Science Bulletin #393. Revised December 1968. Pp. 49–50.

Hamlett, G. W. D. *The Reproductive Cycle of the Coyote*. U.S.D.A. Technical Bulletin #616. Washington, D.C. July 1938.

High Country News. "Snowmobiles Reviewed." January 1973. Reprinted from *Desert News*, December 4, 1972.

Jackson Hole Guide. "Killed Coyotes." April 8, 1971.

Knowlton, F. F. "Aspects of Coyote Predation in South Texas, with Special Reference to White-Tailed Deer." Ph.D. thesis. Purdue University. 1964.

Mech, L. David. *The Wolves of Isle Royale*. National Park Service Fauna Series #7, 1966.

Minnesota Game Research Job Progress Report. Coyote collections, job #14. Grand Rapids, Minn. P. 58.

Murie, Adolph. *Ecology of the Coyote in the Yellowstone, op. cit.*

Schenkel, Rudolf. "Submission: Its Features and Functions in the Wolf and Dog." *American Zoologist*, 7 (2), pp. 319–330.

Scott, John Paul, and Fuller, John L. *Genetics and the Social Behavior of the Dog*. Chicago: The University of Chicago Press. 1965.

White, M. L. "Population Ecology of Some Whitetail Deer in South Texas." Ph.D. thesis. Purdue University. 1967.

Whiteman, Eldon E. "Habits and Pelage Changes in Captive Coyotes." *Journal of Mammalogy*, 21 (4), pp. 435–438.

INTERLUDE

Barnett, S. A. "Rats." *Scientific American* (January 1967), pp. 79–85.

Baynes, E. H. *My Wild Animal Guests*. New York: Macmillan & Co. 1930.

Cole, John N. "Coyotes in Maine?" *National Parks and Conservation Magazine*. November 1973.

Cole, John N. "The Return of the Coyote." *Harper's Magazine*. May 1973.

Coppinger, Raymond P., Sands, M., and Groves, E. "Meet New England's New Wolf." *Massachusetts Wildlife*. May–June 1973.

Dobie, J. Frank, *op. cit.*

Doherty, Paul. "The Northwoodsman." *Berlin* (N. H.) *Reporter*. November 4, 11, 1971.

Fentress, John C. "Observations on the Behavioral Development of a Hand-Reared Male Timber Wolf." *American Zoologist*, 7 (2), pp. 339–351. May 1967.

Gier, H. T., *op. cit.*

Grimes, Richard. "The Coyote That Outfoxed a State." *True*. February 1972.

Koons, Gary. "Food Habits of the Eastern Coyote in New Hampshire." Paper presented at Game Management 1, Forest Resources 737. University of New Hampshire, Institute of Natural and Environmental Resources. January 1972.

Lawrence, B., and Bossert, W. H. "The Cranial Evidence for Hybridization in New England *Canis*." *Brevoria*, 330. Cambridge, Mass. September 15, 1969.

Lawrence, B., and Bossert, W. H. "Multiple Character Analysis of *Canis lupus, latrans* and *familiaris* with a Discussion of the Relationship of *Canis niger*." *American Zoologist*, 7 (2), pp. 223–232. May 1967.

Lovell Chronicle. "Coyote Bites Child." June 1972.

McCarley, Howard. "The Taxonomic Status of Wild *Canis* (Canidae) in the South Central United States." *The Southwest Naturalist,* 7 (3–4), pp. 227–235. December 10, 1962.

Mech, L. David, *op. cit.*

Scott, John Paul, and Fuller, John L., *op. cit.,* pp. 101–116.

Silver, Helenette, and Coons, Gary. "Friend or Foe?" *The New Hampshire Outdoorsman.* March 1972.

Silver, Helenette and Walter. "Growth and Behavior of the Coyote-like Canid of Northern New England with Observations on Canid Hybrids." *Wildlife Monographs,* 17. October 1969.

Van Wormer, Joe. *The World of the Coyote.* Philadelphia: J. B. Lippincott Company. 1964.

Woolpy, Jerome H., and Ginsburg, Benson E. "Wolf Socialization: A Study of Temperament in a Wild Social Species." *American Zoologist,* 7 (2), pp. 357–363. May 1967.

SPRINGTIME

Audubon, John, and Backman, John. *Quadrupeds of America.* New York, 1852, II, pp. 153–154.

Autopsy report on coyote specimen performed at University of Utah. Spring 1973.

Barnett, S. A. "Rats," *op. cit.*

Barnett, S. A. *The Rat: A Study in Behavior.* Aldine Publishing Co. 1963.

Beckoff, Marc. "The Development of Social Interaction, Play and Metacommunication in Mammals: An Ethological Perspective." *The Quarterly Review of Biology,* 47 (4), pp. 412–434. December 1972.

Camenzind, Franz, letters to author. July 18, 1972, and October 10, 1972.

Chesness, Robert, *op. cit.*

Conversations with people in and around Jackson, Wyo., and with employees of National Elk Refuge and Grand Teton National Park.

Dobie, J. Frank, *op. cit.*

Errington, P. L. "Predation and Vertebrate Populations," *op. cit.*

Fox, Michael W., and Clark, A. L. "The Development and Temporal Sequencing of Agonistic Behavior in the Coyote." *Zeitschrift fur Tierpsychologie,* 28 (3), pp. 262–278. 1971.

Gier, H. T., *op. cit.*

Gilbert, Bill. *The Weasels.* New York: Pantheon Books. 1970.

Knowlton, Frederick, letter to author. February 14, 1974.

Krebs, Charles J., and Myers, Judith H. "Population Cycles in Rodents." *Scientific American,* pp. 38–46. June 1974.

Lorenz, Konrad. *On Aggression.* New York: Harcourt, Brace, and World. 1963.

Lorenz, Konrad. "Speaking Freely." *NBC-TV News.* Interview by Edwin Newman. November 20, 1971.

Mech, L. David., *op. cit.*

Murie, Adolph. *Ecology of the Coyote in the Yellowstone, op. cit.*

Murie, Adolph. *The Wolves of Mount McKinley, op. cit.*

Rabb, George B. "How Wolves Became Friends." *Science Service.* August 24, 1966.

Rabb, George B., Woolpy, Jerome H., and Ginsburg, Benson E. "Social Relationships in a Group of Captive Wolves." *American Zoologist,* 7 (2), pp. 305–317. May 1967.

Roche, Frank. "The Coyote That Cried Wolf." *Defenders of Wildlife News.* October 1973.

Schenkel, Rudolf, *op. cit.*

Scott, John Paul, and Fuller, John L., *op. cit.*

Snow, Carol J. "Some Observations on the Behavioral and Morphological Development of Coyote Pups." *American Zoologist,* 7 (2), pp. 353–355. May 1967.

Theberge, John B., and Falls, J. Bruce. "Howling as a Means of Communication in Timber Wolves." *American Zoologist,* 7 (2), pp. 331–338. May 1967.

Van Lawick-Goodall, Hugo and Jane. *Innocent Killers.* Boston: Houghton Mifflin Company. 1971.

THE OUTLOOK

Albuquerque Journal. "Western Governors Vow Greater U.S. Policy Role." August 1, 1974.

Allen, Durward. *Our Wildlife Legacy.* New York: Funk & Wagnalls. Revised 1962.

Amory, Cleveland. "Little Brother of the Wolf." *The American Way.* October 1973.

Annual reports for 1960–70, Bureau of Sports Fisheries and Wildlife, Department of the Interior, Washington, D.C.

Balser, Donald, chief of Predator Research Division of Bureau of Sports Fisheries and Wildlife. Testimony before Senate Subcommittee on Public Lands. June 4, 1973.

Balser, Donald, letter to author. January 15, 1974.

Buys, Christian J. "Predator Control and Ranchers' Attitudes." Psychology Department, New Mexico Institute of Mining and Technology. Socorra, New Mexico.

Cain, Stanley, Dudlec, J., Allen, D., Cooley, R., Hornocker, M., Leopold, A. S., Wagner, F. Report to the Council on Environmental Quality and the Department of the Interior. 1971.

Camenzind, Franz. Testimony before Senate Subcommittee on Public Lands. June 4, 1973.

Chesness, Robert, *op. cit.*

Conversations with Franz Camenzind, Hugh Soest, Will Minor, E. Raymond Hall, James B. Ruch, Cynthia Wilson, Wyoming ranchers and sheep herders.

Crowell, Charles. Testimony before Senate Subcommittee on Public Lands. June 4, 1973, pp. 273–274.

Davis, Raymond Sandy. "Lamb Chops and Cyanide." *Defenders of Wildlife News.* April 1974, pp. 91–96.

Dobie, J. Frank, *op. cit.*

Dorn, Vern, letter to author. December 22, 1972.

Evanson, R. M. "Predator Control and the Sheep-Raising Industry." Dissertation for Doctor of Business Administration. George Washington University. February 22, 1967.

Frome, Mike. "Predators, Prejudice and Politics." *Field and Stream.* December 1967.

Hansen, Senator Clifford, and 20 U.S. senators, letter to Secretary Rogers C. B. Morton. December 12, 1973.

Hearings before House Subcommittee on Public Lands. March 1, 1974.

Hearings before Senate Subcommittee on the Environment. March 27, 29, 1973.

Hearings before Senate Subcommittee on Public Lands. June 1, 4, 1973.

Henderson, F. Robert. Testimony before Senate Subcommittee on the Environment. March 27, 29, 1973, pp. 152–155.

Jackson, Senator Henry, letter to Secretary Rogers C. B. Morton. January 22, 1974.

Javits, Senator Jacob, and 19 U.S. senators, letter to President Richard Nixon. February 8, 1974.

Krutch, Joseph Wood. "Human Life in the Context of Nature." *Friends of Animals.* Fall 1970.

Leopold, A. Starker, Cain, Stanley, Cottam, C., Gabrielson, I. N., and Kimball, T. L. "Predator and Rodent Control in the United States." *Transactions of North American Wildlife Conference* 29, 1963.

Linhart, Samuel B. "Relative Indices of Predator Abundances in the

Western United States." U.S.D.I. Preliminary Report for 1972 and 1973.

Litigation initiated by Defenders of Wildlife against the United States Department of the Interior. U.S. District Court. Washington, D.C. April 1971.

Mansfield, Senator Mike. Statement published in *Congressional Record*. Feb. 4, 1974.

Matthiessen, Peter. *Wildlife in America*. New York: The Viking Press. 1959, pp. 192–202.

McCutchen, Dick, executive director of the Ohio Conservation Foundation, letter to Roger Caras.

McNulty, Faith. *Must They Die?* New York: Audubon/Ballantine Books. 1972.

McNulty, Faith. "War on Wildlife." *National Parks and Conservation Magazine*. March 1971.

Mech, L. David, *op. cit.*

Metcalf, Senator Lee, letter to Secretary Rogers C. B. Morton. February 1, 1974.

National Wildlife Federation Conservation Report. "Wheeler Explains Expanded Predatory Animal Damage Control Program." P. 156.

New York Times. "Idaho Sheepmen Denounce Ban on Poisoning Range Predators." January 7, 1973.

New York Times. "Coyotes, It Seems, Wear Black Hats." January 6, 1974.

New York Times. "Cyanide Gun Due for Coyote Test." January 20, 1974.

New York Times. "Senators Accuse Interior Chief of Ignoring Coyote Peril in West." January 2, 1974.

New York Times. "Idaho Ranchers Declare a Shooting War on Rapidly Increasing Coyote Population." June 30, 1973.

Nixon, President Richard M. Executive Order 11643. February 8, 1972.

Olsen, Jack. *Slaughter the Animals, Poison the Earth*. New York: Simon and Schuster. 1971.

Orent, Sander. Testimony before Senate Subcommittee on Agriculture, Environment and Consumer Protection. December 14, 1971. P. 342.

Perry, Harold. "Predator Control Notes from Arizona." *Defenders of Wildlife News*. January–February–March 1970.

Public Land Statistics 1972, U.S.D.I. Washington, D.C. Government Printing Office.

Randall, Dick. "You Can Hear Them from Quite a Distance." *Defenders of Wildlife News*. April 1974.

Regenstein, Lewis. "Gunfight at the D.C. Corral." *Environmental Action.* February 17, 1973.

Rickover, Admiral H. H. "Can Technology Be Humanized—in Time?" *National Parks and Conservation Magazine.* July 1969.

Schnittker, John A. "Changes Needed in Farm Legislation." Paper submitted to Subcommittee on Priorities and Economy in Government of the Joint Economic Committee, Congress of the U.S. April 30, 1973.

U.S. Department of Agriculture Statistics. 1970.

Van der Veer. "Cisco and Others." *Defenders of Wildlife News.* March, April 1972.

Washington Evening Star. "Cost of Predator Control." August 14, 1973.

Wilson, Cynthia. "Federal Subsidies to the Sheep and Goat Industry." National Audubon Society Paper. March 15, 1973.

Wilson, Cynthia. Testimony presented to the Senate Subcommittee on the Environment. August 8, 1973.

Wynne-Edwards, V. C. "Population Control in Animals." *Scientific American* (1964), pp. 68–74.

POSTSCRIPT

Environmental Protection Agency. "Applications to Register Sodium Cyanide for Use in M-44 Device to Control Predators: Part Four." *Federal Register* 40 (189), pp. 44726–44739. September 29, 1975.

Executive Order 11870. July 22, 1975.

Executive Order 11917. May 28, 1976.

New York Times. "Idaho Ranchers Plan Protest on Coyotes." June 29, 1978.

U.S. Fish and Wildlife Service. "Report on Coyote Management in the West: A Study of Alternatives." Department of the Interior, Washington, D.C. June 12, 1978.

Index